Setting up Community Health Programmes

A practical manual for use in developing countries

Ted Lankester MA, MB, BChir, MRCGP

Director, InterHealth, at the Mildmay Mission Hospital, London
Formerly, Founder-Director, SHARE Community Health Programme, North India

With
a chapter on AIDS by

Ian D. Campbell

Medical Advisor, Salvation Army International Headquarters, London
Formerly, Medical Officer, Chikankata Hospital,
Mozabuka, Zambia

and

Alison D. Rader

AIDS Programme Consultant, Salvation Army
International Headquarters, London

TALC

First published 1992 by
MACMILLAN EDUCATION LTD
London and Basingstoke
Companies and representatives throughout the world

ISBN 0–333–57423–0

14	13	12	11	10	9	8	7	6	5
06	05	04	03	02	01	00	99	98	97

This book is printed on paper suitable for recycling and
made from fully managed and sustained forest sources.

Printed in Malaysia

A catalogue record for this book is available from the
British Library.

Tear Fund is an evangelical Christian relief and development
agency, based in the United Kingdom, supporting people and
programmes in 80 countries worldwide. It publishes *Footsteps*, a
regular development newsletter, in English, French and Spanish.

Further information is available from: Tear Fund, Dept. OD,
100 Church Road, Teddington, Middlesex, TW11 8QE, UK.

Contents

DEDICATION

This book is dedicated to the team members and Village Health Workers of
SHARE Project.

Acknowledgements

The writing and publication of this book has only been possible because of the support of many people.

I would first like to thank the members of SHARE, OPEN and TUSHAR projects for all that I learnt through them, along with the members of the Himalayan villages with whom they work in partnership. I am greatly indebted to Dr Alton Olson and Dr Pat Wakeham for their apprenticeship into community based health care and to other members of the Doon Medical Project.

Mr Lalchuangliana of the Emmanuel Hospital Association has been a long-standing friend and steady inspiration as has Dr Kiran Martin of ASHA programme, Mrs Barbara Deutschmann of TICH, Stanley and Gwen Hawthorne, and Miss Dorothy Holstein.

I am indebted to Professor Andrew Tomkins for his encouragement to proceed with the book, and to Professor David Morley for his helpful comments and for writing the foreword.

A number of people have advised on the text, including Dr Stephen Brown, Drs Richard and Judith Brown, Professor Duncan Vere, Mr Richard Franceys, Dr Malcolm Molyneux and Sir John Crofton.

I am grateful to TEAR Fund for their support in helping to bring the book to publication.

Dr Ian Campbell and Alison Rader deserve special thanks for sharing many of the insights into AIDS control they have developed in the outstanding programme in Zambia for which they have been in large part responsible.

Mrs Helen Green has spent long hours unravelling pages of doctor's writing. Finally I owe a big thankyou to my inspirational family.

Acknowledgements for illustrations

The author and publishers wish to acknowledge with thanks, the following sources:

AHRTAG, 1 London Bridge Street, London SE1 9SG for Figure 9.18 (from *Dialogue on Diarrhoea*).
Camera Press for Figure 2.10.
Richard Franceys/WEDC for Figures 15.9, 15.10 and 15.11 (from *Waterlines* **8**(3): 18–19, 1990).
The Hesperian Foundation for Figures 1.7, 3.3, 3.4, 3.6, 3.7, 3.8, 3.10, 5.4, 5.6, 5.7, 6.13, 7.5, 7.10, 7.18, 8.17, 9.15, 9.17, 11.2, 11.5, 11.8, 13.10, 16.3, 18.7, 19.8 and 19.11 (from *Helping Health Workers Learn*).
John and Penny Hubley for Figures 7.4, 7.6, 7.12, 12.13, and 13.11.
Oxford University Press for Figures 2.8, 10.8 and 19.4 (from *Practising Health for All*) and for Figures 10.2, 10.3, 10.4, 10.5, 10.9, 10.10 and 14.13 (from *Immunization in Practice*).
PANOS Pictures for Figures 5.1 and 12.5.

PATH, Seattle, Washington, USA for Figure 15.6 (Path adaptation from, *Peace Corps Times*).
TALC for Figures 8.7, 8.8, 9.8, 9.10, 9.12, 9.19, 9.21, 13.2, 13.5, 19.6, 19.9 and 19.10.
WHO for Figures 8.3, 9.7, 9.13, 11.6, 11.12, 19.13, 20.1 and 20.5 (WHO photographs); Figures 15.2, 15.3 and 15.8 (from *The Community Health Worker*); and Figures 16.8, 18.1, 18.2, 18.6 and 18.9 (from *On Being in Charge*).
WHO Expanded Programme on Immunization for Figure 10.6.
World Council of Churches for Figure 9.14 (from *Contact* No 111).

Cover photographs courtesy of Dr Ted Lankester.

The publishers have made every effort to trace the copyright holders, but if they have inadvertently overlooked any, they will be pleased to make the necessary arrangements at the first opportunity.

Author to reader

In the early 1980s I left suburban general practice near London, to help set up a community health programme in an area with little effective medical care. This book started as my scribbled field notes and gradually took shape, as together with colleagues and local community members, we developed the initial stages of a health programme. It has finally seen the light of day as I have been encouraged to broaden the scope of the book by including the accumulated experiences of others.

The title itself is rather provocative as there is no one way to set up a health programme. Each community has its own specific needs and solutions and no two programmes can ever be the same. Moreover community health practitioners often hold strong and differing ideas about how programmes should be set up. For these reasons alone, anyone daring to write about 'How to do it' risks immediate protest and rebuff. This manual is therefore an attempt to record some practical ideas which are currently being applied. Please write in with your own ideas and suggestions and let me know of any successful methods you have used.

Health workers of all types from informally trained enthusiasts to community orientated nurses and doctors are increasingly being challenged to meet the vast health needs of the world's poor. My hope is that this book may prove useful to such people eager to respond to community requests in the most appropriate way, but who are unsure about how to set about it.

Although aimed primarily at programme directors and field leaders in non-governmental organisations, I hope this book may also prove useful to those in government programmes, to the organisers of training courses, and to doctors, nurses and other levels of health worker challenged by the Health for All initiative.

Two philosophies of health care continue to do battle world-wide. On the one hand is the model of the Patient as Consumer – consumer of pills, services and procedures, provided to him and for him by doctors, projects and hospitals.

On the other hand is the model of the Community Member as Partner in a locally based health programme where he contributes as well as receives. This book wholeheartedly endorses the second approach but stops short of insisting that all communities should eventually 'own' their health programmes.

Those looking for omissions will find many. Some subjects have not been given the coverage they deserve, and some have been mentioned only in passing. Owing to its wide coverage certain sections may be less relevant to some than to others. Whereas some areas of the world have material and human resources to develop a stable primary health care system, others are disintegrating, as famine, civil strife and AIDS frustrate attempts to provide even basic health care. For some such areas even the simple procedures suggested in this book may be beyond reach.

Some readers may hope for a clear answer on how projects can be sustainable and self-supporting. They will find some ideas but no final answers. The risk of non-sustainability should keep us alert but not frighten us into retreat when the clamour of local needs demand that we take reasoned action.

In the Christian gospels we have an account of how Jesus used what was available – five loaves and two fish to feed a crowd of 5000. May all of us who are committed to the ideal of Health for All not be paralysed into inaction by the size of the task, but dare to believe that by working in partnership with local communities we can indeed make a valid contribution. As the Chinese proverb states with brave simplicity. 'Many little things done in many little places by many little people will change the face of the world'.

Foreword

Over the last 50 years there has been a tremendous change in health care world-wide. On one side we see the increasing sophistication with new technologies and new drugs being available. On the other side we see growing concern over the extent to which health services provide coverage to the communities they serve. In the countries of the South the very poor coverage provided by existing health services has led to much greater emphasis on Community Based Health Care. Here the communities are seen no longer as just consumers but as active partners in the planning, creation and supervision of health care.

Much of the early writing on this has been undertaken by those from outside the medical profession and among these David Werner has pride of place with his books *Where There Is No Doctor, Helping Health Workers Learn* and *Disabled Village Children*. The first of these has been translated into over 40 languages and more than a million copies have been distributed. This movement of health care away from dependence on doctors to a more family and community based health care is illustrated in one of David Werner's diagrams to which a further drawing has been added (Figure). In this last drawing emphasis is placed on the mother in the family who has always played such a major part in traditional as well as Western health care.

Although David Werner has played a leading role in his writings there are many others who, from a relatively lay background, have written on this subject. Dr Lankester, in this book is one of the first doctors to write an extensive manual on Community Based Health Care. As you read this book you will see that much of it is quite unrelated to the traditional training of doctors. The Author has shared his own experience and that of others for the benefit of all health workers who are concerned that the health care they provide should be community based and related to the desires and needs of the population they are serving. Such health care can only be successful when it is preceeded by a dialogue between those being served and the health workers – a dialogue that has to be maintained as

Encourage independence

the health care programme develops. Dr Lankester gives ideas as to how such communication can be achieved.

The book is particularly aimed at non-governmental organisations as they are fortunate in having a greater ability to vary and develop services. Such non-governmental services are however having an increasing influence not only on how governments provide health care, but also in stimulating a more appropriate training of doctors and other health care workers. Perhaps those in developing countries who find the existing training they receive in medical schools irrelevant to the real needs of the country, will also find this a book they can usefully turn to for answers on how to create community based health care.

Thoughts on all forms of health care are in a stage of rapid change but few are developing so fast as in the area of community health. Moreover stages achieved by different communities, even within the same country will vary widely, meaning that no community health manual can ever be 'fully relevant to every stage of every project'. As you discuss and put into practice guidelines given in this book remember that the Author is eager to hear your own suggestions and ideas so that these in turn can be passed on to others.

Professor David Morley
Institute of Child Health
London

Part I
BASIC PRINCIPLES

1

What is Community Based Health Care?

Some years ago a famous author wrote these words:

One thing which is greater than the march of great armies is an **idea** whose time has come.

A large number of health workers world-wide believe that Community Based Health Care (CBHC) is an example of such an idea.

Every year the world has a longer list of qualified doctors and a greater range of medical equipment. And yet every year the majority of the world's poorest and neediest people live and die beyond the range of even basic medical services.

Most of this book gives practical guidelines on how to bring basic health care to those who need it most. But before doing this it is useful to know:

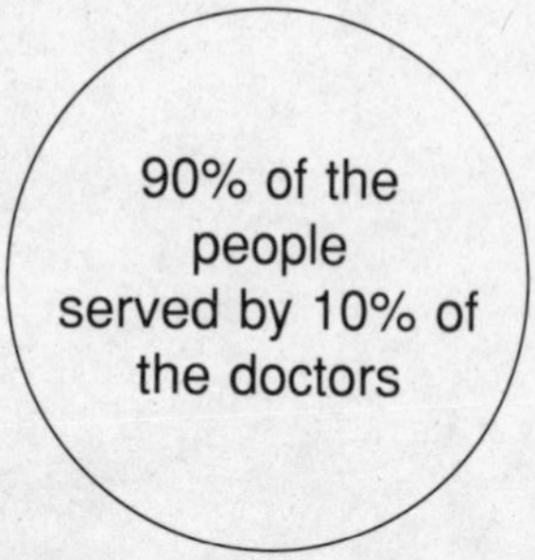

90% of the
people
served by 10% of
the doctors

Figure 1.1   Needed: a new model of health care

1. **What** special features make CBHC different from orthodox health care.
2. **Why** CBHC is so important in the last years of the 20th century.
3. **How**, by including community development, CBHC can help to remove the root cause of ill health – **poverty**.

What are the special features of Community Based Health Care?

The answer to this is summed up in the two words:

Community   and   **Health**.

Community Based Health Care emphasises – *community*

1. CBHC encourages **participation** by the community.

   Community health has been described as 'Health **of** the people, **by** the people, **for** the people'.

   Orthodox health care is provided **by** doctors and health workers **to** the people. **CBHC** is a genuine **partnership** of health workers and community members.
2. **CBHC responds to the needs** of the people.

   Orthodox health care starts with planners, projects and governments. **CBHC** starts with the people, helps them identify their needs, and works with them in finding answers.
3. CBHC leads to **self-reliance**.

   Orthodox health care often introduces two unwanted side effects – a dependence on medicines and on doctors.

   CBHC aims to bring about healthy, self-reliant communities. People become armed with knowledge so they depend less on outsiders.
4. CBHC helps to **encourage community life**.

   Traditional practices are encouraged unless they are positively harmful. New ideas are introduced with sensitivity. The aim of the health worker is always to build up confidence and dignity, never to cause offence or humiliation.

CBHC comes about as all health workers realise that they have as much to learn from the community as they have to teach it.

5. Health care **moves outwards** to where the people are.

   Care, wherever possible, is based in the community, not the clinic or hospital. It is

This tree was rigid

This tree was flexible

© Illustration David Gifford

Figure 1.2 The flexibility of community health programmes enables them to respond to changing needs and situations

Figure 1.3 Community health programmes work in partnership with others whenever possible

decided according to the **needs of the community**, rather than the convenience of the doctor or health worker.

Sick people are treated in their homes or as near to their homes as possible.

6. Health care **moves forwards** to the next generation.

> Children become a focal point of health activities. They are not simply targeted for improved health care but are involved in bringing it about.

Healthy patterns of living absorbed by children today, become the accepted practices of tomorrow.

7. CBHC **creates awareness**.

In doing this CBHC attempts to share ideas and increase understanding, so the people themselves are motivated to follow healthier life-styles.

8. CBHC **includes** all.

The poorest, neediest and most at risk are given priority. Women are given equal status. The elderly and handicapped are cared for. Members of the least popular tribe, the poorest sub-group and minority religion are given full equality. The rich and powerful are included where possible, though never permitted to displace the poor or dominate the process.

A person's need, rather than money or status determines the type of health care received.

9. CBHC **co-operates** and **integrates**.

Wherever possible other doctors, practitioners, and development workers are consulted and included. Other voluntary programmes are welcomed and ideas mutually shared.

Without losing their unique strengths and values community health programmes integrate into the health services of the country.

10. CBHC aims for a **new community order**.

As the community takes initiatives, as health standards improve and as other forms of development emerge, a new order starts to take shape. This is based on:

- **justice**, where the rich are no longer allowed to exploit the poor, nor the strong allowed to oppress the weak;
- **equity**, where all have sufficient, and the differences between rich and poor are reduced; and
- **unity**, where individuals and community groups learn mutual respect, and where by working towards a common goal they overcome tribal, ethnic and other differences.

Community Based Health Care emphasises – *health*

1. CBHC is involved more in **health** care than in **medical** care.

CBHC opposes 'PPNN' – a Pill for every Problem, a Needle for every Need. Instead it emphasises that well-being is largely brought about

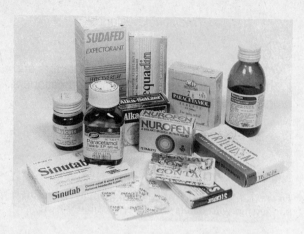

Figure 1.4 Most medicines are unnecessary, some are dangerous, a few are essential. Community based health care selects **essential** drugs and uses them effectively

through healthy living patterns and enlightened attitudes.
2. CBHC emphasises appropriate **cure**.

Included among the vast numbers of medicines and injections used world-wide, are a small number of essential, life-saving drugs.

CBHC health ensures that such drugs are always available and appropriately used.
3. CBHC follows a **comprehensive** model of health care.

It aims to include:
• Health education,
• Mother and child health services,
• Diagnostic and curative care,
• Control of infectious diseases,
• Adequate nutrition,
• Immunisation,
• Improvements in water supply and sanitation,
• Referral systems,
• Monitoring and evaluation.

CBHC leads in turn to other forms of community development.

What Community Based Health Care is NOT

1. CBHC is **not** against doctors and hospitals.

CBHC clearly recognises that both doctors and hospitals have a vital role to play in health care. By concentrating on effective primary care

in the community, it releases doctors to use their training more effectively, and enables hospitals to use their facilities more efficiently.
2. CBHC is **not** simply adding new structures on to old foundations.

CBHC is not an extension of a hospital into the four walls of a village clinic. It is a complete restructuring of the health care system so that the people becomes partners with the providers.
3. CBHC is **not** a second rate health service for the poor, as long as it is correctly set up and **adequately supervised**.

Section Summary

Community Based Health Care is a radical approach to health which aims to put care into the hands of those who need it most. The community rather than the hospital becomes the focal point, health care rather than medical care the main emphasis. Participation becomes the basis of all activities, self-reliance the aim.

In CBHC the community takes increasing responsibility, with the doctor and health worker acting as facilitator and guide. This process has been described as health **of** the people, **by** the people, **for** the people.

Why is Community Based Health Care so important at the present time?

In 1978 health planners from 134 member states of the United Nations met at Alma Ata in the Soviet Union to draw up a health charter aiming to bring basic health services within reach of every community and individual. It was here that the famous phrase was coined, 'Health for All by the Year 2000'.

CBHC is based on principles set out at Alma Ata and increasingly seems to offer the only practical way of bringing about 'Health for All' to the world's poorest people.

In trying to understand why this is so it is helpful to look back and see how health care has changed over the past 50 years.

We can observe three distinct stages: different

The traditional health system is   Convenient
                                       Affordable
          but not very   Effective

The scientific health system is   Inconvenient
                                        Expensive
                                        Effective for the few
                                        who can afford it

Community based health care is   Convenient
                                         Affordable
                                  and   Effective

© Illustration David Gifford

Figure 1.5   The three stages of health care

countries and areas may be at different stages, and sometimes two or more stages may be present at the same time.

Stage 1: The traditional health system

Health care takes place **in the community**, according to the wishes and convenience of people and patients.

Senior family members such as grandmothers are the traditional source of wisdom. In serious situations other health workers are called in. These are usually community members using **traditional** skills or knowledge. Each community has its own trusted healers. Examples include: witch-doctors, shamans, priests, herbalists, traditional midwives and ayurvedic practitioners.

Payment is made in cash or kind, usually but not always at a level which the patient can afford.

This system has value when no better alternative exists, and when people's expectations are low. Today many rural societies still function partly on this system.

Stage 2: The scientific health system

Health care takes place in the **hospital** or **clinic** at the convenience of the doctor or health worker.

The health worker is an **outsider** with specialist and scientific knowledge, who tends to direct and dominate the treatment of the patient. Often he

will demand high fees, which the poor cannot afford.

Although often effective, this approach may be frightening, inconvenient and expensive. **The poor may never use it at all**.

Stage 3: The Community Based Health Care system

Health care returns to the **community**, with referral to clinic or hospital only when necessary.

The health worker, usually a Community Health Worker (CHW), is an **insider** who lives in the community, understands its traditions and provides effective health care at a fee that most can afford.

Stage 3 health care **at its best** combines the finest features of stages 1 and 2. Good quality care is available in the community, from a friendly provider at an affordable cost. A referral system ensures that those who need clinic or hospital care are able to receive it.

Although it may seem that Stage 3 is the most appropriate model, there are many who wish to anchor the process at Stage 2.

Will Health for All actually be achieved? Will Stage 3 ever become the norm?

This will depend on many factors especially how **effective** and **sustainable** CBHC programmes prove to be. **Each successful programme, however small, helps to tilt the balance in favour of Stage 3.**

Section Summary

Since the Alma Ata Conference of 1978 a primary health system with the full involvement of the people has been seen as the key to bringing about Health for All.

As health care progresses from the traditional to the scientific, it must combine the best features from both in a radical community-based model. The success of this 'Stage 3' health care will depend in large part on community health projects demonstrating world-wide that they can bring about effective and sustainable health improvements at reasonable cost.

The outer circle (1) represents poverty in the country
The middle circle (2) represents poverty in the community
The inner circle (3) represents poverty in the family

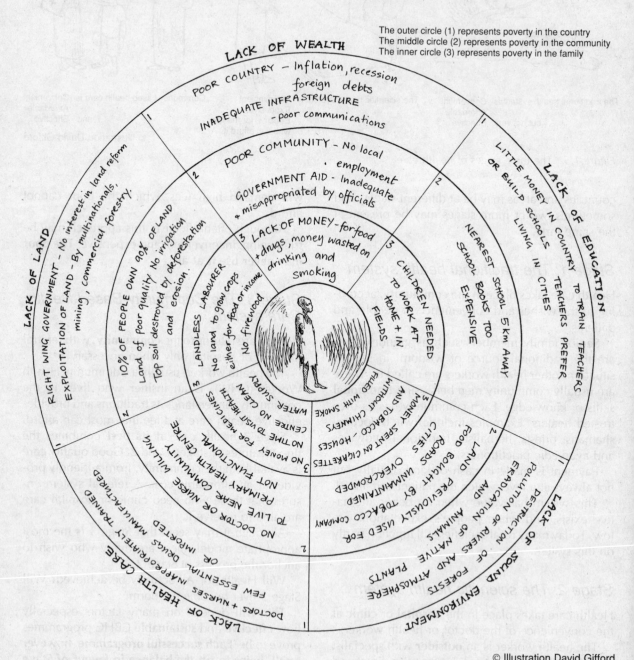

Figure 1.6   The causes and effects of poverty

How can health programmes tackle underlying causes of ill health?

The problem

Health workers soon come to realise that the diseases they see are usually symptoms of a much greater 'illness' which affects their communities.

Much disease in developing countries is a direct result of **poverty**. A poor person has little money, little food, or little power; the rich consider him a 'little person'. He becomes used and abused by those who own more land and more money. Such **exploitation** is always found in association with poverty and both causes it and results from it (see Figure 1.6).

> Poor people and poor communities have the greatest share of illness and malnutrition. As poverty is reduced health improves.

Poverty does **not** usually disappear when a country becomes prosperous. Most commonly the rich become richer still, and the poor stay the same or slide deeper into poverty and dependence.

For example: Recent reports have suggested that the life expectancy of certain groups living in a poor suburb of New York is lower than the average life expectancy in several of the world's poorest countries.

As health workers we must be aware of the forces which act against the poor and lock them into life-styles of poverty. We must come to see how other forms of development which reduce poverty and exploitation may be even more important than the health programmes we help to bring about.

We can look beyond the causes in Figure 1.6 and notice another thread which weaves its way through all the problems listed – human corruptibility. This multiplies still further the problems facing the poor. Here are some examples:

1. **greed** which brings about a wealthy minority at the expense of a poor majority;
2. **dishonesty** where broken promises and pledges are most keenly felt by the poor;
3. **corruption** where those unable to offer a bribe suffer the most; and
4. **pride** where the rich and clever tend to despise the weak and poor, so refusing to assist.

Our approach

In planning our attack on poverty and exploitation we must consciously resist becoming discouraged or intimidated.

Here are some approaches which can be helpful:

1. **Understanding the causes** of poverty.
   This will help us to be more compassionate towards the community and more realistic in our planning.
2. **Realising** that although we can do little by ourselves, we can do a great deal as we work together with others.
3. **Seeing community based health care** as **a multiplication** process, not an addition process.
   Stage 2 health care – where health workers merely treat patients, is an addition process. Someone has described it as trying to empty the ocean with a teaspoon.
   Stage 3 health care is a multiplication process. Health workers teach others, who teach others, who teach others. A stone is set in motion at the top of a hill which moves faster and faster the further it travels.

Figure 1.7

4. **Starting** with the **skills** which we **do** have.

   'We can't start everywhere but we can start somewhere.'

5. **Including community development** as soon as we are able.

   This may either mean expanding our own health programmes or linking the community with other agencies and experts. Agriculture, forestry, education, adult literacy, income generation, appropriate technology, improved housing, urban renewal and housing co-operatives will have a far greater effect on improving the health of our communities than health interventions alone.

6. **Encouraging** people to **claim their rights** under the laws of the country.

   There may be many promises on paper designed to help the poor but little happening in practice. We can help the poor to claim the provisions which are due to them.

7. **Altering** traditional patterns of life as little as possible unless they are positively harmful.

We must make sure that any unwanted side effects of development are kept to the minimum. We should affirm village and community life, and discourage a needless drift to the cities and the adoption of harmful aspects of western lifestyles.

8. **Fighting injustice**, and standing or suffering with the people where important principles are involved.

Section Summary

In poor communities most illness is a direct result of poverty and exploitation. As health workers we need to discover the causes in our community and work with the people in bringing about changes.

This will lead us into a deeper commitment to the communities we serve. We will be encouraged to link them with other development workers, or move into appropriate areas of development ourselves in partnership with the community.

Figure 1.8   Our aim is to affirm appropriate lifestyles

Further Reading

1. *Primary Health Care.* Report of the International Conference on Primary Health Care, Alma Ata, 1978. WHO, 1978.
   Available from: WHO. See Appendix E.
2. *Achieving Health for All by the Year 2000: Midway reports of country experiences.* WHO, 1990.
   Fifteen reports on progress so far.
   Available from: WHO. See Appendix E.
3. *My Name is Today.* D. Morley, H. Lovel. Macmillan, 1986.
   This book gives a powerful analysis of the state of health care in today's world and current priorities, especially for mothers and children.
   Available from: TALC. See Appendix E.
4. *Practising Health for All.* D. Morley, J. Rohde, G. Williams. Oxford, 1983.
   Articles from 17 countries describing primary health care successes and problems.
   Available from: TALC. See Appendix E.
5. *Rural Development: Putting the Last First.* R. Chambers. Longman, 1983.
   Available from: TALC. See Appendix E.
6. *Implementing Primary Health Care: Experiences since Alma Ata.* P. Streeflans, J. Chabot (eds) Royal Tropical Institute, Amsterdam, 1990. A useful overview of the successes and problems of Health for All with useful case studies from different countries.
   Available from: KIT Press, Mauritskade 63, 1092 Amsterdam, Netherlands.

2
Working as Partners with the Community

The **key** to Community Based Health Care (CBHC) is **working in partnership with the community**. This includes, but also goes beyond the idea of **people's participation**.

> As health workers our chief task is to enable communities to set up and manage their own health programmes.

In this chapter we will consider:

1. What we need to **know**
   • Why partnership is important
   • The effects of partnership
   • Partnership as the basis of all programme stages
   • Which factors obstruct partnership
2. What we need to **do**
   • Prepare ourselves for partnership
   • Prepare the community
   • Choose a subject
   • Carry out the process
   • Avoid the pitfalls
   • Understand some models
     – Village health committees
     – Women's Clubs

What we need to know

Why partnership is important

As we saw in Chapter 1 CBHC has come about because other models of health care have failed to bring basic health services to the world's poor.

In developing countries orthodox health care follows a 'top-down' model, is mainly curative, usually dominated by doctors, and often subsidised by donations from governments and outside agencies. People come to expect things to be given **to** them and done **for** them. Although in the pro-

cess they may **gain** a degree of improved health, they often **lose** something far more important – **control over their own lives**. An approach where **people participate** is the exact opposite of this.

> Our aim will be to promote **health care with** the people, not provide **medical care for** the people. The community is the starting point, their leaders the chief partners.

Community involvement is the basis of almost every successful health programme. A recent world-wide study of programmes that really **worked** and really **lasted** showed that participation was the single most important reason for success.

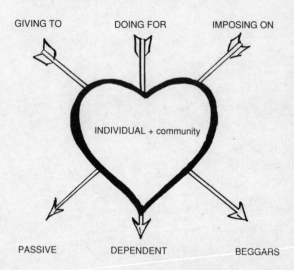

GIVING TO   DOING FOR   IMPOSING ON

INDIVIDUAL + community

PASSIVE   DEPENDENT   BEGGARS

© Illustration David Gifford

Figure 2.1   The effects of 'wrong development'

The effects of partnership

1. It makes a project **permanent**.
   If people themselves learn to **change wrong health patterns and adopt correct ones**, then when the experts go and the funding stops their

THE POOR'S **ARMOUR**:

<u>CONTROL</u> OVER THEIR OWN LIVES

1. Participation in the prograrnme to PROTECT against EXPLOITATION	2. Practical health knowledge to PROTECT against ILLNESS

Figure 2.2   The poor's armour

health will be **permanently improved**.

As a famous book-character once said: 'Why, Tom, **us** people must go on living, when all **these people** are gone.'

2. It helps to **protect** the people.

The poor are always exploited:

- Doctors want them as patients – for a profit.
- Drug companies sell them medicines – also for a profit.
- The rich loan money – for high interest.
- Politicians make false promises – for votes.

Participation acts as armour against these forces.

For example: In the treatment of diarrhoea in poor communities there is little value in **only** teaching mothers to buy packets of oral rehydration salts (ORS) from doctors or drug companies. Supplies will often be exhausted or prices raised.

Mothers in addition should be taught **how to make their own ORS from materials available in the home**. In this way they will be self-sufficient and free from dependence on expensive, unreliable supplies. See also Chapter 11.

3. It gives **dignity** to the **poor**.

People soon realise that they no longer need others to do things for them or give things to them. They come to see **they can do things**, **and obtain things for themselves**.

This new self-reliance gives a sense of value and worth to the poor. Instead of being passive receivers they become active participants.

For example: In many projects it is found that newly selected CHWs tend to cover their faces, look down to the ground and say: 'We are only useful for making bread and carrying water'.

After a few months these same women, armed with practical health knowledge and new self-confidence, will be teaching their communities, and caring for their health needs.

4. Local people become **effective health workers**.

Members of a community already have a great store of wisdom and skills. With good training CHWs can provide more appropriate primary care than doctors: community members can understand local needs better than social workers.

An old Chinese proverb says: 'Outsiders can help, but insiders must do the job.'

5. Participation acts as a '**multiplier**'.

Once local people become excited by what they have achieved they will want to spread the news to others. They themselves will become agents of change, taking new health patterns and new ideas to other communities.

Community participation often seems a slow process at the start. Later this multiplier effect will cause a rapid increase in growth (see Figure 2.3).

6. Equipment is better looked after.

When people feel it is **their** clinic, **their** forestry plantation, **their** water pump, they will take pride in looking after it.

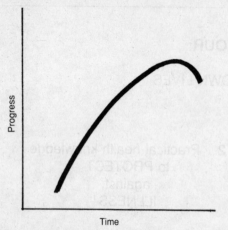

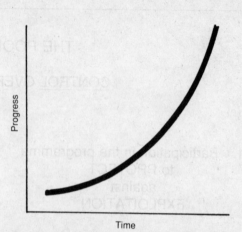

Project A: 'Community passive'. Project itself provides health care, gives to the poor, does things for people.
Result: apparent rapid progress at first – stagnation and decline later.

Project B: 'Community active'. Community participates at every stage. Project a facilitator, not a provider.
Result: slow progress at first – sustained and accelerating progress later.

© Illustration David Gifford

Figure 2.3   Comparison between 'community passive' and 'community active' programmes

Partnership as the basis of all programme stages

All activities and all project stages involve the community – not just as receivers but as partners (see Figure 2.4).

Which factors obstruct partnership

Helping a community to manage a health project is not easy. Being a 'facilitator' requires social skills every bit as challenging as a surgeon's technical skills.

Here are some problems we are likely to face:

1. Blocks within the community.
   Most communities will be used to the 'charity and donation' approach. They will expect us to do things for them and give things to them. If we don't they may lost interest.

2. Blocks from professionals.
   Some doctors and nurses will want to hold on to their knowledge and skills. They may dislike or even oppose any system in which patients and people start learning about health or running a programme.

3. Blocks from the government.
   Although almost all governments support the 1978 Alma Ata declaration which calls for participation, some will be less keen in practice.

4. Blocks within ourselves.
   It is often much easier for health workers to run programmes and clinics for the community rather than work together with them (see below).

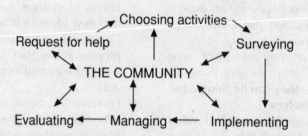

Figure 2.4   The community is central in all programme activities

What we need to do

Prepare ourselves for partnership

We will never work in genuine partnership unless our own minds and attitudes are carefully prepared. We will need to be:

1. Really **committed** to the idea of participation.
2. Ready to **share** knowledge and skills at every opportunity.
3. **Flexible**, being prepared for mistakes, delays and experiments.
4. Ready to **trust** others.
5. Ready to give **respect** and **credit** to others.
   'Our job is not to be heroes ourselves but to make heroes of other people.'
6. Prepared for a **long-term** commitment as facilitator.
7. Willing to **give up control**, and stop being the boss.

© Illustration David Gifford

Figure 2.5 Check your motives

> The biggest block to participation is not the unwillingness of the community. It is the possessive attitude of the health worker wanting to gain credit and keep control.

Prepare the community

Partnership will not just happen if we arrange a few meetings and hope for the best.

Like other community health skills, the ability to bring about participation has to be **learnt** and **practised**. At the beginning many of the poorest, neediest and most exploited communities will not be ready to participate.

How can we 'teach' participation?

1. By building trust and friendship.
2. By making our aims clear.
   The people must see that we are not merely **providers**. If they know we are rich and will easily give handouts their **participation may not be genuine**.
3. By starting discussion groups.
   These can consist of interested community members, CHWs, community leaders or members of a health committee or club.
   A project member can act as facilitator and guide the discussion as follows:
   - **problems** will be raised and real causes identified, *for example*, we can use the 'But why?' approach:
     'The child has an infected foot.'
     'But why?'
     'She stepped on a thorn.'
     'But why?'
     'She has no shoes.'
     'But why?'
     'Her father is a landless worker and cannot afford them.'
   - **solutions** can be discussed.
   - **suggestions** can now be followed up.
   This approach to participation quickly leads on to awareness raising. This is an **essential** part of community **development** and is a valuable tool in community **health** (see Chapter 3 page 24).
4. By arranging visits to other projects.
   'Most visions are caught not taught.'

Visiting a project in which participation is genuine can inspire others to aim for the same. Such a visit may act as an ideal stimulus for our own health team, CHWs or community leaders.

Choose a subject

Partnership does not happen at once. Although our eventual aim is for people to manage the programme this process has to come about in stages, and the technique of participation has to be taught.

The community should first learn how to take an active part in **one** main activity. As soon as possible this can be extended to **others**.

The **community** can **suggest** subjects – either through a discussion group above, or in a meeting of leaders or community members (see Chapter 5 page 54). An obvious time is during the post-survey meeting when we work together on a community plan (see Chapter 6 page 69).

We will need to **guide** the final choices to make sure they are suitable.

A good subject for teaching participation should be:

1. A **need** strongly felt by the community.
   There is no point in 'scratching where there is no itch', in choosing a subject in which the people have no interest.
2. Within **reach**.
   The activity must be easily **within the abilities** of the community. If it is too long or too difficult all will lose interest.
3. Able to bring an **early**, **obvious** benefit.

For example: one project was able to work with the community in sinking tubewells, so bringing drinking water and ridding the community of guinea worm. All were excited and wanted to work together on further activities.

It is important to realise that many changes in community health are **real** but not **obvious**. The community may fail to notice any change unless they are **helped** to **look back** and see how much things have improved since they started.

For example: Improvements in child nutrition may be obvious if a special feeding programme is started. If however mothers are simply taught how to improve their feeding practices at home, changes may be less visible.

In order to maintain interest in correct feeding practices, these changes must be **demonstrated** to the people. This can be done by showing Road to Health Charts with weights before and after new feeding practices were started.

Whatever activity is chosen, it must **work** and it must be **enjoyable**.

Some **suggestions** for 'starter-subjects' include:

- Community survey (see Chapter 6 page 57).
- A community immunisation drive (see Chapter 10 page 147ff).
- Planning and building a community health post (see Chapter 8 page 98ff).
- Running a 'health fair' or baby show.
- Carrying out a CHW training programme (see Chapter 7 page 78ff).
- Improving a water supply (see Chapter 15 page 216ff).

Carry out the process

1. Generate enthusiasm.
   Just as jeeps run on diesel, so projects run on enthusiasm.

Enthusiasm ⟶ Success ⟶ More ⟶ More
                      enthusiasm   success . . .

Figure 2.6

To increase enthusiasm:
- **do** be friendly,
- **do** create an atmosphere where people enjoy working together,
- **do** give people the freedom to share their own ideas and do things their own way,
- **do** give support when things are difficult,
- **do** celebrate successes,
- **do** give training and teaching so people feel they are making personal progress,
- **do** be fair in making decisions and solving disputes,
- **don't** blame people or become easily angered.

2. Hand over tasks to others as soon as possible. The person **least** qualified to do a job well should be given that job to do. In this way everyone's skills are used most effectively (see

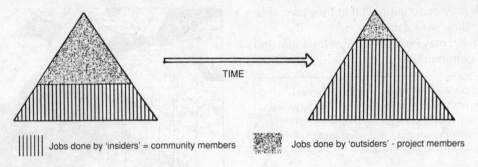

TIME

||||| Jobs done by 'insiders' = community members

▓▓ Jobs done by 'outsiders' - project members

© Illustration David Gifford

Figure 2.7 Skill pyramids

Chapter 18 page 253).

If there is a job which only we know how to do, we should teach someone else to do it as soon as possible.

Make sure that more and more of the skill pyramid is filled by community members (see Figure 2.7).

For example: In teaching CHWs:

- first **we** teach CHWs,
- later CHWs teach each other,
- eventually **senior** CHWs start training new CHWs from new areas.

For example: In running a clinic:

- first **project** members register, weigh, nurse and dispense,
- later **community** members take over these functions,
- eventually **the community** shares in or takes over the management of the health post.

3. Identify interest and abilities in community members.

   Suggest names of people with special interest to the community and if appropriate train them and involve them.

4. Lead from the middle, not from the front.

5. Keep outside money, resources and equipment to the minimum.

6. Be truthful and straightforward.

   Never make promises which cannot be kept, or raise expectations that can't be met.

7. Show respect to everyone **even those it may seem difficult to trust**.

8. Teach generosity and kindness.

9. Stop an activity if it is obviously not going to work.

Avoid the pitfalls

Common ones include:

Partnership is in name, not in practice

Participation may seem to be present but activities are only slanted **towards** the community, not based **in** the community. The community sees the **branches**, but the project keeps the **roots**.

Partnership is often **surface** rather than **deep**. Community members join in, but more as workers than as partners, more on the project's terms rather on their own terms.

Partnership is often a **pretence** rather than **genuine**. This is usually in the hope that a good performance will be rewarded by a nice handout or new job opportunities.

Partnership fades away

We may originally aim for genuine community partnership. When the health committee chairman runs off with the funds we may quickly change our mind.

We must keep encouraging participation even when problems arise and we are tempted to retake control.

Partnership leads to division

Someone has written: 'Participation should release the energy to overcome the problems of poverty.' Although true this process may start going in the wrong direction or get out of control.

- The **poor** may become so angered that they rise up against their exploiters.

- The **rich** may be so cunning that they use problems for their own gains.
- **Issues** raised may be so strong that they split and destroy communities.

> Participation is a powerful process. Carried forward correctly it can help the poor, include the rich and benefit the community. Handled wrongly it can leave a community wounded and unstable.

Understand some models

In order for partnership to succeed there need to be 'vehicles' to carry the process forwards. Two ways in which this can be done are village health committees and women's clubs.

Village health committees (VHCs)

We will consider:

1. The **functions** of the VHC
2. How VHC members are **chosen**
3. The **advantages** and **disadvantages** of VHCs
4. The **training** of VHC members
5. How VHC members **progress in their understanding**

The functions of the VHC

There will be wide differences between projects. Usually a committee will start with one or two functions and learn to do these well. Later it can extend its activities. Here are some common examples of health committee functions:

CHW support
Members can encourage and support the CHW. They can help weigh children, keep records and accompany the CHW on night calls. They can stand with her in the face of any criticisms.

Health centre, post or dispensary: building and upkeep
The committee can help organise the construction of the health post. They can be responsible for its upkeep and repairs.

Health centre: clinic activities
Responsible VHC members can assist in the clinic. They can register patients, weigh children, help the health worker, and assist the dispenser. They

Figure 2.8   The people construct a community health centre

can call patients and organise 'patient-flow'.

Within the community they can make sure that those **needing** to attend the clinic **actually do so**. These will include the under 5s, pregnant women, TB patients and others at risk.

They can accompany sick patients to hospital.

Immunisation campaigns
Committee members can arrange publicity and gather the children. They can assist the CHW and health team on community immunisation days by preparing the site and organising the campaign.

Community survey
Members can visit homes beforehand to explain why the survey is being done. They can work with project members in carrying out the survey. They can explain results to the community after the survey is finished.

Public health activities
Health committees can organise the digging of

soakage pits, construction of latrines, and can take responsibility for community hygiene. They can help build and maintain water storage tanks, pumps and wells.

Contacts with government and outside agencies

They can claim grants and benefits on behalf of the people. They can make sure government plans and promises are actually carried out, and that the poor and underprivileged are treated fairly and receive any subsidies due.

Meetings

Regular meetings are held with the community and the project. These are arranged for liaison, planning and training.

How VHC members are chosen

Who chooses them?

If possible the whole community should be involved following the normal method of decision making used by the people. The process of selection is broadly similar to that use in choosing CHWs (see Chapter 7 page 75ff).

The committee should **not** be chosen only by or from the rich, the powerful or those who speak the loudest.

What size should the committee be?

The committee should be **large** enough to represent the main social groups in the community and **small** enough to keep united and get things done. Six to 12 members is ideal. Smaller 'social action groups' can be appointed in addition.

Each main group in the community should be represented including women, the landless, the low-caste, and member of any minority tribe, sub-group or religion.

> Every health committee, no matter how small, must include at least one woman, and at least one member of the poorest sub-group of the community.

In very small communities each household can send one member.

What sized community should a committee represent?

This varies greatly. Usually each self-contained community such as a village, a plantation or a city slum has its own committee.

This is not always possible: *for example (1)*: When villages are very small or scattered. In this case:

- **either** two or more villages can join together providing they are close enough for joint activities.
- **or** health committees can be set up for each health centre (often serving several villages), rather than for each village.

For example (2): in city slums or large towns. In such cases an appropriate area needs to be defined. This could be a street as in the People's Republic of China, or a cluster of dwellings. Some slums, especially illegal settlements, are often small enough for a single committee.

In mixed slum communities we must make sure that **all** communities and groups are represented.

© Illustration David Gifford

Figure 2.9 Village health committees must represent the whole community

Figure 2.10   Gandhi – a strong supporter of community involvement

Generally it is hard for a health committee to represent more than 2000 people and a much smaller number is preferable.

When should the committee be selected?
There are three possible times:

1. At the start of the project.
   Although this is a common practice people are more likely at this stage to join for the wrong reasons.
2. After a period of 6 months to a year.
   By this time those with a **genuine** interest in health will be known both by the project and by the community.
3. Before a special activity.
   An example of this would be the building of a health post or the improving of a water supply. At such times members have a goal to aim for and are more likely to work effectively.

The advantages and disadvantages of VHCs.

In some projects Village Health Committees have proved successful, in others they have been disappointing.

Their **advantages** include:

1. They are a people's organisation. Their members are chosen by the community and live in the community.
2. They have authority to carry out health related activities.
3. They may have official government recognition.
4. They tie in with the idea of 'community democracy'.

VHCs can also have **disadvantages**:

1. Members join for the wrong reasons.
   They may be more interested in personal prestige than community welfare. They may join because of hoped-for perks and privileges, not because of any interest in health and development.
2. The committee may be slow and bureaucratic.
   Unless committees are small and their members enthusiastic 'A great deal of time can be spent doing a great deal of nothing.'
3. The committee may become politicised.
   Those with political ambitions, either local or national, may 'hijack' the committee for their own personal campaign. Divisions in the com-

munity may be reflected in the committee. Meetings may turn into fights and power struggles. This is a particular risk in urban slums, or in the run-up to elections.

All these problems can be lessened by the careful **choosing** and **training** of VHC members.

In practice VHCs are often most successful when they take responsibility for community development as well as health. Health activities alone may not be sufficient to maintain their interest.

The training of VHC members

> Time taken to teach and sensitise health committee members can have a key effect on the health and development of the community.

How VHC members progress in their understanding

An African health leader has described four stages through which VHCs usually pass:

Stage 1

Members are busy working out their own relationships and seeing which individual or which group will gain control.

Stage 2

Members test out the benefits to which they are entitled. Common ones include: lifts in project vehicles, free medicines, priority in clinics, and special access to the project doctor or director.

During this stage members may **seem** very interested in project activities, but only because of the privileges they are hoping to get.

Stage 3

Members start requesting special things for the community. Common examples are: a resident doctor, a well-equipped hospital, a new vehicle or some special equipment. They may demand free food and handouts, supposedly for the poor.

If **successful** in these demands members may hope to increase their own standing in the community.

If **unsuccessful** or if personal benefits fail to occur, members may lose interest.

Stage 4

Remaining members start working with the project and serving the community with genuine commitment.

© Illustration David Gifford

Figure 2.11   Inappropriate demands of a newly formed health committee

Women's clubs

We will consider:

1. **Advantages** of women's clubs
2. **Which** women might join?
3. **How** clubs are started
4. **Activities** that can be carried out
5. A simple **constitution**
6. **Problems** that have to be faced

Advantages of women's clubs

Clubs have one main advantage over committees: people usually join them out of genuine interest rather than to gain privileges.

Women's involvement in health care has one main advantage over men's: women are usually more interested in the welfare of their family than in personal gain.

> **Women acting together** can be highly effective. Not only can they claim justice for themselves but, if organised and united, they can **help to overturn harmful community practices** or resist exploitation from outside.

Which women might join?

Each project and community should set up its own guidelines. Some will encourage any woman who lives in the community to attend. Others will suggest that each household sends one female member, preferably a mother of small children.

Sometimes upper and lower age limits are set, or only married women are eligible.

How clubs are started

Here are some suggestions:

1. A club should only be started **if the people want it**. However if interest is lacking it is possible to create awareness about the value of such clubs.
2. Appoint a 'project facilitator'. Community members may appreciate having one project member who can work with them, give them guidance and act as their teacher. Such a person will need to be **sensitive**, **enthusiastic**, and **willing to let others lead**. The facilitator's job might include:
   • encouraging interested women to call a first meeting,
   • helping women to come forward with their

© Illustration David Gifford

Figure 2.12 Clubs are more likely to succeed when the people themselves want to start them

own ideas and suggestions,

- enabling women to develop leadership skills,
- giving advice and guidance when it is needed or when asked,
- teaching club members about practical health matters,
- assisting club members to seek loans, or obtain justice.

3. Suggestions for a first meeting:

- Share a common religious observance. This is a good way to start a meeting, but we must make sure it is acceptable to all who are present.
- Discuss a topic of current interest. *For example*: The CHW may have been beaten up the night before by her drunk husband or a friend's child may have died from malaria. As causes and solutions are discussed those present will come to see that such harmful events don't have to happen and that by working together they can often be prevented.

Other suitable topics might include:

- How to prevent and treat common diseases of children such as diarrhoea, measles or malnutrition.
- Family planning.
- How to raise more income for the use of the family.
- How to start a kitchen garden.
- How to prevent the spread of AIDS.
- Start a 'chit fund' or credit co-operative. Members contribute a small amount each month. Later, in turn or according to their needs, members receive a lump sum back.
- Discuss future programmes and activities.

Activities that can be carried out

World-wide, women's clubs carry out a huge variety of activities. Usually they will have started with just one or two activities which they have learnt to do well. Here are some examples:

Health-related activities

> Women's clubs are ideal for giving practical support and encouragement to the CHW. This is especially needed when she first starts working and is finding the job difficult.

In addition women's clubs will often take special interest in the following:

- the health needs and feeding of children,
- immunisation,
- health problems faced by women,
- family planning and child spacing,
- running a community health centre,
- problems in the home.

Social activities

Examples might include:

- running a creche for young children so mothers can work in the fields or earn a living,
- helping to organise festivals or cultural activities,
- starting a sewing circle.

Educational activities

Women's clubs can arrange literacy classes or non-formal education for children or adults.

The club may have a member who is an effective teacher. Alternatively a club member could be sent on a training course and then do the teaching herself.

Economic

These activities should not be started too soon. Club members should first establish trust among themselves and gain experience in club activities. Possibilities might include:

1. Starting a special savings fund into which each member pays a monthly amount. The fund could be used for:

- Emergency grants to any member in special need such as following the death of a husband.
- An item of equipment which could be used by the club or hired out to others.
  For example: One club in Maharashtra, India bought tents and musical instruments used for weddings. These are then available for the families of club members and are hired out to others for a profit.
- Giving repayable loans to members. These could be used for useful items which the family could not otherwise afford. Examples might include a sewing machine, farm animals, or improved seeds or fertilisers.

2. Income generation

Women's clubs are an ideal way for a community to start income generating activities. Money earned in this way may be kept by women to help their families and children. This will make families and the community less dependent on outsiders.

Agricultural

Women's clubs can encourage and teach their members to start kitchen gardens. Nutritious vegetables can be grown on a plot near the house, kept damp by waste water from the kitchen and fertilised by kitchen compost.

Vegetables grown by women are more likely to be used as a food crop for the family, so benefiting the children.

Community action

Once a club is well established women can stand together in joint action against social evils.

For example (1): Action against drunkenness. Women can make a united stand in the community to discourage husbands and other community members from abusing alcohol and drugs.

For example (2): Action to save the environment. Women in the Himalayas have banded together to prevent contractors cutting down trees and ruining the soil. When axemen appear they hug the trees, and when lorries arrive they lie down in the road.

A simple constitution

At the start women can simply meet together, the CHW acting as leader. No formal leadership is needed.

Later the club may wish to appoint a Secretary (usually the CHW) a President and a Treasurer.

Eventually the club may wish to draw up a written constitution and become registered – usually in association with other clubs.

A small yearly membership fee can be paid by each member to cover costs.

Problems that have to be faced

Men oppose the clubs

The **reasons** for this are often because of jealousy and suspicion.

The **remedies** for this are to include and inform partners. Once they understand that activities are to benefit the whole family, the problem is often resolved.

Club members lose interest

The **reason** is often because of wrong expectations. Club members expect great things to happen quickly. When they don't interest drops and women stop coming.

The **remedy** is to start small with low expectations and for club members to know that it takes

© Illustration David Gifford

Figure 2.13   Women can act as effective pressure groups to overcome social evils

time (often about 5 years) to achieve useful results.

Members start to argue, factions develop, the club closes down

At the beginning everyone must know and agree that **learning to work together is the main purpose of the club**, and that if this fails to happen, the club will achieve nothing.

The facilitator may be able to suggest a fair way of solving any serious dispute.

Finally **Young Farmer's Clubs**, **Men's Clubs or Youth Clubs** can be started, either at the same time as the women's clubs or later, following their lead.

These can give valuable support to health and development activities in the community, sharing or replacing some of the functions of the health committees. They too can act as vehicles for community participation in health care.

Summary

The ultimate aim is to hand over management to the community. The active participation of the community in all project activities is the means of bringing this about.

Unless projects include the community in a genuine partnership, health patterns don't change and projects don't last. Participation protects people against exploitation, creating self-dependence and enabling communities to identify problems and devise solutions.

Although participation should be the basis of all project activities, one or two starter-subjects should be chosen at first as a means of teaching the idea of participation to the community.

For participation to succeed health team members must have clear aims and correct attitudes, making sure they give the community the correct training and preparation. Creating enthusiasm and showing trust are keys to bringing this about.

The process can be greatly helped by the setting up of health committees, women's clubs or similar community organisations.

Further Reading

1. *Practising Health for All*. D. Morley, J.E. Rohde, G. Williams (eds). Oxford University Press, 1983.
   Eighteen projects worldwide are described in detail. Part 2 is especially useful.
   Available from: TALC. See Appendix E.
2. *Two Ears of Corn: A Guide to People-centred Agricultural Development*. R. Bunch. World Neighbors, 1982.
   Although mainly concerned with agriculture the principles of participation are excellently described.
   Available from: World Neighbors. See Appendix E.
3. *Health Care Together*. M. P. Johnston, S. B. Rifkin (eds). Macmillan, 1987.
   Available from: TALC. See Appendix E.
4. 'Community-Based or Community-Orientated?' D. Hilton. *Contact* No 106 December 1988.
   This highlights the key issues.
   Available from: Christian Medical Commission. See Appendix E.
5. *Role of Community Participation in Primary Health Care Programmes*. R. S. Arole. Undated paper.
   An exposition by a famous pioneer of community participation.
   Available from: CRHP, Jamkhed, Dist. Ahmednagar, Maharashtra, India.
6. *Training for Transformation*. A. Hope, S. Timmel. The Mambo Press.
   The 'How to' of community participation.
   Available from: PO Box 779. Gweru, Zimbabwe.
7. *Community Involvement in Health Development*. P. Oakley. WHO, 1989.
   This describes current thinking and gives many practical examples.
   Available from: WHO. See Appendix E.
8. 'Community Participation in Research and Action against Alcoholism.' A. and R. Bang. *World Health Forum* **12**: 104–9, 1991.
   A practical description of how a community reduced alcoholism through joint action.
   Available from: WHO. See Appendix E.

3

Raising Health Awareness

In this chapter we will consider:

1. The importance of raising health awareness
   - Health teaching
   - Creating awareness
2. Choosing an appropriate subject
3. Choosing an appropriate method
4. Making preparations
   - Teachers
   - Methods
   - Equipment
   - The community
5. Methods of raising health awareness
   - Group discussions
   - Personal teaching at the point of need
   - Flashcards and flipcharts
   - Flannelgraphs
   - Stories and songs
   - Role play
   - Drama
   - Puppets
   - Live examples
   - Slides and filmstrips
   - Films
   - Radio, TV and video
   - Other forms of health teaching
6. Evaluating progress

The importance of raising health awareness

We must remember:

In Community Based Health Care, teaching is always a two-way process. As we start teaching others about health, we ourselves must be ready to learn from the community. In doing this our understanding will grow, our attitudes will become more sensitive, and our own lives will be enriched.

Creating health awareness includes health teaching but goes beyond it. We will consider each in turn.

Health teaching

Many health programmes spend most of their time running clinics and curing illnesses. They give health education only if there is time left over. Such an approach will never improve the health of a community.

Health teaching with the active involvement of the people is probably the most important of all community health activities. It must be **top** of our priority list, and should take place on all appropriate occasions, not only in clinics, but in schools, in meetings or whenever community members and health workers come together.

Creating awareness

Health awareness results from effective health teaching.

The purpose of health teaching is not simply to increase people's **knowledge** about health. Even if people **know** more, it may not make any difference to what they actually **do**.

A community may have considerable health knowledge, but not be healthy; people may have heard endless health talks but not have changed incorrect practices. *For example*:

A mother may know she **should** wash her hands before preparing food but will not do so because no one has told her **why** it is necessary. Such a person **knows** but is not **aware**.

A person who has been made aware of a particular problem not only knows and understands it, but **sees the importance of doing something about it**. Such a person will be able to say: 'I know, I

Raising awareness ⟶ Knowledge + Understanding ⟶ Motivation ⟶ Action

© Illustration David Gifford

Figure 3.1

understand, I am motivated, I will take action'. *For example*: Consider a childhood immunisation drive:

- An **unaware** community may bring a few children because they have been told to.
- A **partially aware** community may bring several children because they begin to see its importance.
- A **fully aware** community will not only bring their children but may help to arrange the programme and encourage defaulters. They may even have asked for the programme in the first place.

Before starting to create awareness in the community we will need to start with ourselves and our team members. We may assume they are aware already, but this may not be the case, especially if they have worked only in hospitals or institutions.

Choosing an appropriate subject

Creating awareness is not a once and for all process. It starts with one or two concerns already important to the community, and grows from there.

Often such concerns will be known from discussions with the community or may become clear from the community diagnosis (see Chapter 6 page 65ff).

Creating awareness about a **felt** need is usually quite easy. The people already understand the **problem**, now they must be encouraged to come up with **solutions**.

Creating awareness about a **real**, but often unfelt need takes longer. Although the problem may be obvious to the health team, the community may have no understanding of how important it is. *For example*: Consider the case of hidden malnutrition in children. Although the health team know the children are below the Road to Health and therefore more likely to die from childhood illnesses, they may look normal to members of the community, who will fail to understand the extra risks such children face.

Choosing an appropriate method

There are many ways of teaching and creating awareness, see 'Methods of raising health awareness' on page 27. We should learn to use one or two effectively, rather than trying to master them all. Any method chosen should be:

1. Appropriate to the **local culture**
   For example: Story-telling or singing may be part of the local tradition. If so we can use these in our teaching.
   Equally we should **avoid** methods which are strange to the local people or which cause of-

CONGRATULATIONS ON PASSING YOUR EXAMS AND WELCOME TO THE PROJECT. NOW THE FIRST NEW VILLAGE WE PLAN TO WORK IN IS 5 Km FROM THE NEAREST ROAD. PLEASE PUT UP YOUR HAND IF YOU WOULD BE WILLING TO ACT AS SUPERVISOR IN THAT COMMUNITY

© Illustration David Gifford

Figure 3.2   In community based health care, knowledge without enthusiasm has little value

fence or give the wrong message.

For example: Television or videos may be an interesting way to provide health teaching, and may even be appropriate in those areas where families have access to them. However in poor communities where few can afford them, the excitement of the media may drown out the message.

> After watching a TV programme on preparation for birth, instead of queuing up for the next pre-natal clinic, community members may be consulting the local money lenders about raising credit to buy their own TV set.

2. Appropriate to the **subject** we are teaching about
   For example: 'How to overcome drunkenness' is well shown by drama or through puppets. Teaching is enjoyable, the audience feels involved and the message is clear.
   For example: The use of oral rehydration solution is best shown by encouraging a mother to **make it herself** in the home or clinic, then feeding it to her child, and seeing its effect.
3. Appropriate to the level of **education**
   For example: Nurses and doctors may learn from lectures, but others become quickly bored and learn very little. Role play, health games or

other action-based learning is more appropriate especially for those with little education or who have difficulty in reading and writing.

4. Appropriate to the **gifts** of the people
   If there is a natural actor, teacher or story-teller that person's gifts should be used.
5. Appropriate to the **resources** of the project and community
   For example: Some projects consider that using films is an appropriate way of teaching. However they should only start doing this if they have the money, resources, spare parts, fuel and expertise to make it successful.

> Try and use teaching methods which depend more on the gifts of community members than on the resources of the project.

Making preparations

Teaching and creating awareness will only be successful if we are well organised beforehand. We will need to prepare: teachers, materials, equipment and the community itself.

Teachers

This is obviously important if we are presenting a drama or puppet show, but it is equally necessary in leading a discussion or giving a talk with flashcards.

Team members should practise their skills in the classroom in front of each other before 'trying them out' on the community. Above all they must learn to teach in a way that involves the community. Training of Trainers courses (TOTs) can help in this.

Materials

Teaching materials need to be both **chosen** and **prepared** with care.

In **choosing** flashcards or pictures as visual aids remember that many rural people are 'pictorially illiterate'. In other words they may not understand a picture's message even if it seems obvious to us.

Visual aids are best **prepared** by local people. For example we can try and find a community artist to draw flashcards and make posters.

Equipment

Any special equipment such as projectors, genera-

Figure 3.3 Make sure that people understand your pictures

tors or even props for a drama need to be well-organised and checked carefully beforehand.

Make sure that everything **works** and that equipment is **complete**. Make a check list of everything needed and read it through before setting out. Slide shows loose their message when the pictures are upside down and films don't impress the audience when the generator runs out of fuel half-way through the performance.

The community

We should aim to plan all health-teaching activities with the community, encouraging them to choose subjects, organise the programme and gather the people.

> Much energy, time and money has been wasted by the arrival of well-prepared health teams to distant communities whose members were unaware of where, when and why the health team were coming.

Methods of raising health awareness

Group discussions

This activity is carried out in full partnership with the community. Team members can act as facilitators to enable community members both to share problems and suggest solutions.

Practical guidelines:

1. Six to 12 people **gather** together in a circle.
2. A suitable **subject** to suggested – preferably a felt need of the people.
3. **Guidance** is given by the facilitator who takes care never to dominate the discussion, and who makes sure that each person has a chance to speak, especially quieter members.
4. Good ideas are **encouraged** and useful suggestions discussed.
5. People are **helped** to think for themselves. This can be encouraged by asking Who? What? Where? Why? and How? questions.
6. The discussion is **closed** by selecting one or two important points for further discussion and possible action later.

7. **Further meetings** can be arranged for any community members with a special interest in health or development or who show leadership qualities. They themselves can be trained as facilitators who in turn help to extend health awareness in the community.

Discussion groups can also be adapted to a variety of special-need groups such as heavy smokers, TB patients and those at risk from HIV infection.

We must remember:

> Health team members need training in how to lead discussion groups. They must learn how to facilitate and not dominate.

Personal teaching at the point of need

This takes place whenever a community member and health worker get together. The setting may be a clinic or a home, a village path, a city street, a local market, or during a community survey.

People listen best when they have a problem

Figure 3.4 Creating awareness through group discussion

and want to find an answer.

For example: A mother comes to the clinic. She is worried about her child, now dehydrated from 3 days of diarrhoea. She listens and responds to the health worker as he talks **individually** to her about the **immediate problem**.

Such teaching will be more effective than group talks at other times when children are well and mothers less concerned.

Practical guidelines:

1. Make this type of teaching a **priority**.
2. **Congratulate** the patient or mother on any good health practice she has carried out, and build on that.
3. **Talk** in simple, non-medical language to the patient, making sure she understands.
4. **Ask** her to repeat back the main point which has been explained to her.
   In the case of a clinic:
5. Leave the door open so other mothers nearby can 'learn by overhearing'.
6. Teach by repetition. A good example of this is the use of 'Health drills' see Chapter 8.

Flashcards and flipcharts

These are simple and effective ways of teaching but in order to work well have to be used correctly.

Practical guidelines:

Before using them make sure:

1. The message is **relevant** to the audience on the occasion it is being used. *For example*: In an MCH clinic show cards on conditions or problems being seen in the clinic on **that** day.
2. The pictures and script are easily **understood**.

> Use illustrations, ideas and words familiar to the people being taught, and not from another country, tribe or district.

3. The cards are **in the right order**. Check them through and practise holding them and telling the story beforehand.

While using them:

1. **Know** the subject and talk without reading.
2. **Involve** the audience.
   Ask questions, make jokes, and refer to recent events in the community such as a death

from diarrhoea, an injury from drunkenness or a measles epidemic.

After using them:

1. Develop a **discussion**.
2. Invite someone from the audience to **retell the story** or show the flashcards.
3. **Stop** before the people become bored, tired, too hot or too cold.

Flannelgraphs

A flannelgraph consists of two parts:

1. A **board** covered in cloth or flannel and mounted in a frame.
2. **Cut outs** of people and objects, backed with cloth which adhere to the board and can be moved about to develop a health-message.

Ready-made flannelgraphs with story ideas can be bought. Better still the project and community can make their own.

Before using a flannelgraph good health stories must be prepared and practised, using the cut-outs.

© Illustration David Gifford

Figure 3.5

Otherwise follow guidelines for flashcards and flipcharts above.

Stories and songs

These are excellent ways of teaching health especially in communities where story-telling and singing are part of the culture.

> One reason why stories are popular is because they use people, places and events which are familiar and often much loved by the people. Health teaching can be woven into traditional stories or folk-epics or new stories made up using familiar characters and settings.

Practical guidelines:

1. **Select** or **write** a story which tells an important health message. Better still help a community member to write a story.
2. **Tell** the story to everyone gathered, for example to the CHW class.
3. **Divide** people into small groups of four to six and get members to retell the story to their group.
4. **Encourage** groups to act out the story as a drama, now or on another occasion.
5. **Weave** some true event into the story which has happened in the community – either a bad event as a warning, a good event as an example, or an amusing one to help the people remember.
6. **Discuss** issues raised by the story.
7. **Songs** help to remind people of important health messages and can quickly be learnt by others. Set them to catchy or popular tunes. Encourage local people, such as CHWs, to make up their own words. Write a special song to mark an important event. Organise a competition between individuals or villages for the best health song, and arrange a cultural evening to hear and judge them.

Role play

This is a simple form of drama where two people take on the roles of other people and act them out. *For example*: a health worker talks to a TB patient, a CHW talks to a pregnant woman, or a money-lender talks to a poor villager.

> The main value of role play is to help those actually performing it to know **how it feels** to be the people they portray.

Practical guidelines:

1. **Make sure** the members of the group already know and trust each other.
2. **Choose** simple subjects and divide people into twos or threes. If groups of three are used members take turns to observe the two doing the role play, make comments, then later feed back ideas to the class.
3. Give simple **guidelines** to each couple and a few minutes for them to plan.
4. **Allow** each pair 5 to 10 minutes.

BEFORE

AFTER

Taking part in role playing and people's theater helps the 'voiceless poor' gain confidence, courage, and skill to speak their thoughts.

Figure 3.6

5. **Discuss** together at the end ideas and feelings which have been raised.

Role play is often enjoyed most by the more outgoing members of a group. Don't force people to take part unless they wish to.

Drama

> Drama is one of the best ways of all both to teach and to create awareness. It is fun, everyone feels involved and people can relate both to the characters and the things being said.

Short, simple dramas can be used in many situations such as CHW teaching lessons, community meetings, market places, school health lessons, or CHW box-giving ceremonies.

Longer dramas can be used during festivals or at special meetings.

Practical guidelines:

1. **Choose** an appropriate theme.

2. **Prepare** and **practise**, using a script if necessary and leaving plenty of space for improvisation.
3. **Start** by using health team members as main characters. Later involve community members also.
4. **Choose a site** which has enough space both for actors and audience.
5. Make sure the audience can **see** properly. Hang lights blacked out towards the front, but shining on players.
6. Make sure the audience can **hear** properly. Actors must speak out and look forwards. Before starting ask someone to sit at the back to make sure the play can easily be heard.
7. **Use** only simple props and costumes. *For example*: Dress a rich man in a tea shirt marked with a dollar sign, a poor man in rags, a crook can carry a toy gun, a health worker a stethoscope.

Consider dressing up some of the characters as animals: this is nearly always popular.

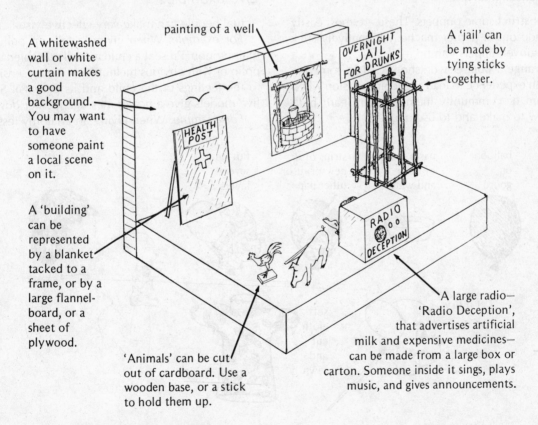

A whitewashed wall or white curtain makes a good background. You may want to have someone paint a local scene on it.

A 'building' can be represented by a blanket tacked to a frame, or by a large flannelboard, or a sheet of plywood.

painting of a well

OVERNIGHT JAIL FOR DRUNKS

A 'jail' can be made by tying sticks together.

HEALTH POST

RADIO DECEPTION

'Animals' can be cut out of cardboard. Use a wooden base, or a stick to hold them up.

A large radio— 'Radio Deception', that advertises artificial milk and expensive medicines— can be made from a large box or carton. Someone inside it sings, plays music, and gives announcements.

Figure 3.7 Props add a sense of reality to a play

8. **Write** explanations and scene descriptions on a piece of cardboard. Hold this up between acts to explain what is going on and where the action is taking place.
9. **Mix** the serious with the funny. *For example*: After an important health or social statement everyone can nod and look wise. After a wrong idea is given other actors can boo or hiss.
10. **Include** songs and teach them to the audience especially any with a useful health message.
11. **Develop** a discussion after the drama is over, or on another occasion to consider the issues raised or to plan community action.
12. **Plan** to repeat the play or perform it in another community if it proves popular.

Puppets

Puppets, like drama, are enjoyable and involve the audience. They can say almost anything, even strong and important points, without offending people.

Practical guidelines:

1. **Construct** some puppets. These are most easily made out of papier mache. Alternatively stick or glove puppets can be made.
2. **Arrange** a puppet workshop. Call in someone with experience to lead a teaching session when team or community members can learn both how to make and to use puppets.

3. **Prepare** and **practise** a story outline leaving plenty of scope for adding in funny or topical extra lines.
4. **Erect** a screen the right height. This can conveniently be a cloth stretched between two poles. The screen should completely hide the people holding the puppets.
5. **Puppets** should **face** the audience, opening their mouths, nodding their heads or making some movement when they speak.
6. A different **voice** should be used for each puppet.
7. Puppets should have **exaggerated** actions and characteristics, for example laughs should be loud, tempers should be bad, noses should be long.
8. **Silences** should be avoided.
9. Puppets can **ask questions** to the audience and encourage them to join in. They can lead a discussion afterwards.

Live examples

Actual people can make very effective visual aids.

For example: When giving a talk on polio or malnutrition: Present a child actually disabled with polio or with obvious malnutrition (being sensitive to the feelings of the child and its parents). Such live models give a health message greater power.

For example: When giving an anatomy lesson:

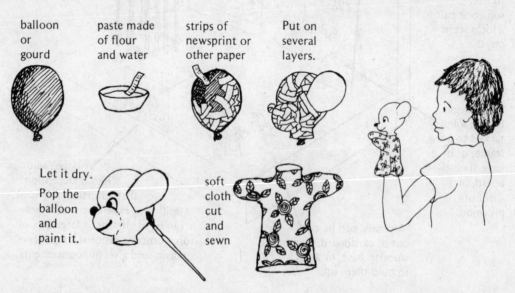

balloon or gourd — paste made of flour and water — strips of newsprint or other paper — Put on several layers.

Let it dry. Pop the balloon and paint it. — soft cloth cut and sewn

Figure 3.8   Making hand puppets out of papier mache

LOOK THAT'S OUR HEALTH WORKER MARI

YES AND THAT'S MY BUFFALO

© Illustration David Gifford

Figure 3.9   Teaching slides taken 'on location' always arouse great interest

Use a young man on which to draw the outlines of organs such as heart, lungs and liver. This will be of greater interest than simply using a chalkboard.

Slides and filmstrips

Although requiring more equipment this is a good way to teach and create interest. People enjoy seeing photos.

Practical guidelines:

1. **Collect** together good-quality, relevant slides. Many different sets of health slides and film strips can be bought. However they may not be appropriate for the project area, and may not cover the exact subject we want to teach (see Appendix A).

Some projects make their own sets of slides. This can be done as follows:
   - **Choose** a pair of health workers in the team with an interest and gift at photography.
   - **Decide** together on the title(s) of the slide sequence to be made. Suitable subjects might be 'Immunise your child'; 'What happens in an MCH clinic'; 'A day in the life of a community health worker.'
   - **List** the subjects and situations for which photographs are needed.
   - **Encourage** the photographers to take **action** and **close-up shots** in the project area.

Each slide should be of a **specific** subject or making a **particular** point. Several slides should be taken of each topic as probably fewer than one in five will be good enough to use.

2. **Link** slides into a teaching sequence. Aim to put about 30 slides together. Each should be clearly numbered, labelled and marked for the correct way of loading into the projector.
3. **Practise** giving the slide show to develop a good technique.
4. **Show** the slides to the audience, using each slide as a discussion starter:
   For example, we could ask:
   - What does this picture show?
   - What is the picture trying to teach us?
   - How could we do this in our community?

Before giving a slide show we should:

1. **Practise** showing the sequence, making sure the slides are in the **right order** and prepared the **right way up**.
2. **Check** the equipment is working and that nothing is left behind. Include a spare bulb.
3. **Visit** the meeting place beforehand, working out how the equipment will be set up and planning a power supply.

If used wrongly slide shows become sleepy entertainment. If used correctly they can arouse much interest and motivate the audience. Their success depends on the skill and enthusiasm of the teacher, and how much the people are involved in dialogue and discussion.

Films

These are good for entertainment but not always good for teaching. People usually go to films for enjoyment, not for learning, unless they understand beforehand the reason they are seeing the film.

One **value** of films is to introduce new ideas on health and development, and show people how others have found solutions to common health problems.

One major **problem** of films is expense and transport. We need to have reliable equipment, a skilled projectionist and plenty of patience. Many health workers have memories of awkward moments trying to mend equipment in front of impatient audiences on dark nights.

Radio, TV and Video

If these are already widely used in the project area then adapt them for health purposes.

Practical guidelines:

1. **Publicise** the times of any regular health-related TV or radio programmes.
2. **Encourage** people to watch in groups.
3. **Arrange** discussions on issues raised either immediately afterwards or within a few days.
4. **Participate** by:
   - Writing to the producer with ideas, questions and suggestions.
   - Sending in a health story or health song.
   - Entering any publicised health competitions.
   - Submitting a health script for radio or making a health video.

Other forms of health teaching

Posters

Buy or encourage the community to design posters with a simple bold text and colourful pictures. Film stars or folk heroes, preferably making an appropriate health quote, are ideal subjects. Place in public places where people wait or stand around such as clinic waiting areas, bus-stops or in the community shop or meeting place.

Calendars

The community can design or buy these, writing in appropriate health texts and making illustrations. They can be placed on the walls of houses where family members will see them every day, and gradually absorb their message. Children can compete in a poster-drawing or calendar-making competition and the best ones can be displayed.

Printed leaflets and handbills

These should be short, well-laid out, easy to read, with catchy illustrations. Comic strips can be used for teaching children (and adults). Leaflets are to remind people of something they have been taught about previously, such as how to make home-made oral rehydration solution (ORS).

Lecturing

Useful for more educated audiences. Maximum time 1 hour. Divide time into thirds – 20 minutes for teaching, 20 minutes for group discussion, 20 minutes for feedback. Alternatively split into two – 30 minutes for teaching, 30 minutes for questions.

Use of chalkboards and overhead projectors

Good for giving a summary of what is being taught. Also helpful in developing a theme where the audience takes part, such as in the use of spider charts (see Chapter 11 p. 162).

Health quizzes and health games

Divide the health team, CHWs or other group into two or more teams. Set carefully worded questions and have a good question-master. Give a prize at the end. This can be enjoyable and is a good way of revising a subject or of testing knowledge. A variety of games can be used or devised by the team or community.

Figure 3.10

Brains trusts

Those with expert knowledge answer questions. Questions are written out before but can also be asked 'from the floor'.

Books and journals

These are helpful for private study and useful for teachers in preparing lessons. Consider setting up a simple project library and show people suitable books and articles to read. The person in charge can mark helpful articles as they arrive with different symbols for levels of difficulty and subject matter and these can be listed out on a noticeboard.

Visits to seminars, conferences and other projects

Arrange for project members, CHWs or community leaders to attend seminars appropriate to their level and interest. Arrange visits to appropriate projects to stimulate interest and generate new ideas.

Finally we can devise our own methods of teaching. Some of the best ways may yet to be discovered.

Evaluating progress

It is helpful to know if our health teaching is effective. Here are some simple ways of finding out:

1. **Talk** with the community.
   We will soon get ideas and suggestions about ways we can improve our methods.
2. Make a **questionnaire**.
   This is good for evaluating CHW teaching or at the end of special courses for health workers.

Ask which sessions or subjects were found to be the most interesting and most important. Discover which forms of teaching were the most enjoyable or helpful. Ask participants to grade their answers from 1 to 5 – 1 being the worst, 5 the best.
Request written suggestions about how teaching could be improved.
If questionnaires are kept unnamed more reliable answers may be given.
3. Set an **examination**.
   This will test how much people have understood, and how much they remember. It tells little about how much knowledge is being put into practice.
4. **Assess progress** in the community.

> The best way of evaluating our teaching will be the participation, enthusiasm and progress both of the health team and the community. Good teaching eventually leads to good statistics.

Summary

Creating health awareness includes teaching but extends beyond it. It is a two-way process in which the community learns about better health practices and the health team comes to appreciate the richness and value of community life.

Before carrying out health activities both team and community members need to be well prepared. They must receive basic health teaching to increase their knowledge, and have their awareness raised to improve motivation.

Communities should be helped to understand about one major issue at a time, using a method that is appropriate both to their culture and to the subject being taught. Many methods are used but the best ones actively involve the community. These include group discussions, the use of story-telling, song, drama and puppets. Slides, films, radio and TV have a growing part to play.

Feedback on the success of health education programmes can be obtained through discussions with the community and by questionnaires. The real mark of success is a healthier community which follows correct health practices.

Further Reading

1. *Health Care Together.* M. Johnstone, S. Rifkin. Macmillan, 1987. Training exercises for health workers in communication.
   Available from: TALC. See Appendix E.
2. *Helping Health Workers Learn.* D. Werner, B. Bower. Hesperian Foundation, 1982.
   This is an outstanding book with practical and valuable information on all aspects of health teaching.
   Available from: TALC. See Appendix E.
3. *Teaching Health Care Workers.* F. Abbatt, R. McMahon. Macmillan, 1985.
   Available from: TALC. See Appendix E.

4. *The Church Health Educator.* I. H. Stober and B. H. Wecker. Macmillan, 1989.
   Available from: Macmillan. See Appendix E.
5. *Education for Health: A Manual on Health Education in Primary Health Care.* WHO, 1988.
   Available from: WHO. See Appendix E.
6. *Facts for Life: A Communication Challenge.* UNICEF/WHO/UNESCO, 1990.
   Vital messages which all community members should know. This book is strongly recommended for all health projects.
   Available from: UNICEF, DIPA, Facts for Life Unit, 3 UN Plaza, New York, NY 10017, USA.
   A resource book on the above known as 'All for Health' is published by UNICEF.
   Available from: TALC. See Appendix E.

Slides

The following teaching slide sets are also available from TALC:

- Communication in Health   Cm
- HIV Infection – Prevention and Health education   HIVe
- A community workers newsletter   NwL

A full list of other slides, all useful for teaching health workers, is available from TALC.

Part II
STARTING A PROGRAMME

4

Initial Tasks

In Community Based Health Care (CBHC), we are helping communities identify and solve their own health problems. In some cases this means setting up health services where nothing appropriate exists. In others it involves developing health services from an existing hospital or health centre at the request of the community.

In order to be effective 'facilitators' we need to be efficient and well organised. This chapter explains the first steps we can take in responding to the needs of a community. The following chapter describes ways in which we can meet the community to set up a working partnership.

There are five 'starter topics' we now need to consider:

1. Choosing a community to work with
2. Choosing a team
3. Obtaining funds
4. Setting up base
5. Ordering supplies

Choosing a community to work with

We should answer these questions:

1. Has the community **requested our help**?
   If the answer is no we should either choose another community or spend time building relationships with community members.
2. Is the community willing to **work with us as partners**?
   Probably few community members will understand this idea at the beginning. As we mix with people and raise awareness they will move from trying to get things **from** us to a willingness to work in partnership **with** us.
3. Do the **leaders** show genuine interest?
   Signs of a good community leader may include:
   • Concern for the people's welfare, especially

that of the poor.
   • Willingness to plan and work together.
   • A reputation for honesty.
   • Respect in the community.
4. Do the **people** seem united?
   Almost all communities have splits and divisions. If these are serious, follow racial or tribal lines or are very long-standing, it is hard to establish a useful partnership.
5. Is there **serious ill-health** present?
   Ask such questions as:
   • Do the people in general seem healthy or sick?
   • Do many of the children die young?
   • Is there year-round clean water?
   • Is there much disability or blindness?
   We can obtain a general picture by visiting the community and talking to the people, a more accurate answer by a sample survey.
6. Are existing **health services** adequate?
   We may find that government services exist but are little used; that private doctors are present but not serving the poor; that other health programmes or hospitals are at work but offering only curative care.
7. Have we **sufficient resources** to help the community set up its health programme?
   • Can we help them to meet their **felt needs**? These are the illnesses people want cured, and the problems the people want answered.
   • Can we help the community identify and solve **actual causes** of ill health, such as contaminated water, wrong feeding practices, lack of food, heavy drinking, **poverty** and **exploitation**.
   • Is there an existing **referral system**, such as a health centre or hospital, for problems we cannot handle ourselves? If not can we help set one up?
8. Is the target area a **suitable size**?
   If it is too small rapid health improvements may

YES, I WOULD BE VERY PLEASED IF THE PROJECT CAME TO WORK IN MY VILLAGE

THINKS: WILL WE GET FREE HANDOUTS? WILL MY FAMILY BENEFIT? WILL IT WIN ME VOTES IN THE NEXT ELECTION?

© Illustration David Gifford

Figure 4.1

Governments are often unable to provide adequate primary health care at community level. Providing we approach them in a co-operative spirit and outline an appropriate plan they will usually welcome our assistance.

It is estimated that at the present time between 30 and 40 per cent of health services in sub-saharan Africa are provided by voluntary (non-governmental) agencies.

Having decided on a community to work alongside we then need to decide whether to serve **all** the people in the target area or just the **neediest groups** within it.

It is generally better to work with the **entire population** but to give special attention to the poor and those with the greatest health needs. There are a few exceptions:

1. Where there is an obvious group that is deprived or different such as refugees, nomads or the landless.
2. In cities there may be needy sub-groups such as beggars, addicts or scavengers.
3. With particular diseases such as TB, leprosy or AIDS, there may be value in targeting special care.

Choosing a team

> The success of a project depends more on the quality of the team than on any other single factor. We should be wise and careful in selection, being prepared to wait for appropriate people.

Who should be selected?

Answer: those best able to respond to the help which the community has asked for.

More specifically this will include:

Those with the right qualities

1. **A real interest** in the job, not just the money.
   Field workers will often work long and hard hours. They are more likely to continue in the project if they possess vision and enthusiasm.
2. A willingness **to learn**.
   It is better to have someone who knows little

occur, but the project will not be cost-effective.

> If the communities we serve are too large we may get swamped with urgent problems and be unable to help the people bring about lasting health improvements.

We should usually confine our work to a single Health District.

9. Does the **government approve** the project plans?
   If our project is not already working closely with the government we will need to contact the District Medical Officer (DMO) and find out:
   - If the government is already doing primary care in the area.
   - If the DMO approves of our plans, feels able to work in partnership or is willing to draw up a written agreement.

but wants to know more than someone who believes he knows everything. **This is especially true of people who have been working in institutions**. They will need careful retraining and re-orientation into the very different world of community health.

3. A readiness to **take on any job**.
A community health worker must be ready to do any task he is asked to do. This includes everything from using clinical skills to cleaning up blood and faeces. No task should be above anyone or below anyone.
A health worker also needs to take initiative and do what needs to be done without always being told.

4. A respect and **appreciation for the poor**.
Many religious teachers have taught special love for the poor. Many of the best health workers are happy to be known as friends of the poor.

5. An ability to **work as part of a team**.
This includes appreciating colleagues from different districts of the country, religions and tribes. It means being slow to become angry and being quick to forgive. Angry words in the community can destroy weeks of work. Hidden anger against a colleague can ruin team relationships.

6. **Good health**.
Strong physical and mental health is important for many jobs. However people with less good health may be given appropriate tasks. This includes those with disability, and where AIDS is common, those who are HIV positive.

Those with the right qualifications.

Generally in community based health care character is more important than qualifications. Most community health skills are best learnt on the job.

In practice non-professional staff have many advantages:

• open minds with which to learn new skills,
• greater closeness to the people,
• a greater willingness to adapt.

Most projects however, will need one or two health professionals. These might include:

THINKS
MUST CHANGE THE WRONG IDEAS OF THESE DIRTY PEOPLE. MUST GET A FIRST CLASS X-RAY MACHINE, SHOULD START A PROPER HOSPITAL, WILL GET SOME MODERN MEDICINES AND INJECTIONS — MAY BE SOME CHANCE TO MAKE A GOOD PROFIT

THINKS
I REALLY WANT TO LEARN HOW TO SERVE THIS COMMUNITY, I THINK TEACHING WILL BE MORE IMPORTANT THAN GIVING LOTS OF MEDICINES, I WONDER WHY MANY OF THE CHILDREN ARE SO THIN, I MUST LEARN THE BEST WAY OF TREATING COMMON ILLNESSES

© Illustration David Gifford

Figure 4.2

A doctor

He can act as adviser, facilitator, teacher and part-time clinician. Many community health programmes work best **with doctors as members rather than directors**.

Any doctor recruited should have experience or interest in community health. Without this there is a danger he will 'hijack' the project, changing it into a curative programme for his own advantage.

A nurse (or medical assistant)

She will be involved in running clinics and giving health teaching. Experience in community health is an advantage. Older nurses who have spent years in hospital often fail to make good nurses in the community.

Where can suitable team members be found?

Here are some possible sources:

1. The local community.
   In genuine CBHC the majority of team members are drawn from the local community. As we mix with the people we can look out for appropriate people.
2. Networks.
   Through networks of friends and contacts suitable workers may be found from a wider area.
3. Training schools and institutions.
4. Voluntary health associations or religious bodies.
5. Transfers from hospitals, sister projects or government programmes, but **only after careful assessment**.
6. Through advertisements in papers and journals. This often attracts inappropriate people merely interested in having employment.

How should team members be selected?

By personal recommendation

These should be from reliable sources. Relatives' comments should be treated with caution.

By interview

Many people seem attractive and talk well at inter-views. It is therefore better to spend time with applicants individually and informally.

By a trial period

This is very useful for non-professional staff. Invite the applicant to spend a week or even a month in the project where he can join in all activities. Assess how he gets on with others and relates to the community.

Situations that require caution

Employing relatives

Existing team members may ask if their relatives can be employed in the project. This is usually unwise. Often such relatives can't get work anywhere else, especially if there is local unemployment. Sometimes two or more members of one family in a project may exert too much influence and cause division in the team.

MEET MY WIFE, THE PROJECT NURSE, MY BROTHER, OUR ACCOUNTANT, MY NEPHEW, OUR LAB. TECHNICIAN AND JUST JOINED TODAY MY WIFE'S COUSIN

INAPPROPRIATE!

© Illustration David Gifford

Figure 4.3

Overloading with members of one tribe or district

This can destroy a team's unity and cause suspicion among the community, especially if most team members are from outside the target area.

Unmarried girls

Any young, single women in the team will need safe working and living conditions. In some countries it is not appropriate to employ them and in others they will need to work in a group or in the company of older married women.

Obtaining funds

Setting up a project is difficult and expensive. It takes many years. It is better not to start at all than to start, then run out of funds and have to stop. The developing world is full of projects that have been abandoned and people whose hopes have been disappointed.

Before making promises and raising hopes plan well ahead and work out how much funding will be needed. This can only be approximate. Our plans will be liable to change as we respond to the needs of the people.

We must make sure that programmes we help to set up can be **sustained** for a number of years ahead.

In obtaining funds we will first **choose** the **source** and secondly **make an application**.

Choosing the source

Before writing off to foreign donors identify sources of funds **within the community** and **within the country**.

It may at least be possible to raise sufficient money to start the project or to cover a proportion of the costs. Foreign funds will not last for ever and from the very beginning the project must aim to become self-sustaining, though this may be hard to achieve in practice (see also page 92).

Main sources of funding include:

Sources within the project itself

Patient fees

One useful source is the fees patients pay for curative services, though this will only amount to a small proportion of the total project budget. 'Revolving drug funds' are an effective way of bringing this about (see page 120). We should aim to get back the full cost of medicines, making sure that the poor are never turned away and are not charged more than they can actually afford.

We may be able to set higher charges for the rich or charge extra for procedures such as deliveries, minor operations and tooth pulling. We can charge higher rates to patients coming from outside the target area (see pages 115–16).

Insurance schemes and income generation

These are relatively difficult to set up but may be possible later (see page 92).

The base hospital

If the project is run by a hospital some funds may be available. If the hospital has a high reputation, funds can flow in from private patients. In practice most hospitals are seriously short of funds and have little to give towards community health care (see page 269).

Local organisations

Try any appropriate sources – churches, temples, mosques, co-operatives, Rotary and Lions clubs, charities, local business associations, the 'generous rich'.

The government – district, state or national

Funds are often available in theory, especially if working in co-operation with the government. However such sources may be unreliable or may have 'strings' attached. In addition to funding, certain supplies may be available, such as immunisations and TB drugs. In many of the poorest countries, government health services have no funds available.

Sources outside the country

Before trying to obtain foreign funds, we must understand the laws concerning foreign contri-

Wise Funding Inc.
Bigtown
Anystate, USA
21 January 1992

Dear Doctor

Thank you for the funding application which you sent on behalf of your organisation, "Cure all People" (CAP).

Although we do have funding available it is our policy only to release this if we have an assurance that all local and national sources have been tried first. We also require outline plans of how your project plans to achieve financial self sufficiency. Kindly therefore . . .

Figure 4.4

butions. Special registration is usually necessary. Sources may include:

Voluntary funding agencies

There are a large number of agencies holding funds to support projects in developing countries. These include missions, aid agencies and other groups, both religious and secular. Most are based in developed countries especially Europe, North America and Australasia. Such groups are often willing to support smaller-scale health and development projects. Lists can be obtained from national or voluntary health associations, and from embassies.

International aid agencies

These include the United Nations Agencies such as WHO, UNICEF, UNDP, but they only rarely support voluntary health programmes. The Euro-

pean Community (EC) has funds available for certain types of project.

Foreign government aid programmes and embassies

Large sums may be available but normally a national of that country needs to be connected with the project. Many voluntary funding agencies receive 1 to 1 matching grants (called co-funding) from their own governments so making more money available.

Before applying for foreign funds we must be aware of possible **disadvantages**:

Dependence

If foreign funds are available community members may expect handouts. They may be less ready to contribute their own time, money and resources

Dependency, suspicion, separation from people as foreign funding increases

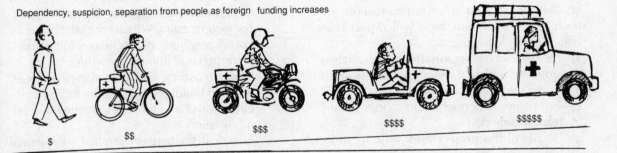

$ $$ $$$ $$$$ $$$$$

© Illustration David Gifford

Figure 4.5 The effect of increased foreign funding

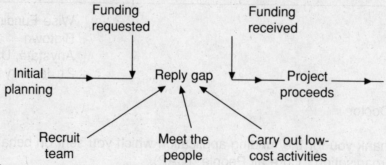

Figure 4.6   The reply gap

if they see foreign jeeps or receive foreign medicines.

Suspicion

In some countries rumours may spread that foreigners attached to projects may be involved in illegal activities or spying.

Applying for funds

Remember that funding takes time. We must start applying just as soon as our plans begin to take shape. In the case of government or foreign funds it may take 6 to 12 months or more before funds are actually received. Follow this procedure:

1. **Write** to the funding source as soon as possible. Include a brief personal introduction and ask for an application form. This is best done through a mutual contact or by asking someone with influence to write in support of the application. Make three copies of the letter. Keep one and send the others to the agency, posted on different dates and from different places because postal services are often unreliable.
2. **Prepare** the material the agency will require. While waiting gather material. Although different agencies request different information and each has its own form, most will expect brief details of the following:
   a) The name of the **organisation** and any larger group to which it belongs: the director's name: the project address.
   b) The names and brief qualifications of any **team members**.
   c) Details of the **project area** – its location, terrain and climate.
   d) Details of the **target population**:
      • Number (approx) of people and villages

or slum colonies to be served.
      • Social structure of the communities, including details of local employment, relative wealth, poor or neglected subgroups etc.
      • Religious makeup of the population.
   e) Details of the **people's health**:
      • Present services available – both government and private.
      • Serious illnesses and health problems present.
   f) Details of the **programme**:
      • Aims and objectives.
      • How these will be achieved.
   Try and give an approximate framework. Details will be worked out later with the community. Mention any surveys planned, and any clinics, teaching or other programmes likely to be carried out.
   g) Relationship with **government**:
      • Details of planned co-operation.
      • Whether written permission has been obtained.
   h) **Budget**:
   Give details of planned income and expenditure. Include detailed budget for 1 year, and an approximate budget for two further years. For income estimate total from other sources. For expenditure divide into capital (non-recurring) and annual (recurring).
   Under recurring include: salaries, services, rent and buildings, supplies including medicines, travel and transport, training and administration.
   Include in the budget items that are essential but do not ask for expensive or unnecessary equipment.
   Other information may be requested, such as

the latest report and accounts of the parent organisation, photographs of the area and people, results of a sample population survey etc.

3. **Maintaining contact** with the agency.

   Having received funds we maintain close and friendly links with the sponsoring organisation:

   a) Write a letter of acknowledgement and thanks.

   b) Send in, on time, any regular reports, budgets or other information requested.

   c) Welcome any visitors from the funding agency.

Setting up base

No project will succeed unless it has a well-organised project base. Before starting a field programme we will need to carry out the following:

Arranging accommodation for team members

This should be adequately equipped, within the project area, appropriate to the worker's level, and available until the member leaves the project.

Draw up an agreement with each worker which includes length of tenure, list of items supplied with the accommodation, details of rent and other charges such as fuel, water and electricity. These should be discussed, agreed, written down and signed by both parties.

In practice team members often live together on a campus or compound. This may be convenient but where team members share work, leisure, worship and accommodation, relationships can easily become strained.

Setting up office and stores

This should ideally be done in close partnership with the community and in the community area. Nothing big or expensive is needed; the simpler this is kept the better. Often three or four rooms will be enough to start with – one for the office, one for the stores, one for meeting, and one for sterilising equipment.

The storeroom will be used for keeping both drugs and equipment. Make sure that this is:

- secure so that people cannot break in,
- dry even during the rainy season,
- large enough and well enough lit for convenience,
- accessible by vehicle for easy loading and
- rat-proof and bat-proof.

© Illustration David Gifford

Figure 4.7 The project storerooms should be well sited and well protected

Ordering supplies

Details on receiving, storing and issuing supplies are found on pages 112 and 254. At this stage we will simply consider what supplies and drugs need to be ordered.

Ordering equipment

1. **List** out what supplies are required (see Appendix B):
   a) Include all items that are **really** necessary.
   b) Decide on what **type** and what **number** of items are needed.
   c) Discuss this list with the leaders of other projects or anyone with suitable experience.
2. **Identify sources** where supplies can be obtained.
   a) Buy locally wherever possible.
   b) For each type of equipment compare **prices** and **quality** of different suppliers.
   c) Build a relationship with the main suppliers. Try and arrange discount prices.
   d) Find an alternative supplier for important items in case the main supplier runs out of stock.
   e) Order supplies **in plenty of time**. There is often a long delay between ordering and receiving.
   f) Avoid poor quality products even if alternatives are more expensive.

   > Only obtain equipment from abroad if supplies are not available or manufactured within the country.

3. Carefully **check** all supplies on arrival, making sure they are complete and intact. See Appendix A for a list of foreign suppliers. See Appendix B for a list of essential supplies.
4. Two **special** pieces of equipment.
   a) A refrigerator. Thousands of people have died worldwide because **vaccines were not kept cold**.
      Buy a good quality fridge in good working order that runs on a power supply or type of fuel which is **locally** available and **always** obtainable.
      Electricity that goes off for 1 or 2 hours may be acceptable but if power failures last longer buy a generator or use a fridge which runs

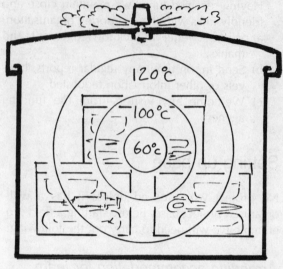

WELL I THINK THOSE INSTRUMENTS WILL BE READY NOW!

120°C
100°C
60°C

© Illustration David Gifford

Figure 4.8   Take care that sterilisation is effective

on kerosene.
   b) A steriliser. Thousands of people die worldwide because of needles and syringes that have not been **adequately sterilised**. AIDS has increased this danger.
      Buy a steam steriliser of suitable size, such as an autoclave or pressure cooker.

Ordering medicines (see also Chapter 16)

1. Decide **which** medicines are needed.
   Together with the project medical adviser draw up a suggested list and then compare it with:
   • the list used by the nearest hospital,
   • the national essential drugs list,
   • the WHO essential drugs list and
   • the suggested list in Appendix C.
   The drugs chosen should be:
   a) Appropriate for the health needs of the area.
   b) Appropriate for the level of health worker who will be using them.
   c) Single component, meaning that in most cases they should contain only a single drug.
   d) Generic, meaning they should be ordered using the scientific, chemical name, and not

the trade name. This saves money and confusion.

e) Good quality. Many bad quality or fake drugs are being made. We should make sure that any drugs used are made by good companies licensed by the government. This can include multinationals. Only use foreign supplies if good quality, essential medicines are not made within the country.

2. Calculate **how much medicine** will be needed. This can be done by working out both the likely number of patients to be seen and by knowing the likely drugs to be prescribed for each.

a) Estimate the likely **number of patients** that may be seen within a 1-year period. One way we can estimate this is by discovering numbers attending clinics in neighbouring projects.

The proportion of a population attending a clinic is extremely variable. An approximate guide for communities with few existing health facilities might be an attendance of between a quarter and a half of the population within the first year for curative care (see also Chapter 8).

b) Estimate the **numbers of each drug** likely to be used per 100 patients seen. To do this look through the records of patients seen in similar clinics or outpatient departments, and list out the **essential** drugs used for each. Total up the numbers of each drug used per

100 patients. Remember that most clinics overprescribe and that patients will only rarely require more than two or three medicines. If there are no such clinics, we can work out from our knowledge of local illnesses, the medicines likely to be needed. Drugs are otherwise ordered and received as with equipment. Expiry dates must be checked.

Ordering a vehicle

> A jeep or ambulance may not be **needed** at the beginning, and may not be **wise** as it suggests a project is wealthy or foreign. For as long as possible we should use local or public transport, a motorbike or foot.

Before ordering a vehicle ask these questions:

1. Are funds available to buy it?
2. Are funds available to maintain it?
3. Are spare parts available to mend it?
4. Is a skilled mechanic available to repair it?
5. Is fuel available to run it?

When **choosing** a vehicle ask these questions:

1. Is it tough enough for the worst roads during the worst weather?
2. Is it large enough to carry project members, community health workers, patients, visitors and

© Illustration David Gifford

Figure 4.9

equipment?

3. Is it suitable for carrying seriously ill patients?
4. Is it cheap to run? In many countries diesel is cheaper than petrol. Some vehicles do many more kilometres per litre than others.
5. Is it dust-proof? Does it start well in cold weather?
6. Is it made in the country and can it be bought locally? Where countries manufacture vehicles, those made within the country are usually more appropriate than foreign models because:
   - They are cheaper to buy.
   - They are cheaper and easier to look after and spare parts may be obtained more easily.
   - They make the project look less foreign.
   - They may be available at a discount for registered charities.
   - There is no need for foreign exchange.

However, locally made vehicles may be less strong or durable than foreign models.

Second hand vehicles should be carefully checked by a skilled mechanic before being bought.

Summary

When a project first receives requests to give help, several activities must be carried out and co-ordinated before field work is actually begun.

This includes selecting an appropriate **commu-nity**, and **selecting** a **suitable team** on which so much of the project's future depends.

Funding needs to be obtained, wherever possible from local and national sources before foreign agencies are approached. The goal of becoming financially self-sufficient should always be kept in mind.

A **base** needs to be established for accommodating team members, for storing supplies and for running the programme. This should be within the target area or as near to it as possible so that the community can be involved in management at an early stage.

Finally a list of **essential equipment** and **drugs** needs to be drawn up and supplies ordered in the correct amount from reliable sources. A refrigerator and steriliser will be needed and at some stage a 4-wheel-drive vehicle will probably become necessary.

Further Reading

1. *Beyond the Dispensary*. R. Shaffer. African Medical and Research Foundation, Undated. 90 pages.
   Useful ideas for starting a programme.
   Obtainable from: AMREF, PO Box 30125, Nairobi Kenya.
2. *Directory of Funding Organizations*. K.K. Kapoor, Information and News Network, Delhi, 1986. 162 pages.

© Illustration David Gifford

Figure 4.10   When choosing a project vehicle consider the worst conditions it may have to encounter

List of international funding agencies, and advice on preparing project proposals.

Obtainable from: INN, 10/142 Gita Colony, Delhi 110031, India.

3. *How to Choose and Make a Cold Box*. A. Battersby. AHRTAG, 1983.

How to Look After a Health Centre Store. A. Battersby. AHRTAG, 1983.

How to Look After a Refrigerator. J. Elford, AHRTAG, 2nd edn 1992.

Useful practical manuals.

Obtainable from: AHRTAG, 1 London Bridge Street, London SE1 9SG, UK.

4. *Management Process in Health Care*. S. Srinavasan. Voluntary Health Association of India, 1982. 517 pages.

Comprehensive and practical manual.

Obtainable from: VHAI. See Appendix E.

5. *On Being in Charge*. R. McMahon, E. Barton, M. Piot. WHO, revised edition 1992.

Definitive manual for project directors and managers.

Obtainable from: WHO. See Appendix E.

6. 'The Pressure Cooker as a Steam Sterilizer.' M. Monson. *Tropical Doctor* **18**: 159–60, 1988.

5

Knowing our Community

In this chapter we will learn about:

1. Preparing ourselves
2. Mixing informally with the community
3. Arranging structured meetings with the community

Preparing ourselves

Many health workers are able to run clinics, give teaching and provide medicines for those who are sick. In CBHC this is not our primary aim. It is **to** bring about lasting changes in the health of the community, and to help the community set up its own programme.

In order to do this we must be prepared to change ourselves. We will need to have both a right **attitude** to the community and a genuine **appreciation** of the community.

A right attitude to the community

We may think we are in some ways superior to those we are serving because we have been to

Figure 5.1 By the year 2000, half the population of developing countries will be living in city communities. The photograph shows Ougadougou, Burkina Faso, on a Friday

WHAT IS THEIR **REAL** REASON FOR COMING TO WORK IN THE VILLAGE

HEALTH TEAM

© Illustration David Gifford

Figure 5.2 After years of exploitation in the past, community members may question the motives of the new health team

school for longer, come from a city rather than a village, or come from a larger tribe or higher caste.

We may tend to look down on some people, even those in our health team, or feel frightened of others, perhaps the team leader or a powerful community member.

We must understand that our attitudes towards others come from different sources, including our homes and parents, our schools and teachers, the people we most admire and the patterns we have seen in our hospitals and training programmes.

As we start to **recognise** the **wrong attitudes** we have towards others, we automatically begin to **adopt** new ones.

A genuine appreciation of the people

As we get to know the people, we start to understand **why** they think and act the way they do. We come to see that although we may be **different** from them we are certainly not **better**.

For example. In many projects team members come to have a deep respect for local women when they see how some, once illiterate and uninformed, now lead their villages as community health workers.

It is helpful to ask ourselves two questions whenever we are tempted to despise someone else. What would that person have achieved if she had been given my opportunities? What would I have achieved if I had suffered her disadvantages?

Mixing informally with the community

As health workers we mix with the people for two reasons: to build trust and friendship and to learn from them.

Trust and friendship

Quite apart from friendship for its own sake we can never act as agents of change unless the community learns to trust both us and our motives. Poor people, after years of being cheated by outsiders, are highly skilled in checking out the latest visitor with his clever promises.

As we make our first visits to a community the people will be asking themselves:

- '**Who** are these people anyway?'
  Are they locals we haven't met before, outsiders, foreigners, government workers, family planning officers, spies?

- '**Why** have they come?'
  Just to do the job they claim, make money out of us, report on us, or because they can't get a better job elsewhere?
- '**What** can **we** get from them?'
  Free handouts, money, a hospital, a resident doctor, tonics for our children, cigarettes, foreign goods, guns?

It is only by mixing with the people that they will learn to **trust us** and we will learn to **appreciate them**.

> This means that at the start of a project, health workers may spend much of their time drinking tea with the villagers, playing with their children or challenging young people at the local sport. This is not time wasted.

Learning from the community

We will learn from the community some of the secrets of living, relating, celebrating or enduring hardship which 'health providers' have often forgotten. As we do this our own lives will be enriched, and the people will realise that we come as **partners and fellow human beings**, not just more outsiders with better ideas than others.

As we start to learn we will spend a lot of time watching, listening and participating. Only when we have earned their trust will we start asking our questions.

There will be plenty of answers to find out including some of the following. Most of these we will learn as we mix, others can be discovered later through the community survey (see Chapter 6).

1. **Family structure**. Marriage customs including age at marriage, whether multiple partners, dowry customs. Authority figures in the family. Attitudes to the elderly, to in-laws and to children. Connections with tribe and extended family.
2. **Social patterns**. Power structures in the community. Leadership, formal and informal. Political, religious and economic groupings in the community. Caste, tribal grouping and its practical results. Ways by which disputes are sorted out. How the community makes a joint decision. Status and what determines it – wealth, land, education or tradition.
3. **Religion**. Beliefs and how they affect life-styles, attitudes to others, to the environment and to health and nutrition. Local and national festivals; how and when they are celebrated.
4. **Daily routines**. Ways in which different members of the family spend their day. How work is divided among family members. School-going among the children and attitudes towards it. Employment patterns of men, women and children.
5. **Relation to nearest city or large town**. Whether used for employment, leisure or crime. Whether young people are leaving or wishing to leave their village or community.
6. **Health-related beliefs and practices**. Traditional beliefs about what (or who) causes and cures illness. Attitudes to traditional healers and remedies, and towards modern medicines and health workers. Whether health needs are considered a priority.

It can be a helpful exercise to give each team member the task of discovering one particular area of knowledge about a community when he spends a day visiting. Information gathered can then be shared and discussed in a team meeting. The team needs to be trained how to enquire about customs without giving offence or causing suspicion.

Whether we watch or we ask we must come to understand the community before we are able to help its members identify their real needs and suggest appropriate solutions.

Listen, → Offer to help, → and then, only after a relationship of trust and friendship has been formed, → Gather information

Figure 5.3

Twelve practical guidelines for when we enter a new community are listed here:

1. Before going we find out first about any custom expected from us as a visitor.
2. On arrival we meet the leaders and explain who we are.
3. We are friendly and open, using the local greeting.
4. We dress appropriately and modestly wearing local-style clothes if possible.
5. We make the differences between ourselves and the people as small as possible, being careful not to show off expensive equipment.
6. We accept hospitality, eating and drinking with the people where possible.
7. We play and joke with the children.
8. We listen and learn, being slow to ask too many questions at the start.
9. We don't make plans or promises which we may not be able to keep.
10. We praise and encourage good customs and practices.
11. We avoid argument or criticism both through our words and through our manner.
12. We don't take sides in any family or village dispute.

Arranging structured meetings with the community

The time soon comes when structured meetings will be necessary. We can suggest these ourselves but it is better if the community takes the initiative.

Any meeting should be at a **time** and **place** convenient for the community.

With whom should we meet?

With community leaders

The elected or **formal** leaders should be present if possible.

Informal leaders can also attend such as teachers, priests or others who have genuine local power or a sense of community welfare.

The **real** leaders may be different again. These are the community members who actually wield power. In practice these are often the rich, the 'bullies' or the upper class. We will need much wisdom in knowing which if any of these should attend. Such people often 'hijack' meetings using them for their own personal ends or to strengthen their power base.

Usually it is better to let the community decide who should attend.

With community members

We should try and encourage the whole community to come along, including women, and members of the poorest sub-group or caste. If this is not possible each household can send a representative. In some societies women will need their own separate meeting.

Often meetings are quite easy to arrange, but in remote or backward communities it may be hard to get people together. We must keep trying. There is no value in a health programme unless the community itself is involved and informed at every stage.

An example: Himalayan projects often have distant and scattered target villages. In one such project the health team were getting discouraged because after many hours driving few villagers came to the meetings.

Figure 5.4

A solution was eventually found. A health film was shown at the beginning to draw and sensitise the people, and a humorous one was shown at the end to encourage them to stay. In the middle a useful dialogue was held with the whole village about the health problems they faced and how they might be solved.

What should we talk about?

Some communities may be ready to lead the meeting themselves and invite us to participate. More often, especially for the first meetings in a community, we will need to be ready with an outline agenda.

In planning the meeting we need to make sure:

1. The meeting is not too long. Farmers who have worked hard all day and drunk beer with their supper will soon fall asleep.
2. The meeting doesn't try to discuss too many things.
3. The meeting doesn't raise hopes which can't be met.
4. There is plenty of chance for people to talk.
5. Someone writes down what is decided. A member of both community and project can take notes.

Above all:

When meeting with the people we must learn from them, question them and welcome their answers and suggestions. We must avoid making long speeches, showing off our knowledge or giving too many of our own ideas.

Following the principles above we can now draft an **agenda** appropriate for each particular situation.

Agendas for the meetings with leaders and with community members may differ. Having first met with the leaders, they may be willing to help, lead, explain and suggest answers when we meet with the community members. It is important however that the leaders are not able to insist on their own way, and that the whole community is involved in discussing and planning.

Here is a suggested **agenda**:

1. **Greetings** and introductions.
   * We **say** how glad we are to be present in their community.
   * We **introduce** team members by name.
   * We **explain** about the local organisation we are from, and why we have come.
2. Discussing **needs**. (Needs and answers will often be expressed together. To help us think clearly about both we will list the two separately on the agenda.)
   * We **listen** for the real needs of the people,

I'M SO GLAD YOU HAVE AGREED TO GIVE US A NEW HOSPITAL, A NEW WATER PUMP AND A VILLAGE AMBULANCE

DID WE SAY THAT?

© Illustration David Gifford

Figure 5.5   Ideas discussed in meetings are often taken as promises by the community

being slow to make suggestions. At this stage the discussion should be free-ranging even if non-health needs are mentioned. We make sure the quieter people have a chance to share their ideas.

- We **steer** the discussion **away** from those needs and answers which are not appropriate. *For example*: The community may suggest needs for which they want expensive equipment or highly trained people. They may list problems for which they will ask for resident doctors and fully equipped hospitals.
- We **steer** the discussion **towards** needs which are suitable for joint action and for which the project has the resources and people to help.
- We **select** one or two needs which are both important and suitable for working on together, and which are likely to lead to early success (see Chapter 2).

3. Exploring **answers**.

After selecting needs we can now discuss answers. We may be tempted at this stage to start planning answers **for** the people, rather than helping the community find its own answers. Sometimes through a question and answer dialogue the community can be encouraged to suggest solutions.

For example: The leaders or community members explain that many of their children die from diarrhoea and from coughs, but the local doctors live too far away and charge too much money.

Figure 5.6

'Could you send a doctor to live in our village?'
'I'm glad you want help looking after your children, and I know you need someone well trained who can care for them when they are ill. Many children living in this area of the country have these problems. Unfortunately there is only one doctor to look after them all. He could only make occasional visits.'
'What use would that be if our children got sick on the days when the doctor wasn't visiting?'
'Not very much! Have you any other ideas of how your children could be cared for?'
'Well, we did hear that in some villages nurses have been teaching village people how they themselves can treat illnesses. Would that work for us?'

It is now possible to take up **their** idea and explain about community health workers. Because they made the suggestion it is more likely to be successful than if we had suggested it to them.

4. Making **plans**.

After answers have been agreed careful planning will be necessary. If there is time and everyone is still alert, broad plan outlines can be made now. Alternatively another meeting can be called a few days later either for the whole community or for an elected planning group or health committee.

In practice the community, with the project's help will often decide to start with one of the following:

- A house-to-house survey to find out more detailed health information and identify families at risk (see Chapter 6).
- Selection and training of community health workers (see Chapter 7).
- Selection and setting up of village health committee (see Chapter 2).
- Setting up a community health centre or village health post (see Chapter 8).
- Improving community sanitation or water supplies (see Chapter 15).

5. Saying **farewells**.

Before leaving we must make sure that:

- Everyone knows what has been decided.
- People know what they have to do.
- Someone has written down the main points of the meeting.
- Plans for next meeting have been discussed.

Figure 5.7

We leave on a friendly note, taking time to talk and share jokes with those present after the meeting.

> In all our contacts with community members our aim is to help them to discover their **needs**, identify their **solutions** and carry out their plans. In this way they will begin to understand it is **their** programme.

Sometimes several meetings may be necessary before a community programme can actually be started.

Summary

Before becoming effective health workers, we need first to **prepare ourselves**. We need to exchange wrong and unhelpful attitudes for new, enlightened ones. In this process we come to experience a genuine appreciation of the people we are serving.

As health workers we should start **mixing with the people** as soon as possible. This helps the community to trust us and helps us in turn to better understand the community. As we do this we be-

gin finding out details about customs, patterns of living and health needs.

After preparing ourselves and mixing with the people we will be ready for **structured meetings**. These will need to be arranged first with community leaders and later with community members. During these meetings, needs, solutions and plans will be discussed, the community taking a leading part at every stage.

Further Reading

1. *Beyond the Dispensary*. R. Shaffer. African Medical and Research Foundation, undated. 90 pages.
   This includes a great number of practical and useful ideas.
   Available from: AMREF. See Appendix E.
2. *Helping Health Workers Learn*. D. Werner, B. Bower. Hesperian Foundation, 1982.
   Part 1 chapter 6 is especially useful.
   Obtainable from: TALC. See Appendix E.
3. *Learning from the Rural Poor*. H. Volken, A. Kumar, S. Kaithathasa. Indian Social Institute, 1982.
   This is a practical and inspirational book.
   Available from: 151, Lodi Road, New Delhi, 110003, India.

6

Community Survey, Diagnosis and Plan

This chapter is divided into three main sections: the community survey, the community diagnosis and the community plan. Having met with the community to discover problems and discuss solutions, the time comes for joint action. This is often an appropriate stage to carry out a community survey.

THE COMMUNITY SURVEY

In this section we shall consider:

ALTHOUGH THIS HOUSE LOOKED OUTWARDLY CLEAN AND HEALTHY IN A FAMILY OF 12, 3 CHILDREN HAD MODERATE MALNUTRITION, NONE HAD STARTED IMMUNIZATIONS, 2 ADULTS HAD SUSPECTED TB AND THE FATHER WAS SLEEPING OFF HIS DRINK IN AN INSIDE ROOM. YOU CAN'T DEPEND ON OUTWARD APPEARANCES.

© Illustration David Gifford

Figure 6.1 Health workers must learn to 'look beyond appearances'

1. What we need to **know**
   - Why a survey is necessary
   - Types of survey that can be done
   - Who should do the survey
   - When the survey should be done
2. What we need to **do**
   - Prepare materials
   - Train the survey team
   - Carry out the survey
   - Use the results

What we need to know

Why a survey is necessary

There are several reasons for doing surveys:

1. To discover the main health needs of the **community**.
   Accurate, baseline information on the community's health and population structure is obtained **before** we help to bring solutions. Then by resurveying **after** a period of time, say 3 or 5 years later, we can estimate how much progress has been made.
2. To discover those **individuals** and **families** with the greatest health needs.

> In hospitals and clinics we treat those who come to us. In CBHC we identify and help those who needs are greatest.

They will usually include:
- Children under 5 especially those below the Road to Health.
- Pregnant and lactating women.
- Those with serious, chronic illnesses such as TB, leprosy and AIDS.
- The physically and mentally disabled: the elderly.

- Any group, family or individual who is socially outcast, or very poor.
3. To build relationships.
   A survey done in a relaxed and friendly manner will help to build friendships and create trust. It will prove a good 'starter subject' for community participation (see Chapter 2).
4. To teach and sensitise.
   We will have a chance to discuss health problems with individual families and create awareness about how they can be solved.

Types of survey that can be done

There are several types of survey that can be carried out in CBHC, for example surveys designed for evaluation (see Chapter 17). This chapter describes basic community surveys. These include:

1. **Comprehensive** surveys.
   Every home is visited and questions are asked concerning all family members.
   The main **advantages** are that all individuals at risk can be discovered and comprehensive care

I THINK WE SHOULD HAVE WAITED FOR THE DRY SEASON

QUESTIONNAIRE

QUESTIONNAIRE

© Illustration David Gifford

Figure 6.2

can be started without delay. Information obtained is also more complete.
   The main **disadvantage** is the length of time it takes.
2. **Sample** surveys.
   Some, but not all households are visited. Every 5th or 10th house can be chosen or houses selected at random.
   Sample surveys are used either if numbers in the project are very large or if a quick, initial survey at the time of fund-raising is needed (see Chapter 4 page 44).
3. **Mixed** surveys.
   Here we may visit **each** house to record certain important information such as the weight or upper arm circumference of the children, but only **some** houses to record other details such as socioeconomic data (see section on page 64).
4. **Pilot** surveys.
   These are small scale surveys carried out at the start of a project, either to estimate the needs of the people, obtain an approximate census or to pretest a surveying technique.

Who should do the survey?

Project and community members should work together. *For example*: a project member can **record** answers, a community member **find out** information.

The **project member** will need to be:

- open and friendly in manner,
- exact and neat in recording.

The **community member** could be one of the following:

- a community health worker,
- a health committee member or
- any community member with a genuine interest and wanting to help for the **right reasons**.

Usually the community should select the surveyor.

When the survey should be done

This will need to be:
1. When the **community** is ready for it.
   We should make sure the community under-

stands the reason for the survey and is ready to participate. A suspicious or unwilling community may give inaccurate answers.

> We can reduce suspicion by always working with the community – in planning the survey, carrying it out and acting on results.

2. When the **project** has enough resources.
   At the very least we will need:
   - Team member(s) who have been trained in surveying.
   - Survey materials including forms or family folders.
   - Time to do the job properly.
   - The ability to work with the community in response to the needs discovered.
3. At a **time of day** and a **time of year** when most people are at home, and not too busy with other activities, such as harvesting or seasonal employment.

What we need to do

Prepare materials

Follow these guidelines:

1. Decide what **information** needs to be gathered.

Such information should be:
- Useful.
  Will it help in making plans?
  Can it be used to bring about improvements?

> Great care must be taken that when doing surveys we do not falsely raise the people's expectations nor create hopes which cannot be met. Surveying a community carries with it an obligation to work with that community on the problems which are discovered (see pages 68–71).

- Easily gathered.
  Questions should be simple to ask and easy to record. Where possible answers should be Yes, No, A Number or a Single Word. This makes it much easier to analyse the data (see below).
2. Study and adapt existing **survey forms**.
   Find out if the government or voluntary health association have materials available. See what nearby projects are using. Study the sample form given in Appendix G. Forms already in use can probably be used or adapted.
   If we are planning to do research or a detailed evaluation later it is worth consulting a doctor or statistician at this stage.
3. Collect the **materials** needed.
   Each surveyor must have:
   - A list of **questions**.

THOSE QUESTIONS THEY ASKED PUT ALL SORTS OF IDEAS INTO MY MIND

YES DO YOU THINK WE WILL GET OUR OWN HEALTH CLINIC, BETTER QUALITY BUFFALOES AND IRRIGATION FOR OUR FIELDS?

© Illustration David Gifford

Figure 6.3 Surveys can easily raise false hopes amongst the community

These will need to be carefully worded so that the answers obtained are **valid**.

For example:

If we are enquiring about cough in a suspected TB patient, there are many ways we could ask a question:

– Do you have a cough?
– Do you cough often?
– Have you been coughing for a long time?
– Have you been coughing for more than a month?

The last of these will give the most **valid** or **useful** answer in trying to discover which people have TB.

In order for all answers to be **consistent** the same question must be asked to each community member with the same **wording**. If different team members use different questions, as about cough above, answers cannot be compared and the results will not be accurate.

• **A family folder**.

This is made of stout paper and details about family members are filled in on the front. Other details e.g. on socioeconomic conditions can be recorded on the back or the inside. Each family has its own folder (see Appendix G for an example).

• **Insert cards**.

These will be needed for comprehensive surveys.

Whenever a family member is found whose health is at risk, details are recorded on an insert card which is then placed in the family folder (see page 108).

In order to keep forms tidy it is better to record answers in pencil first and ink them in later when the survey is complete and folders have been checked.

Train the survey team

Surveyors should be trained in two basic skills:

1. **Relating** to the community.

The surveyor must be:

• **Friendly** so that he will be able to build lasting relationships with the families he visits.
• **Tactful** so that he can ask questions without causing offence.

• **Persistent** so that he obtains the answers he needs.
• **Discreet** so that he does not gossip about the health problems of those he visits.

> Before asking questions the surveyor will need to explain **who** he is, **where** he is from and **why** he is doing the survey. This will be much easier if a community member is doing the survey with him, and if the community has been involved in planning the survey from the start.

Survey skills are best taught by role play in the classroom (see page 30).

2. **Obtaining** the information.

The surveyor will need to learn:

• **Questioning**, both what questions to ask and how to word them. He should have a list in front of him until he has memorised the correct wording of each question.
• **Recording**, making sure that each answer is written down correctly (see below).
• **Measuring** the mid-upper arm circumference (MAC), child's weight or anything else required.

Skills should be practised until mistakes are no longer made.

The training described above will take place **before** the survey is started in the community.

During the survey the supervisor should accompany the surveyor until he is confident and accurate.

> **After** the survey the supervisor should check through the survey cards. Any mistakes should be discussed with the surveyor. If accurate answers have not been obtained he should be asked to resurvey the family in question.

Team members, unless carefully trained will tend to make many mistakes in surveying. We should start by training several team and community members and then select those who show the greatest interest and ability to become future 'survey specialists'.

Carry out the survey

The stages are as follows:

1. First arrange a day well in advance, inform the

Figure 6.4 Co-ordinate your numbering system before the survey

© Illustration David Gifford

people and co-ordinate with community partners.

2. Work in pairs, a team member and community volunteer working together.

3. Decide on a numbering system for the houses with the survey teams **before starting**. If this is forgotten several houses can end up with the same code number.

Numbering often causes problems. Frequently houses have no numbers or else numbers change as extra houses are built. If a permanent numbering system exists, use that. If there is no such system devise one and make sure each family records and remembers its health survey number. Mark the number on the outside of the house for the convenience of visiting health workers.

4. At the start allow at least 5 minutes per family member. This may be shortened later.

5. Then do the survey.

The model described here can be used or shortened. Each project should adapt methods and forms to suit its own situation.

Data to be gathered

The following information is recorded (Letters in text headings correspond to those on sample folder in Appendix G):

(a) Name, address etc.

1. **Name**, **address**, and **occupation** of the head of the family.

2. **Code number** of the family.

A useful method is to construct a code with three sets of digits. The first set represents the health centre code, the second the community code and the third the house code. *For example*: 03/10/46. A fourth set can be added to define individuals. *For example* 03/10/46/01 would be the code number of the head of the family of the 46th house in the 10th community of the target area of the 3rd health centre.

(b) Felt problems

What are the main problems affecting your family? This is probably the best wording to use and is asked as the very first question of the survey before the answers have been influenced by other health-related questions.

(c) Family profile

1. **Names** of family members.

Enter these in a logical order by starting with the head of the family, his wife, the oldest son, his wife and children, the second oldest son etc.

FAMILY PROFILE

No.	Name	Age/DoB	Sex	Relation to head	Relation to each other
01	MOHAMMED	65	M		
02	HASSAN	34	M	Son	
03	FATIMA	25	F	Daughter in law	Wife of 02
04	ALI	4 OCT '88	M	Grandson	Eldest son of 02 + 03

© Illustration David Gifford

Figure 6.5   Family profile section of survey form

Elderly relatives can be added either at the beginning or the end.

In many communities this can be surprisingly difficult. Children may be known by several different names, or only given a permanent name after a certain age.

2. **Ages**.

Children under 5 should have the month and year of their birth recorded **accurately** to help in preparing Growth Charts. Those over 5 years can simply have their age recorded.

If ages cannot be easily remembered make a 'local events calendar' where seasons and annual events are marked to help parents remember the time of year their children were born. Check that the age the parents give, broadly corresponds with the appearance of the child.

3. **Sexes**.
4. **Relationships**.

These can be written in two columns:

The **first** records the relationship to the head of the family.

The **second** need only be used for large or extended families. It records how different members are related to each other. For example which wife belongs to which husband, or which child belongs to which father etc.

				DISEASES				IMMUNISATION				
No.	Name	Age/DoB		TB	Lep	Eye	Nutrition under 5	BCG	DPT	Polio	Measles	Tet tox
01	MOHAMMED	65		1	0	0	0	0	0	0	0	0
02	HASSAN	34		0	0	1	0	0	0	0	0	0
03	FATIMA	25		0	0	0	0	0	0	0	0	1
04	ALI	4 OCT '88		0	0	0	1	1	0	0	0	0

© Illustration David Gifford

Figure 6.6   Disease and immunisation sections of survey form

(d) Diseases

1. **Suspected infection** with **TB**, **leprosy**.
   Other locally serious diseases can be included. We will need tact where people are sensitive about a disease and be careful not to offend.
2. **Nutritional status of under 5s**.
   This can only be found out by careful **measuring**. There is little value in simply asking questions or just looking at the child.
   Children can either be weighed or have their mid-upper arm circumference (MAC) measured with a coloured strip (see Chapter 9 page 128).

(e) Immunisation

This will include the original six diseases covered by WHO's Expanded Programme on Immunization (EPI):

1. **BCG** (for TB), **DPT** (diphtheria, pertussis, tetanus), **polio**, **measles** – for children.
2. **Tetanus toxoid** – for women of child-bearing age.

Other diseases for which immunisation is given locally can also be included e.g. hepatitis B, typhoid, yellow fever.

Only record positive answers if certain that the **complete** course has been given. It is helpful to record the year in which each immunisation was completed. BCG scars can be looked for.

Many parents will be unable to give accurate answers. Where immunisation has already been started by the project, the immunisation register can be used to help fill in this part of the survey (see Chapter 10 page 151).

(f) Family planning

This is often a sensitive subject in which case it can be done later, when trust has been established and a Family Planning Worker trained (see Chapter 13).

1. Record year of **tubectomy** or **vasectomy**.
2. Record whether **O/C pill**, **coil**, **barrier** or **other** method is being used now.
3. Record if **currently pregnant**.
   This is useful to know only if prenatal care is being offered. Sensitivity is obviously needed.
4. Record if **eligible** for **family planning**.
   Those eligible are usually defined as (married) women from 15 to 44 who have not had a tubectomy or whose regular partner has not had a vasectomy.

(g) Addiction

This covers **smoking**, **drinking**, or other **drug abuse**. Define the lower age limit e.g. 12 or 15 in rural areas, 8 or 12 in cities. Ask about every family member over that age.

No.	Name	Age/DoB	FAMILY PLANNING							ADDICTION		EDUCATION		Remarks
			Tub	Vas	O/C pill	Coil	If preg nant	Eligible FP	Alcohol ↓ Tobacco		Adult literacy	School	
01	MOHAMMED	65	O	O	O	O	O	O	O	1	1	O	Stroke 2 yrs ago - can walk in house
02	HASSAN	34	O	O	O	O	O	O	O	1	1	O	
03	FATIMA	25	O	O	O	O	1	1	O	O	O	O	
04	ALI	4 OCT '88	O	O	O	O	O	O	O	O	O	1	Twin brother died at birth

© Illustration David Gifford

Figure 6.7 Family planning, addiction and education sections of survey form

(h) Education

1. **Adult literacy**
   This is defined as those aged 15 or over who can read or write. Male and female will later be separated in the tally (see page 66).
2. **School attendance**
   This commonly applies to children aged between 5 and 19 inclusive. Record the grade attended now (or the highest grade attained).

The level of education, especially female literacy has an important effect on health.

(i) Deaths in the previous 12 months

Record **age**, **sex** and **cause of death**. This needs to be as accurate a cause or description as possible.

> Deaths in the past year are often under-reported. The family may not want to talk about them, they may not consider deaths in the first few days of life worth mentioning or they may only report the deaths of sons.

This means that if we are using verbal reports of deaths within the last year to calculate mortality rates before the project starts, we will need to ensure they are accurately reported. If under-recorded the original state of health of the community will seem better than it really is, meaning that any improvements brought about through the project will be underestimated.

(j) Use of existing services

1. **Who** and **where** does the family attend when sick?
2. **Who delivers babies?**

(k) Water supply

1. **Type**, **distance** and **number of months** functioning in year of main water supply (and alternative).
2. **How much water** collected daily per person or household.

(l) Sanitation

Method of human waste disposal used by the family.

(m) Diet:

For each main food source:

1. **Number** of **months eaten** per year.
2. **Number of months grown by family**, and **number of months bought** by family from outside.

Estimated socioeconomic status

1 is the richest subgroup, 5 the poorest. Try and estimate this for each family, or ask questions such as:

1. **Type** of **housing** and **number** of **rooms**
2. **Types** and **numbers** of **animals**
3. **Area** and **quality** of **land** owned.

This information helps us later to target resources to those most in need and shows which families might be eligible for reduced rates or subsidies.

For details on how to complete 'Vital Events Since Survey' (see Chapter 8 page 114).

Symbols used in recording

There is no value in asking carefully worded questions unless the answers are also recorded accurately. Each surveyor must record with care and use the same symbols.

0 can be placed for a negative answer or where the question does not apply.

1 can be placed for a positive answer.

? can be written if an answer is not known or a family member was absent. This can later be altered when the answer is known.

Numbers can be written e.g. for school grade attained.

Dates can be written e.g. for year tubectomy performed or year an immunisation was completed.

No space should be left blank as this can mean one of two things – **either** that the question could not be asked (e.g. because a family member was absent) **or** that the questioner forgot to fill in the answer. When blanks are left, statistics, e.g. for child nutrition, quickly become inaccurate.

Where an answer is descriptive as in 'Felt problems' above, the key words or ideas can be recorded.

Use the results

Having completed the survey the results **must now be used**, not stored away and forgotten.

The results are analysed to make a **community**

Figure 6.8

diagnosis (see below) and then discussed with the community to draw up a **community plan** (see pages 68–71).

COMMUNITY DIAGNOSIS

In this section we shall consider:

1. What we need to **know**
   • What community diagnosis means
   • Sources of information which are needed
2. What we need to **do**
   • Tally
   • Tabulate
   • Present
   • List problems

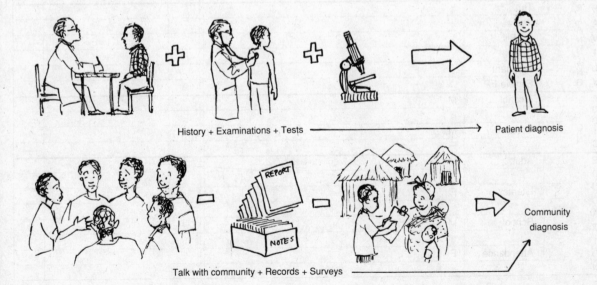

Figure 6.9 Community diagnosis

TALLY SHEET

Name of Village   Date of survey   Name of surveyor

....

Total population .... M .... F ....

				First Total	This column for later adjustments	Final Total
AGE OF POPULATION		0 – 1	M / F			
		1 – 4	M / F			
		5 – 9	M / F			
		10 – 19	M / F			
		20 – 29	M / F			
		30 – 39	M / F			
		40 – 49	M / F			
		50 – 59	M / F			
		60 – 69	M / F			
		70 – 79	M / F			
		80 – 89	M / F			
DISEASES	**& NUTR 1–4**	TB				
		Leprosy				
		Eyes				
	M A C	Don't know				
		Green				
		Yellow				
		Red				
IMMUNI	**SATION**	BCG				
		DPT/Polio				
		Measles				
		Tet Tox				
FAMILY	**PLANNING**	Tub.				
		Vas.				
		o/c Pill				
		Coil				
		Pregnant				
		Eligible FP				
ADDIC	**TION**	Alcohol	M			
			F			
		Tobacco	M			
			F			
EDUCATION		Adult	M			
		Literacy	F			
		School	M			
		Attendance	F			

Figure 6.10 Community tally sheet

COMMUNITY DIAGNOSIS FORM

Name of village .... Name of CHW ....

Name of supervisor .... Name of Chief ....

Names of VHC members ....

....

INFORMATION FROM FIRST HOUSE TO HOUSE SURVEY   DATE _____

(a) *Basic statistics*

	Actual	Numbers Eligible	Percentage
Total population			
No. male			
No. female			
Total number of families			
Suspected tuberculosis			
Suspected leprosy			
Current eye problems			
Under 5 malnutrition (Red MAC)			
(Yellow MAC)			
No. BCG			
No. completed DPT, Polio			
No. measles			
No. completed Tet Tox			
No. tubectomy			
No. vasectomy			
No. o/c pill			
No. coil			
No. pregnant			
No. Eligible for Family Planning			
No. 8 and over drinking			
No. 8 and over smoking			
Total number literate (15 and over)			
No. male literate 15 and over			
No. female literate 15 and over			
Total number at school (5–19)			
No. boys at school 5–19			
No. girls at school 5–19			

Deaths in the last 12 months

	Age	Cause
1.		
2.		
3.		
4.		
5.		

(b) *Problems mentioned by villagers*   Number who mention

1. _____
2. _____
3. _____
4. _____
5. _____
6. _____
7. _____

(c) *Surveyors observations*

_____
_____
_____
_____
_____
_____
_____

Figure 6.11 Community diagnosis form

What we need to know

What community diagnosis means

Just as we question and examine a patient to help find a diagnosis, so we can do the same for a community. In this way we can discover its main health **problems**, their underlying **causes**, and explore possible **solutions** with community members.

Sources of information which are needed

The **main** sources are the community survey and the observations of the health team concerning the community's beliefs about the cause, cure and prevention of disease.

   Other sources might include:

1. Clinic and hospital records concerning prevalence of local diseases, causes of death, and estimated birth and death rates.
2. Written reports, books and films about the area may give useful background information.

What we need to do

Tally

A tally is a simple method of adding up. From each family folder, the totals for each subject are marked on the tally. ⧣ equals 5 (see Figure 6.10). These are then added to give the total for the community.

Tabulate

The totals from the tally are now tabulated out on to a Community Diagnosis Form (see Figure 6.11).

   For example: For each community we will need to know the total number of malnourished children under 5. This will be the **numerator** (N) or actual number.

   We will also want to know the total number of children under 5 (both malnourished and well-nourished together). This will be the **denominator** (D) or eligible number.

   Percentages ($100N/D$) convey the **most useful** information. They give a picture of how serious a problem is at any one time. By comparing percent-

ages over a period of time we are able to tell how much improvement has occurred.

Present

We will soon need to present information to others such as community members, donors or government. This can be done through graphs, bar charts, pictograms and pie charts.

   Literate community members may understand percentages, bar charts and graphs. However it is important to make sure that **illiterate** members also understand the results of the survey. *For example*: Percentages can be described as cents in the dollar or pennies in the pound etc.

List problems

This involves drawing up a list of serious problems for each community surveyed. This is best done by the surveyor(s) in discussion with the team leader.

   The Community Diagnosis form contains space both for **figures** from the tally, and **written observations** from the surveyor. Both are taken into account when drawing up the problem list.

COMMUNITY PLAN

What we need to do

Prepare with the team

Before discussing the survey results with the whole

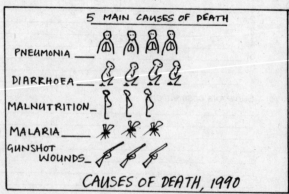

© Illustration David Gifford

Figure 6.12   Pictogram to show causes of death

community, the health team and all those involved in the survey will need to consult together. The purpose is to:

1. **Understand** the results.

> Spend time with all the surveyors explaining what has been discovered about the health of the community. Help them to understand the significance of the findings. This helps each person to be informed, involved and interested.

2. **Prioritise** the problems.
This means rewriting the problem list already made **in order of priority** with the most important health problems at the top.
To do this we can ask four different questions about each problem.
- How **serious** is the problem?
- How **widespread** is the problem?
- How **important** is the problem to the community?
- How **suitable** is it for joint project/community action?

The team can now rate answers to each of the above questions from 1 to 3 making a maximum possible total of 12. Problems are then prioritised in order of their score see Table 6.1. In the example shown the resulting order of priority is: water 11, tetanus 10, drinking 8, malaria 6.

This is a method of informing and preparing the team before they explain to the community. It is **not a list to be imposed on the community by the team**.

Plan with the community

It is helpful first to meet with the **whole community** for sharing results and ideas, and then with a **VHC** or **planning group** to draw up specific action plans.

Meeting with the whole community

We will probably already have held at least one previous meeting with the community (see Chapter 5). Now we have an exciting chance to present the findings of the survey and diagnosis. Those who were involved in this can make a joint presentation and lead the discussions.

This meeting should be held as soon as possible after the survey has been completed, while matters are still fresh in peoples' minds.

The **agenda** of the meeting will include:

Presenting the findings

The community will want to know the results of the questions they were asked during the survey.

Keep this simple. Explain the **main** problems found in a way that can be easily understood. The more talk-back and questions the better. Our purpose is not merely to inform but to sensitise and motivate so that community members both **understand** and **feel** the seriousness of their problems and the urgency to find solutions.

For example, one of the main findings commonly found is under-5 malnutrition. The community may not even believe there is serious malnutrition, because all the children look much the same. Explain that weighing and measuring is the only accurate way to discover 'hidden malnutrition'.

Table 6.1 Prioritising problems

Problem	How serious	How widespread	How important to community	How suitable joint action	Total
Lack of clean water	3	3	2	3	11
Occasional malaria in wet season	2	1	1	2	6
Many deaths from neonatal tetanus	3	2	2	3	10
Heavy drinking among men	2	3	1	2	8

Tell them how doctors have found that children with hidden malnutrition are many times more likely to die from common illnesses such as diarrhoea, measles and pneumonia than those who are on the road to health. Help them to understand that **feeding children properly is the best way to stop them dying or becoming seriously ill**.

Agreeing priority problems for joint action

During the meeting we will talk about serious problems suitable for working on together. We will already have prepared our priority list (see above) but we must be flexible and ready to change if other priorities emerge.

Make sure that any problems chosen for joint action are:

1. Within the resources of the project (both budget and expertise).
2. Are suitable for a joint community/project approach.
3. Are likely to bring early (and successful) results (see also Chapter 2).

Meeting with the VHC or planning group

For each problem discussed or selected with the whole community, detailed action plans are now drawn up. Further ideas on how this is done are found in the relevant chapters later in the book.

For examples of two problems and how they might be solved see Tables 6.2 and 6.3.

Before the community or committee meeting closes make sure:

Table 6.2   Problem: 40% children with third degree malnutrition

	What causes	How solved	Who will solve	When to start
1	Lack of knowledge about correct feeding practices	House to house health teaching Health education in clinics	CHWs and health team members	As soon as CHWs start training As soon as MCH clinic starts
2	Irrigation channels broken and blocked	Repair of channels	Community health committee with government development officer	Liaise with government office now Start repairs after harvest

Table 6.3   Problem: 5% of population with suspected TB

	What causes	How solved	Who will solve	When to start
1	Lack of understanding	Health education	CHWs Folk-drama group	When CHWs have completed basic training
2	No medicine available or affordable	Ensure regular low-cost drugs	Project director liaising with District Medical Officer	At once
3	Smoke from cigarettes and cooking hearths	Health education Install simple chimneys	Representative from each house with instruction from health team member	Prepare now for community-wide project after rainy season
4	Associated and made worse by AIDS	Health education HIV Testing	Plan to be drawn up with health team and community leaders	At once

Figure 6.13 Before the meeting closes make sure everyone knows what is to be done next and who is to do it

1. Action decided on has been understood and recorded.
2. Everyone knows **what** is to be done next, **who** is to do it and **when** the next meeting or joint activity is planned.

Some practical situations

These are examples of situations that commonly occur in practice:

1. **Health** problems are not a community priority: **non-health** problems often are.

   We must decide at an early stage whether we are able to offer help in other development sectors such as forestry, agriculture, or income generation. If we ourselves cannot help, it may still be possible to link the community with those who can, so stimulating an 'intersectoral approach'.

   In either case the community must know at an early stage to what extent we will be able to respond to the needs which they voice. Probably at the beginning we will restrict ourselves to health-related problems.
2. Gifts of community members need to be used. Normally we start with community needs and think of solutions. Sometimes it is better to start

with special gifts or abilities in a community or individual and see how they can be used in health care.

Examples might include gifts in drama, singing, teaching, caring for the handicapped or organising youth activities.

> One of the skills of health workers is to identify and use the gifts and abilities of community members, if necessary designing certain aspects of the project to enable this to happen.

3. Activities in different project communities need to be integrated.

   After a short time we may be working with several different communities at the same time, each of which has its own list of needs and priorities.

   This calls for careful forward planning to make sure that plans and promises made are always followed up.

Summary

Both community survey, diagnosis and plan are carried out jointly by the project and community.

The main purpose of the **community survey** is to gather information for a community diagnosis. It can also be used to discover all community members whose health is at risk for subsequent targeting of healthcare.

The **community diagnosis** reveals the main problems affecting a community and is based largely on information from the survey and the observations of team and community members.

A **community plan** is drawn up on the basis of these findings. After the team has been fully briefed on the issues involved, the results of the survey and diagnosis are explained to the whole community. Detailed action-plans are then worked through with a VHC or planning group.

Further Reading

1. 'Health surveys.' *World Health Statistics Quarterly* **38**(1), 1985. 126 pages.

   Various articles on the theory and practice of health surveys.

Available from: WHO. See Appendix E.

2. *Partners in Evaluation*. M. T. Feuerstein. Macmillan, 1986.
   Useful and practical information on surveys.
   Available from: TALC. See Appendix E.

3. *Beyond the Dispensary*. R. Shaffer. AMREF, undated.
   Helpful ideas, especially pages 52, 53.
   Available from: AMREF. See Appendix E.

4. 'Making the community diagnosis – the point of departure for community health programmes.' H. Gideon. *Contact Special Series* No 1. WCC, April, 1979.
   A 'classic' and useful description of community diagnosis.
   Available from: CMC. See Appendix E.

5. 'Look, listen and learn – preparing the ground for primary health care.' S. Buzzard. *World Health Forum* **6**: 361–4, 1985.
   Available from: WHO. See Appendix E.

7

The Community Health Worker

In this chapter we will try and answer the following questions:

1. What is a Community Health Worker (CHW)?
2. What are the roles and functions of the CHW?
3. How is a CHW selected?
4. How is a CHW trained?
5. The CHW's medical kit
6. How does a CHW keep records?
7. How is a CHW supported?
8. Should a CHW be paid at all?
9. By whom should a CHW be paid?
10. How much should a CHW be paid?
11. Practical hints if payment is essential.

What is a Community Health Worker?

As Community Based Health Care (CBHC) becomes an increasing world-wide movement, the Community Health Worker (CHW) is emerging as a key health worker in many developing countries.

CHWs are known by a bewildering number of different names of which Village Health Worker is probably the commonest. CHWs may be either men or women. In this chapter for the sake of convenience we shall refer to the CHW as female.

> The CHW is **selected** by the community and is ideally **trained** in the community. She **lives** in the community, **serves** the community and may be **paid** by the community. She belongs **primarily to the community** and **not** to the project or the government.

The CHW has several **advantages** over other primary health workers:

1. She is **accepted** by the community because they have chosen her.
2. She is **available** to the community because she lives in it.
3. She is **cost-effective** to health planners and governments, because she is inexpensive to train and can do many of the jobs traditionally done

I AM TRAINED ON THE JOB, LIVE IN THE COMMUNITY AND UNDERSTAND THE PEOPLE I SERVE. I CAN REACH 85% OF THE POPULATION AND AM COST EFFECTIVE TO THE GOVERNMENT

I AM TRAINED IN A HOSPITAL AND LIVE NEAR MY CLINIC. I CAN REACH 15% OF THE POPULATION AND FOR THE COST OF MY EDUCATION 100 COMMUNITY WORKERS COULD BE TRAINED.

© Illustration David Gifford

Figure 7.1

by doctors, nurses and social workers.

4. She **covers populations** where other health workers are often unwilling or unable to serve.

A CHW can however have certain **disadvantages**:

1. She may be **tempted** by money or status to separate herself from the people she is serving.
2. She may provide **poor quality** care unless she is well trained and well-supervised.
3. Any **payment** she receives may be hard to maintain, unless the community itself are willing to provide it.
4. She may be **wrongly selected** and therefore ineffective.
5. She may be **uneducated** or **illiterate**, though with appropriate training this is usually unimportant.

This means in practice:

> A CHW programme which is well **set-up** and **well maintained** can be highly successful, but a programme with poor planning and supervision is of little value. The future usefulness of any CHW will depend on how well she is selected, trained, supervised and supported.

What are the roles and functions of the CHW?

The roles of the CHW

The CHW has a triple **role** in her community as **health educator**, **health provider** and **agent of change**.

As **educator** she will teach the whole community how to improve health and prevent illness.

As **health provider** she will treat common illnesses early, **before they become serious**.

As **agent of change** she will help community members change their knowledge, attitudes and practice so that they lead healthier lives.

The functions of the CHW

The **functions** of the Community Health Worker will vary greatly depending on:

Figure 7.2   The CHWs will teach at every opportunity

- the **needs** of the community,
- the **availability** of other health care nearby,
- the **plans** and **policy** of the government and
- the **aims** of the project.

The list below is a comprehensive list of a CHW's functions and each project will need to adapt, and probably shorten this for its own use. A CHW will:

1. Be **available**.
   She must be willing to give appropriate care and advice to **any** community member, regardless of wealth, tribe, caste, or religion, **whenever** she is needed.
2. Be a **teacher**.
   She must be continually passing on knowledge in a practical and helpful way whenever the opportunity arises, both to individuals and to groups.
3. **Care** for **children**.
   a) By promoting good **nutrition**.
   The CHW can measure the weight (or mid-upper arm circumference) of under-5 children once per month, filling in a growth chart, or other record card.
   She can give practical feeding advice to parents, emphasising the value of breast-feeding and appropriate weaning. She may help to arrange feeding programmes or set up kitchen gardens.
   b) By demonstrating the use of oral rehydration solution (ORS) so that all community

members know how and when to use this in the treatment of diarrhoea.

c) By promoting immunisation of all children.

d) By distributing vitamin A and worm medicine to children between 1 and 5 years where these are health priorities.

4. **Care** for **mothers**.

a) By promoting **pre-natal care**.
The CHW will motivate women to attend clinics or will carry out checks herself. She will distribute iron and folic acid to pregnant and lactating women and promote tetanus immunisation.

b) By carrying out **deliveries**.
The CHW may do this herself or work alongside the Traditional Birth Attendant (TBA) to use safe and sterile methods of delivery. She will refer women likely to have problems at delivery, before they occur.

c) By giving **post-natal** advice and care.

5. Promote **child spacing** and **family planning**.

6. Care for those with **chronic infectious diseases** including those with tuberculosis, leprosy, AIDS and other locally important illnesses. This will include motivating patients for treatment and encouraging them to complete courses of medicine.

7. Care for the **blind**, **handicapped** and **disabled**.

8. **Treat simple illnesses** and **give first aid**.
Most CHWs will keep a stock of simple, effective medicines, using them to treat common illnesses or severe symptoms.

9. **Refer**.
The CHW will learn to recognise and refer serious illnesses and those she cannot treat herself. She will care for those discharged from hospital.

10. Develop **public health activities**.
With the support of the health team or committee, the CHW may promote waste disposal, safe water, smokeless cooking hearths and other valid improvements to home and environment.

11. **Keep records**.

12. **Work** alongside her supervisor or other members of the health team. This may include taking part in surveys, immunisation, care of school children, teaching and supervision, health centre activities and community projects.

13. Form **community clubs**.
Female CHWs may help to set up women's groups or teach female literacy. Male CHWs can set up young farmers' clubs or youth activities.

14. Encourage parents to **send children to school**.

15. Carry out **other** activities requested by the community or health team.

How is a CHW selected?

It is common to see programmes where some villages make great improvements while others seem to stand still. The reason is often because one will have a more effective CHW than the other.

> The correct selection of a CHW is of critical importance to the whole future success of the programme.

Who should choose the CHW?

The CHW should be chosen by the community. This can only happen if the whole community thoroughly understands what functions a CHW will carry out, and therefore what type of person she should be. In order for the community leaders and members to grasp this, two or even three meetings or discussions may be necessary.

For example. Many communities may assume that a CHW is a low-grade and unimportant health

Figure 7.3 The community often judges a CHW by how well her medicines seem to work

Figure 7.4   An effective CHW often holds the secret to a community's progress

aide only to be called on if no proper doctor or other health worker is available. With such a wrong idea they may choose an unsuitable person, whom it may be hard to change later.

> Time taken in explanation is never time wasted. The more community members understand, the more they will come to trust, use and support their CHW.

Each community has its own way of reaching a decision. Although the health team should not usually interfere in this, they must ensure that the CHW is acceptable to the majority of community members, **including women and the poor**.

They should try and ensure that the local chief has not chosen his own relative or friend in order to gain power, money or influence.

Sometimes a community will put forward several candidates and allow the health team to make the final choice after seeing which one(s) prove the most suitable.

In some instances the health team may notice

and suggest a community member who appears very appropriate.

A part-time CHW can cover at the most 100 families and ideally not more than 50. There is often value in choosing two CHWs to work in pairs

Figure 7.5

especially where they are working as unpaid volunteers (see page 91).

We must remember:

> Both projects and government programmes must take special care to allow the people themselves to choose their own CHWs and **not** force candidates on the community against their wishes.

What type of person should be selected?

Male or female?

There are no absolute rules. Men are more appropriate in some communities, women in others. Sometimes there is value in having one of each. Here are some principles which will help us to decide:

Advantages of choosing **men**:

- They may be less busy than women.
- They may be better educated and more literate.
- They may find it easier to liaise with government officials and with agencies.
- They may be less hesitant at the beginning and more willing to take initiatives.
- Some societies may insist that health workers are male.

Advantages of choosing **women**:

- They may be more appropriate in mother and child health care.

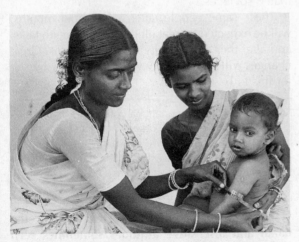

Figure 7.6 A community health worker in south India measures mid-upper arm circumference

- They are often less eager to make money or to set up as private practitioners.
- They are more likely to be resident and available in the community.
- They may be more compassionate and sensitive to people's needs.
- Some societies may insist that only women look after the health needs of other women and children.

A well-respected community member

A CHW should be:

- friendly,
- concerned for the welfare of others,
- able to keep confidence and avoid gossip,
- uninterested in status or money,
- hard-working,
- respected as a good parent, and
- willing to visit any community member.

Such community members may include those of any religion, caste, tribe or status.

Intelligent and willing to learn

This does **not** mean that CHWs need to be literate or educated, though this is sometimes an advantage.

It **does** mean they must be able to learn fresh ideas and gain new skills. Older CHWs may find this more difficult.

Interested in the job.

> CHWs must have both a genuine interest in the work and an unselfish desire to serve.

In good health

CHWs need to be healthy and strong in body and mind. They will usually continue their other jobs in home or community, in addition to serving as CHWs.

Those suffering from **active** TB or leprosy should not be chosen though cured TB and leprosy patients are often suitable as may be those with a degree of disability.

Mature in age and outlook

Younger people are often quick to learn. They are

however more likely to marry and move away, or have young children which will make them less available. They may also lack maturity or command less respect.

Those aged between 25 and 45 are usually the most appropriate.

Backed up by her family

This is especially important for female CHWs. Husbands, mothers-in-law and other family members must understand and give support.

> A common reason for female CHWs dropping out is because family members do not accept their new roles and resent the extra work in home or farm which now needs to be done by others.

Already engaged in health work

Traditional Birth Attendants (TBAs, Dais) often make

Figure 7.7   TBA in a remote mountain village. Such women, when appropriately trained may make excellent CHWs

excellent CHWs, providing they are ready to learn new ways. Their communities already know them, use their services and usually respect them.

Other traditional practitioners can become good health workers but there is a risk that after training they may use their new knowledge to increase their earnings, or be so interested in curative care that they take little interest in other health activities.

How is a CHW trained?

Many good books and guidelines have been written on this and some are listed at the end of the chapter. We should try and obtain one which is appropriate for the area or which is published in our country.

In this section we shall be considering:

1. The personal development of the CHW
2. **Where** the training should be held
3. **How long** the training should continue
4. **Who** should do the training
5. **How** the training should be done
6. **What** the curriculum should include
7. **What** supervision should be carried out

The personal development of the CHW

CHWs often come from poor backgrounds. When first chosen they may severely lack self-confidence. This is especially true for women in male-dominated societies.

These same people, after a few brief months, will be expected to treat illnesses, give health talks, and alter their community's health patterns. Great changes will be necessary within the CHW herself for this to be possible.

> The single most important part of CHW training is to develop the health worker's personality so that she becomes confident in her manner and caring in her approach. This will come about largely by the attitude of the health team and the way in which she is treated.

There is no place in CHW teaching for the harsh and insensitive attitudes sometimes seen from over-worked hospital staff. Such attitudes frighten and stifle CHWs who in turn learn to treat

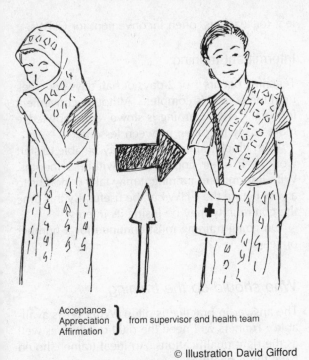

Acceptance
Appreciation } from supervisor and health team
Affirmation

© Illustration David Gifford

Figure 7.8 Community health workers need to be accepted, appreciated and affirmed

their patients in the same manner.

All health team members, but especially the trainer, will need to be **accepting**, **appreciative** and **affirmative**.

They will **accept** the way the CHW is, her per-sonality, her beliefs and her fears. They will never despise or judge her for any ideas which may be wrong, or for customs and habits she may follow.

They will **appreciate** the CHW and take an interest in her family, her community and her tra-ditions. This will involve **learning from her** and adopting good ideas from her own traditions and background.

They will **affirm** the CHW, always looking for ways to encourage her.

This process of conferring dignity will happen both in lessons and in the community. The health team must always show the CHW respect, espe-cially in front of others. She must not be ordered to do menial tasks such as sweeping floors or be expected to act as the unpaid personal servant of male team members.

Where the training should be held

Different programmes will choose different places. A few will choose hospitals or central training sites; most will prefer local health centres or com-munity rooms.

Although it may be less convenient for trainers, there are many advantages in training CHWs **as near as possible to their own communities**:

1. It is more convenient for the CHWs.

In poor rural areas it may be hard for busy women to leave home for training. They may

THINKS: IF I FIND MY OLD VILLAGE TOO DULL I CAN ALWAYS RETURN TO THE CITY WHERE I TRAINED AND SET UP A HEALTH SHOP

THINKS: DOES HE STILL BELONG HERE AND WILL HE STILL UNDERSTAND OUR VILLAGE PROBLEMS

© Illustration David Gifford

Figure 7.9 Disadvantages of training health workers away from their own communities

not be allowed to sleep away from their community.

2. CHWs can relate what they have learnt to actual problems in their community. They can take part in a community survey as part of their training.
3. Trainers can themselves learn about the CHWs lifestyle and the day-to-day problems they are likely to face.
4. Practical work and supervision in the field can be done more easily.

There are also important reasons why rural CHWs should **not** be taken for residential teaching to towns and cities.

These problems are often seen with male trainees in Africa. The more they learn in town-based training programmes the more distant they feel from their villages. As one health educator wrote: 'All that is achieved in the end is just another set of unproductive workers in government service'.

How long the training should continue

This will depend on:

1. The educational level of the CHW.
   Illiterate, uneducated or older CHWs may take a long time to learn basic knowledge and skills.
2. The time the CHW has available.
   Most female CHWs from rural areas are also mothers and farmers. The length of training must fit in with their home commitments.

Each programme should design its own time scale and pattern of training.

Here are examples of two commonly used training models:

Block training

Teaching initially occurs each day for a period of from 1 week to 3 months. Three weeks is often an appropriate length. Regular lessons then continue once per week or once every 2 weeks until the full course is completed.

This method helps trainees develop fresh attitudes and gain new knowledge which is reinforced every day.

When this system is used training often takes place in a hospital or central training site, conven-

ient for teachers, often inconvenient for CHWs.

Intermittent training

Teaching occurs 1 or 2 days or half days per week until the course is complete. Although convenient for rural CHWs learning is slower and knowledge more easily forgotten between lessons.

With **block** training CHWs may be able to start working in their communities within 3 months. With **intermittent** training it may take 6 months to a year before the CHW can be useful. By this time the community may be losing its interest.

On-going training must continue for a number of years

Who should do the training

The answer in practice is often 'Whoever is available'. Trainers will need the right qualities as well as the right qualifications. An ideal trainer should have these **qualities**:

1. The right gifts.
   She should be lively, humorous, enthusiastic and good at explaining and encouraging participation.
2. The right cultural background.
   The smaller the language and cultural gap between trainer and trainees, the more effective will be the teaching.

For example. In many mountain areas of the world, hill people are taught by those from the lowlands with higher qualifications. Although such trainers may be very knowledgeable they often make poor teachers because they are unable to understand the lifestyle and thought patterns of the people.

Hill people themselves with simple, appropriate training often prove to be better teachers than more highly qualified people from the plains.

An ideal trainer will have these **qualifications**:

* practical experience in community health,
* nursing, paramedical or teachers' training.

In practice trainers will come from a great variety of backgrounds and will include doctors, nurses, lab-technicians, teachers, medical assistants, multipurpose health workers (MPWs) and social workers.

Figure 7.10 Teaching should **not** be like this

Community Health Nurses, MPWs and senior CHWs often make the best trainers. Already established CHWs may need training from doctors or senior nurses.

Although personal qualities are of greater importance than academic qualifications, CHW trainers should be encouraged to attend Training of Trainers (TOT) Courses being set up in many areas.

How the training should be done

We will consider this under **method** and **plan**.

Method

Our method should be:

Pupil-centred

Traditional teaching is usually done by a dominant person, who stands at the front, looks down on the class, and teaches facts to his pupils. Such pupils, learn by rote, fail to understand, never participate and are scared to ask questions. The training of community health workers should be the opposite of this.

All sit in a circle. The teacher learns from the pupils and the pupils learn from her and from each other. 'Teaching is not a one-way, nor a two-way but an all-way process.' Each class member is encouraged to take part, share ideas and ask questions. No one's ideas are mocked.

Problem solving

Lessons will start, **not** with the teacher's knowledge, but with the pupil's problems and the community's concerns.

For example: Many teachers traditionally start their health course with a lesson on human anatomy. But the CHWs may be wondering what they can do about the latest outbreak of eye infection or recent deaths from malaria. A good teacher will choose a lesson which is **relevant to the** CHW's **current concerns**, and not simply follow the manual in order from lesson 1 through to the end.

> In the context of community health the purpose of knowledge is to help find effective answers to practical problems.

Starting with trainee's own knowledge

Before starting to teach a subject we first discover what the trainees know already, what their attitude is towards it and what they normally do about it. Discussing Knowledge, Attitude and Practice (KAP) can be rewarding both for trainees and for the trainer.

WE HAVE AN OUTBREAK OF MEASLES IN OUR VILLAGE — COULD WE LEARN ABOUT THAT TODAY

THAT'S A GOOD IDEA. COULD YOU START BY TELLING US YOUR OWN BELIEFS ABOUT MEASLES AND THE WAY THAT YOU WOULD TREAT IT?

© Illustration David Gifford

Figure 7.11   Good teaching builds on the trainee's own knowledge

For example: In many parts of the world pregnant women believe they should eat less food, so that their babies will be small. In this way delivery is easier and the baby is less likely to get stuck during delivery.

A good teacher will **accept** this logic but gently **correct** the wrong idea on which it is based.

> **Correct** ideas are approved and built upon.
> **Neutral** ideas are left alone.
> **Wrong** ideas are corrected and altered.
> **All** ideas are listened to and respected.

Encouraging, friendly and enjoyable

We should **encourage**, not criticise in our teaching, especially when CHWs may be unwilling to accept ideas which go against their own beliefs and traditions.

The more CHWs **enjoy** the lesson the more they will learn, and the more likely they are to make their own teaching to the community enjoyable and interesting.

Repetitive

A large tree is more quickly felled by three axes falling at different angles than by one axe always hitting at the same angle. We should teach each subject using different methods and different examples.

At the end of each lesson ask the pupils to give a summary of what they have learnt. Make sure they really know and understand one subject before going on to the next.

Use different senses so that trainees can:

- **Hear** what is being said,
- **See** what is being shown,
- **Touch** what is being presented.

Plan

Our plan for each lesson should include:

1. Greetings, welcome and introductions.
2. Discussion on problems CHWs have recently come across in the community. Minor points can be discussed at the time, more major ones can form the basis of the day's lesson or be postponed till later.
3. Review of the previous lesson.
4. Introduction of the day's subject.
   Trainees should first share their own Knowledge, Attitude and Practice (KAP) on the topic for the day's lesson.
5. Consolidation of the day's topic.
   This is the main part of the lesson. Use imaginative methods so the topic is really understood and learnt. Repeat-back, role play, story telling, drama, song, quiz, interview etc. can be used (see Chapter 3).
6. Practical use of the day's topic.

There may be a **skill** to learn in the classroom such as bandaging or weighing. There may be a **practical** assignment to do in the community such as teaching a lesson or checking for a symptom such as night blindness or chronic cough.

7. Review and giving of **reminder cards**.

   After reviewing the main points of the lesson the CHWs are given special cards. These reminder cards summarise the main points – in words if the trainees can read, in pictures if they are unable to.

The curriculum

The **trainer** will know the important subjects to cover according to his manual or his own experience.

Figure 7.12 The community health worker has taught this mother how to use oral rehydration salts

The **trainee** will know the most useful things to know for her own community.

> The curriculum is best worked out by trainer and trainee discussing together at the start of the course.

Try and obtain a training manual either through the government, voluntary health association or hospital. Make sure this manual has both the **right approach** and the **right content** for the community.

Most projects will be able to **adopt** and **adapt** existing manuals. Some may want to field test an existing one before adopting it. Projects working in remote areas may need to write their own.

> As the trainer uses the manual she should be continually writing in new ideas and new information. In this way the manual becomes increasingly useful for each new batch of trainees.

A suggested syllabus is shown in Table 7.1.

Notes on the curriculum

1. Subjects included.

   This list is a guide only and each project will develop its own curriculum.

2. Order of lessons.

   It is **not** necessary to follow a strict order as found in this list or in a training manual.

   Start with subjects of interest to the trainees or relevant to the community. **Mix** teaching on diseases (often enjoyed most by the trainees) with other subjects, to keep the course balanced.

3. Number of lessons per subject.

   Some subjects can be easily covered in one lesson, others such as pre-natal care, may need several.

4. Length of lessons.

   Aim for about 2–3 hours per lesson providing there is plenty of variety and the trainees participate. Arrange breaks during the lesson for chat, refreshment or games.

> Learn to recognise boredom. If pupils get bored, we should stop the lesson, change our approach or set up an activity. Bored people don't learn.

Table 7.1   Suggested syllabus

Care of under 5s.
1. How to recognise a sick child.
2. How to care for a sick child.
3. How to weigh children and use growth charts: how to measure the mid-upper arm circumference (MAC).
4. Malnutrition: types and causes.
5. Malnutrition: prevention and treatment through correct feeding.
6. Hygiene.
7. Immunisations.
8. Diarrhoea and the use of oral rehydration salts (ORS).
9. Acute respiratory infection (ARI) and its treatment.
10. AIDS: its recognition and management (in areas where prevalent).

Care of pregnant mothers
1. Human reproduction.
2. Pre-natal care: normal and abnormal signs: food supplements: preparation for delivery.
3. Birth of the child: stages of labour, normal and abnormal deliveries, use of delivery kit.
4. Post-natal care.
5. Care of new born; breastfeeding.
6. Family planning and child spacing.

Parts of the body and how they work (anatomy and physiology)

Prevention and treatment of common illnesses
1. Diarrhoea and worms.
2. Abdominal pain.
3. Chest infections.
4. Tuberculosis.
5. Malaria.
6. Typhoid and cholera.
7. Measles.
8. Leprosy.
9. Sexually transmitted diseases (STD) and AIDS.
10. Anaemia.
11. Eye diseases.
12. Ear diseases.
13. Mouth and tooth problems.
14. Problems of menstruation.
15. Skin problems.
16. Other locally important diseases and symptoms.
17. Mental illness.
18. Care of the handicapped.

First aid
1. Cuts and bruises: bandaging.
2. Burns.
3. Bone injuries.
4. Serious soft tissue injuries: shock.
5. Animal bites and injuries.
6. Snake and scorpion bites.
7. Drowning.
8. Poisoning.
9. The unconscious patient.
10. Cardiopulmonary resuscitation.
11. Prevention of common accidents in home and community.
12. Treatment of drug reactions, and collapse after injection.

Environmental health
1. Clean water.
2. Sanitation and waste disposal.
3. Clean house and clean community.
4. Housing improvements: smokeless hearths.
5. Tobacco, alcohol and drug abuse.
6. Kitchen gardens.
7. Appropriate development.

General
1. The role and function of the CHW.
2. How a hospital works.
3. How and when to refer patients (see Chapter 8).
4. Record keeping and simple accounting.
5. Healthy living.
6. Keeping and using a medical kit.
7. Methods of teaching and communicating.
8. Leading discussion groups: raising awareness.
9. Details of the health project to which they belong.
10. National health problems and programmes.
11. Co-operating with others.
12. Health for All: WHO and UNICEF

---

5. Hospital experience.

Whether or not a hospital is used as the teaching centre, CHWs will need to understand what a hospital does, and how a hospital works. This is best done by introducing them in turn to each department and its staff. As well as benefiting CHWs, this will have two helpful results for patients:

- They can be given useful, informed advice by CHWs before being referred to hospital.
- They will receive better care in the hospital because staff will have personally met their CHW.

6. Further training.
After the basic curriculum has been covered CHWs will need further teaching. This might include:
- **Revision** and update on important subjects.
- **Teaching** on new health topics.
- **Introduction** to wider development issues.
- **Adult literacy**.
- **Training** so that CHWs themselves can become trainers and supervisors.

7. Examinations.
CHWs should have frequent oral tests.
Before medical kits are presented an outside examiner should be called in to test each candidate. Take care that this is both **fair** and **thorough**. CHWs should especially be tested on their use of medicines, and how well they recognise common and important illnesses.

© Illustration David Gifford

Figure 7.13 Trainers should point out mistakes in private, **not** in front of the CHW's community

What supervision should be arranged

There is no value in training a CHW, sending her back to the community and forgetting her. The real value of a CHW to the community will depend on **how well she is encouraged and supervised**.

The supervisor will often be the same person as the trainer or teacher. Her main jobs will include:

1. Encouragement, support and training.
This is the supervisor's **main purpose**.
2. Pastoral care.
The CHW will value her supervisor's advice about practical problems she faces in the community. She may need help with personal troubles also especially if these arise from her work as the CHW. The supervisor must be willing to support and advise but be careful not to encourage dependence.
3. Discipline.

> If the CHW needs correcting, disciplining or warning, the supervisor should do this, **gently**, **privately** and **fairly**. There should be ten words of praise for every one word of criticism.

CHWs **should never be disciplined in front of community members**.

4. Payments.
When appropriate the supervisor should make sure each CHW receives the **right** payment **on time**.

A point to emphasise:

> A supervisor's job is not simply to 'tell off and pay off'. Supervisors should make frequent community visits both to understand its needs and to support CHWs in their work.

The CHW's medical kit

Although some CHWs will be involved only in teaching and prevention, the offer of **curative** care helps to make a CHW more popular and more effective as a health promoter.

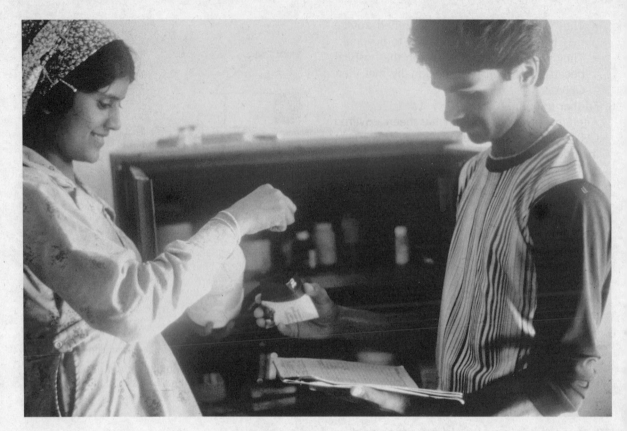

Figure 7.14   CHWs need to become expert in the use of simple medicines

What should a kit contain

Medicines

Choice of medicines is a top-level decision and a **doctor should advise** on contents. In case of misuse or serious reactions he will be responsible.

Medicines chosen should be: **effective**, **simple**, **safe**, **cheap**, and **easy to obtain** (see also Chapter 16).

A suggested list is shown in Table 7.2.

Notes on medicines

1. Medicines should be carefully **packed** into secure, damp-proof, containers. Liquid medicines such as gentian violet must be stored in leakproof bottles.
2. Medicines must be clearly **labelled**. If CHWs are illiterate this can be done through symbols or pictures (for example chloroquine can be labelled with the drawing of a mosquito). Normal doses can be recorded as a reminder.
3. Supplies must be regularly **restocked**. When seeing a sick villager the CHW should never have to confess that her stocks have run out.
4. The kit should be safely **stored**. It should be kept locked and in a safe place.
5. **Ordering**. A system should be set up with the supervisor (see also pages 16–17 and 112–13).

Equipment

Keep this simple. It might include:

- Bandages, tape and cotton wool.
- Scissors.
- Envelopes for pills (can be home-made from magazines).

Table 7.2 Suggested list of medicines for CHW's medical kit (see note opposite page)

Disease/symptom	Medicine†	Comments
1. Pain, fever	Paracetamol Aspirin	Aspirin not suitable if stomach ulcers common, and not to be used in children under 12.
2. Stomach ache/indigestion	Magnesium trisilicate Co Belladonna	Belladonna also good for pain of menstruation.
3. Worms	Mebendazole Piperazine	Treatment of choice for pinworm, roundworm, hookworm, whipworm. Good for pinworm, roundworm.
4. Malaria	Chloroquine	Areas with high resistance need specialised advice.
5. Anaemia and for use in pregnant and lactating mothers	Iron sulphate or fumarate + folic acid	Warn that stools may turn black.
6. Serious bacterial infections*	Co-trimoxazole (sulphamethoxazole + trimethoprim) or Sulphonamides or Ampicillin	Life-saving in pneumonia. Valuable in many situations. Care needed in prescribing.
7. Allergy and itching: insect bites	Chlorpheniramine or pheniramine	Warn about drowsiness.
8. Vitamin A deficiency	Vitamin A tabs or syrup	Use only if this illness locally present. Give 200 000 units 6 monthly for prevention.
9. Eye infections	Tetracycline eye ointment 1%	Cures most eye infections including trachoma if used early and correctly.
10. Scabies	Benzyl benzoate Gamma benzene hexachloride	May be alternative local remedy.
11. Sores, cuts, skin infections	Gentian violet Mercurochrome	GV also good for thrush. Some communities won't accept.
12. Rub for muscles, bruises, headache, etc.	Local liniment or balm e.g. Vicks, menthol	Usually popular.
13. Antiseptic for cleansing skin	Savlon or local equivalent: soap	Use before injecting and for cleaning skin infections/wounds.

* These include chest infections such as pneumonia and bronchitis, severe ear and skin infections, tooth abscess, severe sore throat or sinusitis, urinary infection, dysentery with fever and some forms of STD.
† Other commonly used drugs include: aminophylline (asthma); griseofulvin tabs or Whitfield ointment (fungal skin infections); ergometrine (blood loss after abortion or delivery); laxative preparation (constipation); metronidazole (amoeba, giardia, trichomonas); multivitamins (famine conditions only); phenobarbitone (epilepsy).

- Flashcards or teaching aids.
- Mid-arm measurer or tubular scale.
- Ballpoint pen or pencil.
- Simple health booklets.
- Delivery kits if used (see Chapter 12).
- Record book.

Both medicines and equipment can be kept in a **box** which should be:

- **Large** enough to contain all supplies.
- **Small** enough to carry.
- **Strong** enough for constant use.
- **Waterproof** in wet climates.
- **Divided** into two or three sections, either arranged side-by-side, or one on top of the other.
- **Marked** with a red cross or crescent.
- **Fitted** with a handle and shoulder strap.

How should the kit be given?

> The health kit should be handed over to the CHW in a **special presentation** or passing out ceremony. The CHW is encouraged and affirmed in front of her people: the **community** has an opportunity to learn more about health care: the **project** has a chance to teach and raise community awareness.

Before the presentation, make careful plans with the community. Encourage them to choose a respected leader or official to be guest of honour, and to invite the whole community.

The **presentation itself** should be festive, and can include cultural items such as health songs or a short drama. **Community leaders** can say a few words (preferably not make political speeches). A **guest of honour** can present both the boxes and certificates, each CHW being photographed in turn.

Figure 7.15   The community health worker's box

Figure 7.16   A community health worker receiving her box

The **health committee chairman** or Programme Director can help the community understand more about the work of the CHW. He can explain again what she can and cannot do. He can ask them to give her encouragement and forgive any mistakes she makes when she first starts work.

How does a CHW keep records?

What records need to be kept

The system described is appropriate if a CHW is literate or can work with a literate friend or colleague. Where this is not possible a book with pictograms or symbols can be designed.

A list of patients seen and treatment given

A possible layout on a double page is shown in Table 7.3.

Under 'Treatment' always record the type of any medicine used along with dose and total number of pills given.

An updated list of all 'at-risk' patients or families who need regular visiting

This is the CHWs' list of those for whom she needs to take special care and who need regular visiting. It includes:

- Under 5 children below the road to health.
- Under 5 children with any acute or chronic illness, and those who have not completed immunisations.

Table 7.3

Date	Patient's Name & No	Problem	Treatment	Outcome	Money taken
April 4th	Jose Lopez 01/04/19	Malaria	Chloroquine 4+2+2+2	Recovery 24 hours	30 cents

Table 7.4

Date	Patient's Name & No	Risk category	Treatment	Date next visit
Feb 22 1992	Mary 12/03/49	Pregnant 40 weeks	Check	March 1st if not delivered

Table 7.5

For **births** include:

Date of birth	Name	Head of family	House No	Live, still	Name of midwife

For **deaths** include:

Date of death	Name	Head of family	House No	Age	Probable cause

For **movements** include:

Name	Head of family	House No	Age	In or Out	Reason

- Pregnant and post-natal women.
- Patients suspected of having TB, leprosy, AIDS or other serious or infectious illnesses.
- The handicapped, very old or socially outcast.
- Those recently discharged from hospital.

It can also include those needing regular birth control supplies.

A separate section can be kept for each category or they can be lumped together. Whichever system is used include the details as in Table 7.4.

An alternative system is to use a diary, recording patients' names on the date they are due to be seen. The two systems can be used together.

Vital events record (Table 7.5)

Births, deaths and permanent movement in and out of the community (e.g. for marriage).

Daily activity list

Some CHWs also keep a list of daily activities carried out, both for their own interest or to show their supervisor.

Books used should be strong with tough bindings, and should fit into the CHW's box. Each of the above records can be kept in different sections of the same book. The supervisor can help to prepare this.

Why are records kept?

> The main reason for keeping records is to help the CHW do her job efficiently, and to make sure that those needing her care are not left out or forgotten.

In addition the **supervisor** will use the record book to help guide the CHW: the **project** will need it for records. The record book can be shown to **com-**

© Illustration David Gifford

Figure 7.17   Newly qualified community health workers face big challenges

munity members to help them understand what the CHW is doing, and to **visiting students** for teaching.

How is a CHW supported?

In this section support does not include payment.

> In order for the CHW to become effective she will need both **confidence** in herself, and **credibility** in her community. She will only succeed or survive if she has an effective support system.

This support will come from various sources:

The health team

When first trained the CHW will rely heavily on the health team and on her supervisor. The community may not believe in her, her family may misunderstand her, she may scarcely believe in herself.

The CHW will continue to receive regular lessons where questions and worries can be dealt with, and encouragement given. She can receive advice on how to deal with difficult people or puzzling cases.

The supervisor or other health team members must visit the CHW in her community, at least once every 2 weeks or once per month.

Other CHWs

'A problem shared is a problem halved'

By meeting together regularly CHWs can share their problems and come to see that others are facing similar situations. More mature CHWs can give encouragement and practical advice.

The CHW's own family

The family may **feel proud** that one of its own members has been chosen by the community. It may **resent** the time she spends away and the extra work that others have to do when she is absent.

> It is important to encourage and involve the family so that they in turn can support the CHW. **The husband's support is especially important**. The supervisor should aim to build friendships with members of the CHW's family.

The community

At the beginning the community may seem more a threat than a support. As the CHW gains confidence and her treatment and advice are seen to work the community will come to respect and support her. Often through the health committee they will be able to support and encourage the CHW. Committee members will need training and guidance to do this in an appropriate way.

Figure 7.18 The community health worker has less protection than most doctors and thus needs more support

Women's clubs or young farmers' clubs can play an active role in giving support. They can give practical help in her work and stand with her when others criticise or complain.

The CHW herself

As she gains in maturity and knowledge the CHW will learn self-dependence, and outside support systems will become less necessary.

It is helpful to consider each CHW as needing ten support points in order to develop as an effective health worker. Table 7.6 shows two examples of how they may add up.

Should a CHW be paid at all?

This is one of the hardest questions to answer in Community Based Health Care (CBHC) and the future of the CHW model will depend partly on finding practical answers.

The dilemma is this: CBHCs using CHWs need to be financially self-sufficient so they can be sustained into the future. CHWs often demand to be paid. Programmes faced with increasing CHW salaries become unsustainable.

Arguments over CHW salaries and excessive payment demands are one of the commonest causes of failure in CBHC programmes.

Wherever possible we should aim to set up CHW programmes in partnership with the community where CHWs are unpaid.

Although difficult to achieve this may be possible under the following circumstances:

1. Where CHWs work a maximum of 2 days per week, ideally half to 1 day per week.
   This is in turn means each CHW will be able to care for 50 families or less. Programmes based on unpaid volunteers will therefore use a larger number of part time CHWs rather than a smaller number of full timers.
2. Where CHWs possess a strong sense of social service or religious motivation.
3. Where CHWs receive their support and encouragement in ways other than through payment. Job satisfaction, and the appreciation of the community are common examples.
4. Where at the start of the programme everyone – both community and CHWs – understand that payments will not be provided and that CHWs will work out of service to their community.

It needs to be made clear that appointment as a CHW is not a path to fame and fortune either for the CHW or her family.

Table 7.6 CHW's support points

	Health team	Other CHWs	Family	Community	Self
1st month	++++	+++	+	+	+
After 1 year	+	++	+	+++	+++

Figure 7.19   This CHW is popular, but is she so popular that the community is willing to pay her?

By whom should the CHW be paid?

If payment appears to be essential funding may be obtainable through the community, the government or funding agencies.

The common AIM:
To reduce illness
in the community –
shared by Project,
Community and
by CHW

The secret wish of the CHW: to keep a pool of illness so she can continue to use her medicines

Figure 7.20   Conflict of aims when CHWs are paid by patients for each medicine dispensed

The community itself

Possible methods include: through a health committee, through an insurance scheme and payment by individuals.

Payment through a **health committee**

This will work only if:

1. The community so values their CHW that they are willing to pay her.
2. The community is able to work out a fair, honest and efficient way of collecting the money.

Few poor communities are able to do this at the start but **may be able to later on** as faith in the CHW grows and community organisation improves.
For example. Such a change has been made by the Comprehensive Rural Health Programme in Jamkhed, western India. CHWs were initially paid by the project but have become so widely appreciated that the community now provides their support.

Payment through an **insurance scheme**

Community members each pay a fixed amount into a fund and receive certain health services free in return. The CHW is paid out of this fund.
Schemes of this sort demand a good level of local organisation in order to be effective, and in particular require a sensitised and honest health committee.

Payment from **each individual** as he is treated

This is the system often used by TBAs and traditional practitioners who are paid in cash or kind for the services they provide. The local community are often familiar with this approach and can apply it to their new CHW.
For example. The CHW can charge a fixed amount per consultation or per medicine given, **as agreed with the project** or **health committee**. She can then keep part or all of this as payment or return it to a pool from which fixed payments are made monthly to CHWs.
There is one disadvantage to this approach. The more medicines a CHW uses, the more she earns. This conflicts with one of the chief roles of the CHW – to be an Agent of Change in the commu-

nity so that illnesses become less common and medicines become less necessary.

The government

This should be used **only if community funding is not possible**. Funds though promised may not come in time, not come in the right amount, or not come at all. The government may try to exercise an unhelpful form of control over the project or the CHWs, so reducing their flexibility and usefulness.

To overcome these problems consider:

1. Using government funds when available but not depending on them.
2. Requesting government funds to be channelled through the project or health committee, **rather than being paid direct to the CHWs**.

Funding agencies

This may seem the simplest or indeed the only solution at the start.

The danger is that of a car running down hill out of control. It keeps going faster and faster and becomes increasingly hard to stop.

Quite apart from the agency having ever larger bills to pay there is a further disadvantage. The CHW may be seen as an employee of the project or agency rather than as a community member answerable to a health committee.

How much should CHWs be paid?

This is worked out in discussion with the community, but it must be understood that outside funds will not be available for long-term payments to CHWs.

The amount paid depends on:

The expectation of the CHW, her family and the community

Effective CHWs often serve because of their social concern, interest in the job and personal commitment. On the other hand CHWs usually come from poor backgrounds and their families may depend on the work they do at home, in the field

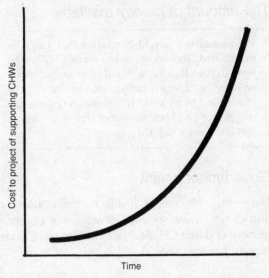

© Illustration David Gifford

Figure 7.21   Projects which both increase their coverage and give regular pay rises to CHWs become unsustainable

or as job earners. It is unreasonable for such CHWs to serve for more than 1 or 2 days per week and receive nothing in return.

> We must therefore find a balance between paying a CHW too much on the one hand and too little on the other, **both of which may take away her sense of service**.

If **too much** is paid this sequence occurs:

1. The CHW's family starts thinking of her simply as another wage-earner.
2. Comparisons are made with salaries received by others. Higher wages may then be demanded and 'unionisation' may occur.
3. Money now replaces service as the reason for working. The quality of care starts to fall. The project (or government) is unable to pay the salaries.

If **too little** is paid this sequence occurs:

1. The CHW and her family become discouraged or resentful.
2. The CHW spends less time in the community and more time doing jobs in the home.
3. The CHW starts charging or overcharging for her services. Quality of care again starts to fall.

The amount of money available

> **We should not pay high salaries that can't be maintained**. The world has too many CHWs who were paid well at the start and have now stopped working because the programme has run out of money. It is better for CHWs to start receiving low wages that can continue rather than high wages that have to be stopped.

Government policy

There may be agreed levels in the country or district which we should follow. Some countries recommend that CHWs should not be paid, others expect that they should.

Practical hints if payment is essential

1. Avoid the term wages, salaries or income.
   Use instead the name or idea of an honorarium, contribution, or compensation for time lost. Make sure that the payment method used does not break national labour laws.
2. Payments must be punctual.
   If CHWs are to be paid make sure payments are not irregular, late, or incomplete.
3. CHWs should sign for payments received.
   This saves argument later and will be needed by the project auditor or health committee accountant.
4. Training expenses can be reimbursed.
5. Modest pay increases can gradually be given as agreed with the health committee.
6. Equivalent grades of CHW are paid the same amount.
   Where possible use similar rates to those paid by neighbouring projects. Any differences may be quickly exploited in bargaining for higher wages.
7. Encourage the health committee to be responsible for payments as soon as it is able to do this reliably and honestly.

Summary

In many countries CHWs are becoming the key health workers in community based programmes.

CHWs should be well respected members of a community, often but not always women aged between 25 and 45, who are chosen by the community itself. They are trained appropriately using a comprehensive and practical syllabus in centres as near to their homes as possible.

When basic training is completed CHWs are given an examination and may then be presented with a medical kit. They now start serving in the community where their tasks include giving health teaching, acting as agents of change and providing curative care. They also care for all community members whose health is at risk liaising with the health team, to whom they refer serious cases. They are encouraged to keep accurate records.

When CHWs start work they need much encouragement and support from the project, from the community and from fellow CHWs.

CHWs ideally serve out of social concern, or through religious motivation, but some receive payment when this is available, especially if they work more than 1 or 2 days per week. The best source of payment is the community and only when such sources are not available should the government or an outside agency be approached.

The future of the CHW model will be ensured only when it proves to be sustainable and when CHWs are sufficiently well chosen, trained and supervised that community members when sick have full confidence in using them.

Further Reading

1. *The Community Health Worker*. WHO, Geneva, 1987.
   A definitive guide for training CHWs.
   Available from: WHO. See Appendix E.
2. *Helping Health Workers Learn*. D. Werner B. Bower. Hesperian Foundation, 1982.
   Now in various editions and languages. Much useful advice on all aspects of CHW programmes.
   Available from: TALC. See Appendix E.
3. Guidelines for Training Community Health Workers in Nutrition. 2nd edn. WHO, 1986 reprinted 1991.
   Available from: WHO. See Appendix E.
4. *A Manual for the Training of Village Health Workers*. P. Wakeham. Emmanuel Hospital Association, 1986.
   An effective manual for use in South Asia.
   Obtainable from: EHA, 808/92, Nehru Place, New

Delhi 110019, India.

5 *Community Health Workers: The Tanzanian Experience.* K. Heggenhougen *et al.* Oxford University Press, 1987.
   Useful overview of experience with CHWs in one African country.
   Available from: Oxford University Press, Walton Street, Oxford, OX2 6DP, UK.

6. *Teaching Health Care Workers.* F. Abbatt, R. McMahon. Macmillan, 1985.
   A simple and well illustrated practical guide.
   Available from: TALC. See Appendix E.

7. *Community Health Workers Manual.* E. Wood. African Medical and Research Foundation, 1983.
   Appropriate and useful book, especially for East Africa.
   Available from: AMREF. See Appendix E.

8. *Community Health Workers in National Programmes – Just Another Pair of Hands?* G. Walsh. (ed.) Open University, 1990.
   A discussion and evaluation of CHWs worldwide. A very useful book for programme managers.
   Available from: Open University, Milton Keynes, UK.

In addition to the above many countries now produce their own guidelines and manuals for selecting, training and supervising CHWs.

Part III

SPECIFIC PROGRAMMES

8

Setting up a Community Health Clinic

In this chapter we shall consider:

1. What we need to **know**
   - Why start a clinic?
   - What type of clinic should be set up?
   - Who will use the clinic?
   - How many people should the clinic serve?
   - Where should the clinic be held?
   - When should the clinic start?
2. What we need to **do**:
   - Design and equip the centre
   - Set up the clinic stations
   - Keep accurate records
   - Decide on a system of payment
   - Set up a referral system
   - Concentrate on teaching

What we need to know

In this section we shall answer the questions below.

Why start a clinic?

The reason may seem simple: **people** are sick: **health workers** can make them better: the **community** requests it.

But we need to look at the reasons more carefully, and see what different expectations people and health workers may have (see Figure 8.1).

> Our aim in running a clinic is to offer cure for people's **felt** needs, while at the same time giving care for their **real** needs.

© Illustration David Gifford

Figure 8.1 A case of differing expectations

If curative care alone is provided this situation occurs:

> The **same** patient with the **same** illness comes back to the **same** clinic to get the **same** medicine to return to the **same** environment to get the **same** illness. . . .

The community may in the long term be worse off than before, still just as sick and now newly dependent.

What type of clinic should be set up?

This should be decided in partnership with the community.

Some projects will run **general** clinics where any person can attend with any problem. Others will run **separate** clinics for different problems such as Mother and Child Health (MCH) clinics on one day of the week, TB clinics on another.

General clinics are usually more convenient for patients unless access is exceptionally easy. **All patients** can be dealt with at the same time – grandmother with toothache, father with indigestion, mother pregnant again, and the twins with malnutrition.

Moreover **each individual** can use the same visit to have all problems seen on one single occasion. *For example*: a mother with sore eyes, having a chronic cough, needing a final pre-natal check, and requesting advice about family planning.

Separate clinics are sometimes appropriate, each being run on a different day of the week. These can be used where access is very easy, or patient numbers large, as when a clinic first starts, or when chronic poverty causes much illness.

> Health team members must **never run clinics at the expense of being involved at the community level**. It is far more useful to spend half the week teaching CHWs or improving a community water supply than spending 5 days within the walls of the health centre.

Who will use the clinic?

Unless the clinic is part of a genuine community programme: the **least needy** may use it **most**, the **most needy** may use it **least**. This is known as the 'inverse care law'.

© Illustration David Gifford

Figure 8.2 The least needy may use the clinic most, the most needy may use it least

The least needy who use it most

These may include:

1. Those with **minor health needs** wanting injections and pills.
2. Those **ill a long time** who have already seen many doctors, and arrive clutching sheafs of reports.
3. Those **living nearby** who can easily attend.
4. Those **well enough** to reach the clinic or who have relatives able and willing to bring them.
5. **Men**, who in poor communities often have more time to attend, and are often less willing than women to tolerate pain.

The most needy who use it least

These may include:

1. The **poor**, the distant and the frightened.
2. **Women,** unable to leave home.
3. **Children** too sick to walk, or with no one to carry them.
4. The **very ill**, the very old, the disabled.

Our project must run clinics in such a way that the inverse care law is reversed. Clinics must therefore be **priced** sensibly and **sited** correctly, be **user-friendly**, and run in **partnership** with the community.

How many people should the clinic serve?

There are several factors to consider:

The 'natural community'

A clinic may serve one large village, one cluster of smaller villages, a plantation, a factory or a refugee camp. It may serve a certain section of a city slum.

Usually the clinic will tie in with our survey area, CHW training programme, and other community activities. It will serve the 'target' area and population.

The number of effectively working CHWs

> The more CHWs that are trained and the more skilled they become the fewer the number of patients who will need to attend clinics.

The length of time the clinic has been running

If our clinic is serving a definite target area and CHWs are working effectively numbers attending **may actually decline**, and we may later be able to reduce clinic frequency.

This effect is **not** seen in clinics open to anyone with no CHW back up. In such cases clinics may actually increase their numbers as others come to hear of good (or cheap) treatment available.

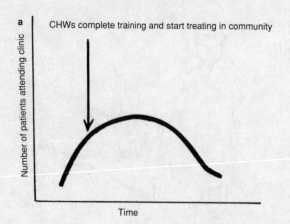
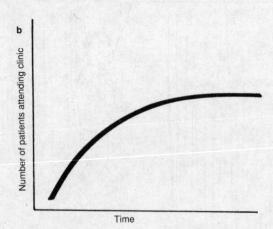

© Illustration David Gifford

Figure 8.3   Clinic attendance rates. **a** With effective CHWs at community level. **b** With no effective functioning of CHWs

An approximate guide for the population a clinic can serve is as follows:

A team of five health workers (see below) **able to spend adequate time with each patient** can manage up to 50 or 100 patients per day. This might represent a target population of up to 5000. Later as CHWs are trained and the community becomes healthier, larger populations can be served or clinics can be held less often.

In some countries, clinics run by voluntary programmes need to link in with government plans. Governments usually plan Primary Health Centres for population blocks of 5000, 10 000, 20 000 or 50 000 depending on resources available, with sub-centres, dispensaries or village health posts serving smaller numbers.

Where should the clinic be held?

1. Close to the community

> Clinics should be set up within the community or as near to it as possible. No one should need to travel more than one hour's easy journey.

2. In an acceptable location for all.

If one clinic serves different villages, tribal groups, religions or castes, it must be in a 'neutral' place where all community members are happy to attend. A roadside or pathside building is often appropriate.

The clinic and its waiting area must be safe for children.

When should the clinic start?

This should be discussed with community leaders. It may have to be started **before** training CHWs or carrying out any other community activity. Remote or poor communities may have so much illness or so little understanding of community involvement that they are not prepared to work in partnership with us until basic health services are provided.

If possible wait to start a clinic until **after** CHWs are trained. In this way the community understands that CHWs are the **front line health workers** whom they go to see first.

> Once people become used to visiting a clinic for day-to-day health problems they may later ignore their newly trained CHW.

If we do delay starting a clinic there must be some nearby health centre or hospital where sick people can attend and to which serious cases can be referred.

What we need to do

Design and equip the centre

Doctors, project directors and community leaders may want impressive and expensive health centres. The local community, especially the poor may want a simple building, as much like home as

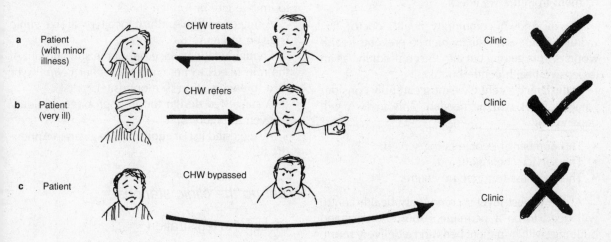

© Illustration David Gifford

Figure 8.4 The right (**a** and **b**) and wrong (**c**) relationship of the CHW and clinic

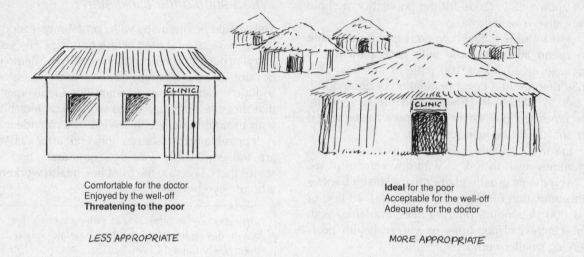

Comfortable for the doctor
Enjoyed by the well-off
Threatening to the poor

LESS APPROPRIATE

Ideal for the poor
Acceptable for the well-off
Adequate for the doctor

MORE APPROPRIATE

© Illustration David Gifford

Figure 8.5

possible, which they feel is **their place** rather than **the doctor's palace**.

> We should rent or construct the simplest building which is able to support the services we are planning to give.

In doing this we must remember the main functions of a health centre building:

1. To enable patients to receive good-quality health care.
2. To protect patients, health workers and equipment from the weather.

A well known community health doctor has written: 'There is nothing which so prevents health workers from getting out into the community, as an expensive health centre building.'

In **designing** a centre we must carefully consider what facilities will be needed. This in turn will depend on:

- The number of people being served.
- The services being offered.
- The nearness to a referral centre.

At the **largest level** a community health centre will need to be a permanent, purpose-designed building, with in-patient beds and a delivery room.

At the **smallest** level, a room or the verandah of a CHW's house may be all that is needed.

At the **middle** level – appropriate for most small-scale projects – a simple building with three or four rooms and a careful 'flow-pattern' will be adequate.

> Health centres should ideally be made of local materials and should follow local building styles. They can be purpose-built by the project and community. Alternatively an appropriate local building can be adapted and used.

Health centres do **not** need to be made of concrete with corrugated iron roofs; nor do they need to imitate city or foreign styles.

A suggested **flow-pattern** for a typical size clinic is given in Figure 8.6.

Enough waiting space out of the sun and out of the rain needs to be available, either centrally or next to each station (see opposite).

A suggested **design** for an appropriate building is given in Figure 8.7.

A suggested list of **equipment** is given in Appendix B.

Set up the clinic stations

Station 1: Registration

The Registrar has two main jobs: **to welcome** and **to register**.

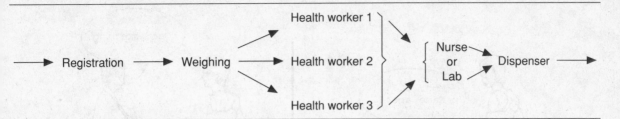

Figure 8.6 Flow-pattern for a typical size clinic

To welcome

To do his job well the registrar must understand the way patients may be feeling. Imagine the feelings of a patient who has never visited the centre before:

> . . . She has got up early, walked a long way in the sun and is carrying a sick child. She is worried. She does not know what to expect, or how the clinic works. She is not sure if she can afford the charges. When she does arrive there are many people before her – all looking anxious. There is a notice giving information but she is unable to read it. . . .

> A friendly smile or a welcoming word from the registrar can be extremely reassuring to a sick or anxious patient.

The registrar looks out for very sick children or other patients and makes sure the health worker sees them as soon as possible.

To record details

Each project will need to work out an appropriate system. Here is a method which can be adapted:

1. Registrar **arrives in plenty of time**, and gets organised before patients arrive.
2. **Patients** arrive to register.
   Various methods can now be followed:
   - **either** Former patients place their cards on the desk, sit down and wait until their name is called. New patients report to the registrar.
   - **or** Patients queue, standing or sitting.

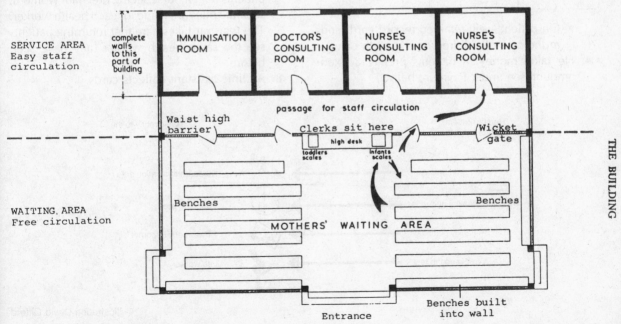

Figure 8.7 Plan of an under-fives' clinic

Figure 8.8   Registration is the first and perhaps the most important contact with the health service

- **or** When large numbers attend, patients take a number on arrival, sit down and wait until the registrar calls out their number.
3. Registrar **records details**:
   - In clinic register as follows:

Patient name	Name Head Fam.	Patient No	Age	Sex	Village	Money paid

- On patient's self-retained record card, and in the case of children on a growth chart.
4. He **takes money**, if patients prepay a fixed amount (see under Payment below).

5. He gives patient a **number**, placing this visibly within the envelope which covers the self-retained card.
6. He extracts the **family folder**.
7. He **places** self-retained notes and family folder together, in a pile (with first arrival on top, latest on the bottom).
   If different health workers are seeing different patients (e.g. a nurse seeing pregnant women), separate piles are made for each health worker. The registrar takes care that returning patients see the same health worker they have seen before.
8. A clinic assistant **collects** cards.

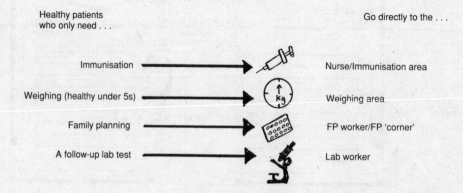

© Illustration David Gifford

Figure 8.9   Saving everyone's time in a busy general clinic

She takes piles of cards from the registrar's desk and places them on the health worker's desk calling out names in turn.

9. Meanwhile **patients sit down** awaiting their turn **except** for certain categories (see Figure 8.9).
10. Registrar **completes his books** after patients have stopped arriving. Any money taken is totalled up and handed over to the person in charge. Finally the registrar checks he has enough supplies for the next clinic.

All MPWs should be trained to register patients. Any with special gifts can take on the job more permanently. **Community members** make good registrars providing they are fair and friendly.

Station 2: Weighing

Those who will need weighing
- Under 5 children.
- Pregnant women.
- TB patients.
- People with AIDS or known to be HIV positive.

A suitable place for weighing
This can be a separate room, a convenient place near the registrar, a verandah or under a tree.

Suitable equipment
Good types include round-faced spring balances or tubular scales. New and experimental methods of weighing and recording are available from TALC (see Appendix A).

Stirrups or trousers are needed for children under 3, baskets for new-born babies.

A suitable person to do it
As in all community health activities, the least qualified person who can do the job well should be given the task.

With careful training family members such as parents or older siblings can do the weighing. MPWs and CHWs should be able to weigh accurately. Nurses can teach others but should not do it permanently themselves.

A suitable system for weighing children
1. The child sits on the parent's lap and the weighing trousers are put on.

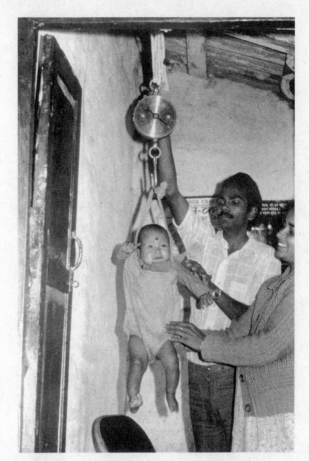

Figure 8.10 Family members weigh their own children

2. The parent lifts the child by the body, not by the straps, and hangs him on the weighing scales.
3. The child hangs **just long enough** for an accurate weight to be measured, and is then lifted down.
4. The weight is plotted on the growth chart.
5. **The card is explained to the parent**. Feeding advice is given where necessary.
6. Any child making good progress can be shown as an example to waiting parents.
7. Children over 3 can hang with their hands.
8. Children very young or very frightened can be weighed with their mother on an adult scale, the mother's own weight then being subtracted: this method is less accurate.

Common mistakes in weighing
1. Many children are waiting but there is only one pair of trousers.

2. Frightened children are left to hang while adults and onlookers unsuccessfully try and cheer them up.
3. Weights are misread through carelessness, because the child is bouncing, or because the mother fails to leave go. Weights that don't seem correct should be rechecked.
4. Growth charts are wrongly filled in (see page 130).
5. The community culture is not understood.

In some rural areas people think that weighing children is wrong or dangerous. Such beliefs should be understood and **gently** corrected. Clinic weighing should not be allowed to replace weighing in the home by mother or CHW.

Station 3: The consultation

> **Those people with the greatest health needs often live in areas where doctors are unwilling to provide primary care.** For this reason many of the world's neediest people will continue to be seen by CHWs at community level, backed up by appropriately trained health workers at clinic level.

Health workers who see patients must be carefully trained and supervised by doctors. They should also follow careful guidelines such as Standing Orders or Treatment Schedules, where the symptoms and treatment of common diseases are clearly set out.

Here is a system which can be followed by any trained health worker who see patients.

1. Health worker warmly **greets** the patient.
2. Health worker **consults** patient's records.
   He notes the patient's village or background, caste or tribe. He looks for details of any previous illness or treatment.
   If a family folder is being used he takes note of the size, structure and socioeconomic status of the family.
3. Health worker takes **history**.
   a) He asks the patient what the problem is – listening carefully without interrupting.
   b) For any important symptom he now asks questions as follows:
      • For **diarrhoea**:
      How many stools per day?
      How many days have you had it?

Is there fever? blood? mucus? vomiting? excess flatus?
   • For **pain**:
   Where is the pain?
   How long have you had it?
   Have you ever had it before?
   What makes it better or worse?
   • For **cough**:
   How long have you had it?
   Is there sputum, blood, fever or chest pain?
   Have you ever had TB treatment?
   • For **fever**:
   How long have you had it?
   Is it continuous or does it come and go?
   Is there sweating, shivering, vomiting or headache?
   • For **cuts, bites, accidents**:
   When did it happen?
   How did it happen?
   • For any **other symptom**:
   How long have you had it?
   Have you had it before?
   Any other suitable questions.
   • For **malnutrition**: obtain full details (see Chapter 9 pages 122–3)
   • For **prenatal patients**: obtain full details (see Chapter 12 page 178ff)
   • For **women of child-bearing** age we should **ask** whether pregnant. This is both so we can offer prenatal care and also so we can know what medicines are safe to prescribe.
   • **Where TB is common** we ask whether there has been cough for more than 4 weeks.
   • **Where AIDS is common** we ask appropriate questions.
   c) Other questions **if** diagnosis still unclear
   • **Ears**: any pain or discharge?
   • **Eyes**: any pain or trouble seeing?
   • **Throat**: any soreness or loss of voice?
   • **Chest**: any other symptoms?
   • **Bowels**: any other symptoms?
   • **Urination**: pain, frequency or trouble in passing? Any discharge?
   • **Periods**: pain, heavy loss, discharge? bleeding between periods?
   • **Skin**: any sores, itching, rash or swellings?

talking

and only then by **examining**

looking

or **investigating**

© Illustration David Gifford

Figure 8.11   Learn to diagnose patients mainly by . . .

- **Bones, joints, muscles**; any swelling, pain or stiffness?
- **Mind**: any sadness, agitation or fits?
- **Any other symptoms** not mentioned?

4. Health worker **examines** patient:
   a) By **looking**.
      - General appearance: anything unusual?
      - Well or ill?
      - Thin or dehydrated?
      - Normal colour? Pale? Yellow? Flushed with fever?
      - Breathing normally? Child with breathing rate of 50 or more per minute? (If so suspect pneumonia.)
      - Eyes: Infection? Pale mucous membranes? Yellow? Vitamin A deficiency?
      - Tongue: Pale? Dry? Sore or smooth?
      - Part of body where symptom located: Anything to see?
   b) By **touching** and **feeling**.
      - Pulse: Rate? Regular? Strong?
      - Part of body where symptom located: any swelling, warmth, pain or tenderness?
   c) By **listening** if problem is chest.
      - Any unusual or added sounds over lung? Any heart murmur?
   d) By **measuring** temperature and blood pressure if necessary.

5. Health worker **diagnoses** the problem.
   Before doing this he may need to order a laboratory test. He then makes the diagnosis, aided by any laboratory results and the Standing Orders.
   If he is uncertain **what** the problem is or **how** serious it is he refers to the supervisor, nurse or doctor.
6. Health worker now **searches** for any **real** need of the **patient**.
   Patients nearly always come because of **felt** needs – some pain, problem or irritation for which they want a cure.

> Trying to find **real** needs is **our most important task**. A **real** need can be thought of as a problem, disease, or lack of health which **seriously affects the long-term health of the patient, the family or the community**.

Chief real needs will include:
a) **Malnutrition** found by weighing.
b) Lack of **childhood immunisations** and tetanus toxoid innoculation found by questioning and looking at notes.
c) Presence of **serious** illness such as **TB**, **AIDS** or **leprosy** – especially if patient undiagnosed or defaulted from treatment.
d) **Pregnancy** with the need for prenatal care.

e) The need for **family planning**.
f) Recent **discharge** from hospital especially if due to an infectious or serious disease.

The health worker can discover these real needs by:

a) Questioning the patient.
b) Checking the patient's record card and in particular the **family folder** and **insert cards**. **This gives a quick and easy way of discovering real needs**.

7. Health worker checks for any **real need of any other family member**.

For example: If a **child** is accompanying the patient, he makes sure that the child has been recently weighed and completed immunisations. If a **mother** is a accompanying a patient, could she be pregnant and if so is she having prenatal care? If a coughing **father** is accompanying, has he himself been tested for TB? **The family folder and insert cards should be checked to make sure immunisations are complete and that any important follow-up to previous problems has been carried out.**

Any family members needing to be seen can be brought to the next clinic.

THINKS: THIS PATIENT CAME WITH BACKACHE, BUT WHAT ARE THE REAL NEEDS OF THE PATIENT AND HER FAMILY

© Illustration David Gifford

Figure 8.12

When clinics first start **or cover too large a population** there may be such a rush of patients that there may be little time to search for real needs. Remember however:

> Health projects should be set up in such a way that CHWs deal with routine problems in the community. This frees clinics for treating serious illness and caring for the real needs of patients. **Unless this is guaranteed clinics spend all their time treating minor, felt needs and the real needs of the individual and community remain unmet.**

8. Health worker **treats** the patient.
   a) He **prescribes** any medicine necessary. He writes down the generic name, the dose, how often the medicine should be taken and how long it should be taken for. He mentions any precautions, special instructions or side effects.
   b) He **advises** the patient how he himself can help to cure his present condition and prevent it from recurring.
   For example: A method which has proved successful in some projects is the use of 'health drills'. These are carefully worded summaries of health advice which are listed alphabetically for each common health problem. The health worker seeing patients, the nurse and dispenser all have copies. The health worker explains the relevant health drill to the patient, then 'prescribes' it in the notes. When the patient later sees the nurse or dispenser she will give identical instructions so reinforcing the teaching.
   c) He **arranges any procedure** such as bandaging, tooth extraction or immunisation.
   d) He **refers** the patient to a more senior health worker if he is not sure of the diagnosis or treatment.

9. Health worker makes sure the **patient understands**, asking the patient to repeat back any important instructions. He recognises if the patient does not seem satisfied and tries to discover the reason.
   He tells the patient when to return to the clinic.

10. Health worker **records** important information on the patient's record card, the family folder insert card, and any relevant register (see below).

© Illustration David Gifford

Figure 8.13 If in doubt about a diagnosis refer, don't guess

Five suggestions when seeing patients:

1. **Patients learn as they wait**.
   In Mother and Child Health clinics patients can wait **in** the consultation room, or just outside it, so that they 'learn by overhearing'. CHWs can gather groups of waiting mothers and give appropriate teaching (see Chapter 3, page 28).
2. **Each one teach one**. Use the consultation as a time to teach other health workers especially CHWs. Encourage other health team members to pass on their knowledge and skills whenever they have a chance.
3. **Respect patients' beliefs**. Patients may have ideas which seem strange or wrong to us. They may be more interested in **who** caused the disease than in **what** caused it. We should instruct gently without causing a patient to lose his dignity, or feel offended.
4. **The same patient sees the same health worker**. The more a patient comes to know and trust one particular health worker the more likely she will follow the advice given, and return for follow-up.
5. **Respect the need for privacy**.
   In many busy clinics patients are seen with others waiting or watching nearby. If this is the case make sure there is strict privacy when

necessary, for example when diseases such as TB, leprosy, AIDS or STD are suspected, or family planning is discussed.

Station 4: The field laboratory

A small field laboratory is quite easy to set up and **greatly adds to the value of a community clinic**:

Advantages:

1. It confirms the diagnosis, meaning that clinics can concentrate on **curing illness** rather than on **treating symptoms**.
2. It makes health care more accurate especially when paramedics are seeing patients.
3. It gives 'customer satisfaction'.
4. It is quick and cost-effective. By reducing the number of visits to hospital it saves the patient time, and saves the project money.

Types of test available

Here are examples of tests which can easily be handled by a field laboratory with **simple** equipment, and manned by a worker with **basic** training.

1. **Blood** tests: haemoglobin, white cell count and differential, erythrocyte sedimentation rate (ESR), malaria smear, HIV test.
2. **Sputum** tests: for acid-fast bacilli (AFB) in tuberculosis.
   This is the correct way to confirm TB. Treatment should not normally be started unless a patient is sputum positive (see Chapter 14, page 205).
3. **Stool** tests: for worms (e.g. hook, round, whip, tape), protozoa (e.g. *Amoeba*, *Giardia*) and *Schistosoma* ova.
4. **Urine** tests: microscopy for pus cells, bacteria and *Schistosoma* ova.
   Dip stick (or other method) for sugar, protein, bile and blood.
5. **Skin** tests: slit skin for leprosy, scrape for fungus.
6. **Vaginal swabs** for *Gonococcus*, *Trichomonas*, or *Monilia*.

The laboratory worker

Tests can either be done by a qualified laboratory worker with basic training, or by a multi-purpose worker carefully trained in simple laboratory skills.
   Laboratory workers must be:

- accurate, reliable and thorough, and
- aware of their own limitations.

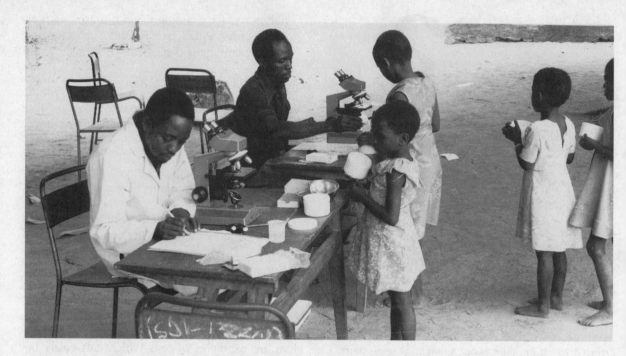

Figure 8.14   A simple field laboratory helps a clinic to treat causes rather than symptoms

Unless carefully trained and supervised, workers may be tempted to 'fudge results' especially if they are rushed for time or lacking confidence, or want to record a result which will please the doctor.

Equipment needed

Needles and **syringes** which are **reliably sterile** must be used and supervisors should make regular spot-checks. A suggested list of equipment appears in Appendix B.

Procedure for patients

Patients needing laboratory tests will be referred by the health worker. They will proceed to the laboratory, bringing either their self-retained card or a separate laboratory request slip, on which the result will be recorded.

They will wait their turn, both for the test and the result, and then report back to the health worker.

Station 5: The clinic nurse

The nurse herself

Larger clinics may have fully qualified nurses. Smaller clinics will often use MPWs, who after appropriate training will carry out nursing duties.

> Nurses who have been trained in hospitals and then join community health projects will need a complete reorientation in their approach and outlook. In practice MPWs trained on the job are often more suitable than trained nurses who wish they were back in the hospital.

The nurse's function

This will include the following:
- Giving injections (see Chapter 10, page 151).
- Dressing and bandaging.
- Cleaning skin infections and wounds.
- Lancing abscesses.
- Giving family planning advice and supplies.
- Running an ORS corner (see page 159).
- Assisting the doctor or the health worker.
- Taking temperatures, weights and blood pressures.
- Teaching.
Nurses may also be involved in consultation.

Station 6: The dispenser or pharmacist

Any MPW with a particular gift or interest can be trained as a dispenser, be put in charge of the dispensary and teach others.

© Illustration David Gifford

Figure 8.15 Mistakes are easy to make when a doctor's writing is unclear or a dispenser is over-worked

The dispenser is usually the last health worker whom the patient will see. His smile, or sharp words, may linger in the patient's mind, affecting future compliance.

> It is good practice in smaller health centres for all MPWs to be trained in dispensing. In this way the job can be shared out so that no one person has to count pills and give instructions for hours at a time.

The dispenser's job includes **dispensing** and **stock-keeping**.

Dispensing

This includes:

1. Reading the doctor's or health workers handwriting. This may be difficult! If in doubt he **should ask, not guess**. If a medicine has run out or is not available he should ask the health worker or doctor if an alternative can be used.

2. Counting. The **exact** number of pills must be given. This is especially important in TB and leprosy treatment and when using antibiotics and anti-malarials.

   Any broken, dirty, or discoloured medicines should be thrown away. Medicines past their expiry date should not normally be used unless there is a genuine shortage of supplies (see Chapter 16, pages 232–3).

3. Explaining. For each medicine the patient will need to know:
   • How many?
   • How often?
   • How long for?
   • How? e.g. with water, before or after food?
   • What side effects?
   • What food, drink or activity needs to be avoided?

   In the case of eye drops, ear drops, ORS packets, or capsules that have to be opened and mixed on a spoon for children, the dispenser should be ready to **show** how it is done, as well as giving verbal instructions. Before leaving, the patient should repeat back the instructions, to make sure he has understood.

> Many patients who leave clinics clutching pills and medicines will not take them as instructed. They may fail to understand the instructions given, forget what they have been told or think their own ideas are better than the health worker's instructions.

© Illustration David Gifford

Figure 8.16

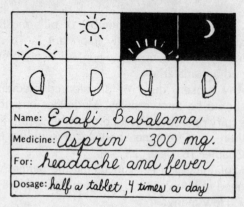

Name: *Edafi Babalama*

Medicine: *Asprin   300 mg.*

For: *headache and fever*

Dosage: *half a tablet, 4 times a day*

Figure 8.17   If patients cannot read use pictures to explain amount and timing of pills and medicines

For example. A doctor greeted a leprosy patient by the roadside who one month previously had been diagnosed at a clinic and given 30 white dapsone tablets. The dispenser had instructed him to take one per day. Asked now how he was feeling the patient replied: 'Fine Doc, I took the tablets – all 30 together and now I feel well.' Other patients may not be so fortunate.

4. Labelling the packet or bottle.
   Any container, or envelope must be well labelled. If the patient is illiterate, we should use symbols.
   For example: One aspirin to be taken four times a day can be represented as shown in Figure 8.17. Even these symbols must be explained.

5. Repeating the health drill (see page 108).

Stock-keeping
This includes:

1. Checking levels
   The dispenser will need to:
   • **check** all drugs:
     – For **quantity** remaining, at least once monthly.
     – For **expiry** dates at least once quarterly.
   • Use a **stock list** made out alphabetically as shown below, so that his check can be systematic.

> The purpose of this system is to re-order in plenty of time so that **stocks never run out unless there is a national shortage of drugs**. Health centres must always keep in stock an adequate supply of essential drugs.

2. Re-ordering supplies.
   The dispenser will need to use a **re-order sheet** made out as shown below.
   Two copies are made:
   Copy 1 is sent with the order. Central stores returns the form with the new supply, filling in (b). The dispenser then writes down the amount actually received in (c).
   Copy 2 is put directly into the dispenser's file and is attached to Copy 1 when this is returned.

3. Labelling supplies.
   Drug names are confusing. Each drug may have several different **brand** names but only one **generic** name. The generic name should therefore always be used, even though it may be longer and harder to remember.
   The stockkeeper in central supplies should always send out supplies with labels attached (see Chapter 18, page 254).

Stock list

Drug name	Code No	Unit of issue	Full stock level	Stock level when re-order necessary
Aspirin	P 04	Bottle 100	2000	500

Re-order sheet

Name of health centre ....   Date ordered..................   Date received ....

List of items needed	Code Nos	No ordered (a)	No sent (b)	No received (c)	Remarks

The label can include these details:

Generic name of drug	Code No.	Number when full

In new, or smaller clinics and where supplies are sent out in bottles labelled by drug companies a bold ring or circle can be made around the generic name instead of sticking a new label on to each bottle.

When semi-literate CHWs help in dispensing, colour codes can be used e.g. green labels for antibiotics, orange for anti-malarials etc.

4. Storing supplies in the clinic cupboard.

Supplies should be arranged **neatly**, in **alphabetical generic order** with the newest supplies at the back of the shelf. The front of the shelf itself can be labelled either with the drug name or with a letter of the alphabet.

In practice it is easy for new supplies to be put at the front and for old supplies to get pushed to the back and expire. Huge amounts of drugs can be wasted in this way.

The following system can prevent this:

For each drug, storage space is divided into two sections, side by side:

A B	A B	A B	A B
Drug 1	Drug 2	Drug 3	Drug 4

At the beginning A is existing stock and B is empty. When the amount remaining in A reaches the re-order level, new supplies are requested and these are put in B. These new supplies are not used until all of A has been used up. Then when B gets low new stock is put in A but not used until supplies in B are finished.

5. Prepacking

In busy clinics much time can be saved if standard courses of commonly used drugs are prepacked and prelabelled.

If possible use bottles or plastic envelopes, especially during the rainy season.

Keep accurate records

Each project will develop its own system of records (see Appendix F). Most centres can use patient-retained record cards, the family folder and insert cards, and clinic registers.

Patient-retained record cards

There will be separate designs for adults, and under-5 children. Those with chronic diseases, e.g. TB and leprosy, can in addition have a specially designed card.

Patients keep their own cards in plastic envelopes (if available) and bring them **whenever** they come to **any** clinic, see the CHW or go to hospital.

Health workers make entries on these cards as follows:

1. The **registrar** writes down the date (and, where relevant) the amount of money paid,
2. The person **weighing** children fills in the growth chart.
3. The **health worker** seeing patients will make brief but accurate notes.

Examples of the notes he could make for two different patients are shown in Table 8.1

If the **health worker** himself carries out part of the management he places a tick to show it has been done.

When writing medicines the health worker must include the following:

- generic name of medicine,
- dose,
- number of times per day and
- any **special** instructions.

(The dispenser will be responsible for **routine** instructions about the use of each drug he gives out.)

The **nurse** places a tick in the notes after any procedure she has carried out.

The **laboratory worker** writes in the results of any tests (or records it on the attached request slip).

The **dispenser** ticks each medicine he gives out. If the medicine requested is finished he writes down any alternative that has been sanctioned.

The family folder and insert card

The family folder itself

With the exception given below **nothing** is written

Table 8.1   Examples of health worker's entries in patient's notes

Adult	6-year-old child
Symptoms and how long they have been present	*Symptoms and how long they have been present*
Cough with blood 3 months	Diarrhoea with mucus 6 times daily for 2 days: no fever
Findings on examination	*Findings on examination*
Patient very thin, crackles in both lungs. Temperature 38°C	General condition good, lips dry, skin elastic
Diagnosis	*Diagnosis*
Suspected TB	Amoebic dysentery with mild dehydration
Management	*Management*
Refer for sputum test on arrival next week Meanwhile ampicillin 500 mg t.i.d. 5 days 'Cough drill' given	Demonstrate use of ORS (nurse) Metronidazole 200 mg t.i.d. for 5 days Return in 1 week if no better

on the **family folder** itself unless a mistake is discovered. The folder is a record of the state of health of the family **on the day of the survey** (see Chapter 6, pages 60–4).

If the folder has a section 'vital events since survey' this can be filled in if any new family member has been born, if anyone has died, or if anyone has permanently joined or left the family.

The insert cards

In the case of **serious illness** or an important **real need** need, make a brief note on the insert card. A similar or simpler pattern to that used on the self-

retained card can be followed, but in addition a date should be recorded by which the patient must be seen again.

Self-limiting or trivial problems should not be recorded on the insert card, otherwise valuable time is wasted.

Clinic registers

These should be kept as simple as possible.

The **health worker** seeing patients fills in any TB, leprosy or special disease register.

The **nurse** fills in the immunisation or family planning register.

INSERT CARD

Date	Problem	Action	Date to be seen again
1st April 1990	Cough with blood 1 month	Sputum test next visit Co-trimoxazole two b.d. 1 wk	8th April 1990

Figure 8.18   Example of an entry on an insert card

© Illustration David Gifford

Figure 8.19 A problem of charging too much

© Illustration David Gifford

Figure 8.20 A problem or charging too little

A note of patients referred will be kept (see below). Disease tallies can sometimes be useful.

The **registrar** keeps a note of patients seen and money received.

Decide on a system of payment

How much should be charged?

Patients should always pay at least some contribution for the services and medicines they receive.

This is in the interest of the **patient**. He values the treatment more and does not come to expect free handouts.

It is necessary for the **project** which should try to cover its drug supply costs. Fixing a fair scale requires much care:

1. If too **much** is charged:
   - The poor cannot afford it and may not attend, indicating we are not providing a comprehensive service to those who most need it.
2. If too **little** is charged:
   - Patients may think the clinic or the medicine is poor quality.
   - People may suspect our motives, or abuse our services by demanding medicines for minor problems.
   - The project will fail to cover its costs.

Payment levels therefore need to be **just**, **acceptable** to most of the community and **affordable** by the poor.

Despite setting up an appropriate system some patients may still claim they are unable to pay.

When this happens we have several options:

1. We can check the socioeconomic status on the family folder, and give a concession to those genuinely poor.
2. We can ask for advice from the CHW or Health Committee member helping in the clinic, who will probably know the patient's **real** situation.
3. We can encourage the patient to pay as much as he is able, or to pay in kind.

What system of payment should be used?

Fixed prepayment to the registrar

A fixed amount is paid to the registrar at the time of registration. Patients must understand this is to pay for services given, **whether or not any medicine is prescribed**. Children pay less than adults. Certain categories are free such as children needing only to be weighed and immunised, women attending for pre-natal checks or family planning, and in some programmes TB patients.

Two variations on this system can be used:

Example 1.
Patients coming to a health centre from villages who have their own CHW pay a lower rate or 'A' rate. Patients coming from villages who have not sent CHWs for training pay a higher rate or

'B' rate. This encourages 'B' villages to send a CHW for training or if the village is too distant, to request a health centre with CHW training for their area.

Example 2.

In communities who have fully trained CHWs a double rate or 'B' rate is charged to any patient **who has not first seen the CHW** and brought a referral slip. This encourages patients to use CHWs for routine problems, and to attend the clinic only if referred.

When using a pre-payment system the final four columns in the Registration Book can be prepared as follows:

Rate	Amount paid	Amount refunded	Total

Payment by item of service

This system is commonly used in hospital out-patients and can be adapted for larger clinics.

Patients are charged for each service they receive and each medicine they need, the amounts being written on a registration slip and totals paid to the cashier, dispenser or registrar before the patient leaves.

In practice charges per patient tend to work out higher, making it more difficult for the poor. It also takes more time.

The use of Revolving Drug Funds can be useful in setting up a payment system (see Further reading page 120).

Set up a referral system

Without a good referral system, CBHC can be dangerous and inefficient. In addition **patients** can waste a huge amount of money and **health workers** a great deal of time.

> Unless a good referral system is set up, patients may wander from one doctor or health worker to another, collecting ever increasing amounts of medicine, advice and reports. Because patients receive **partial** treatment from many doctors, they often receive **effective** treatment from none.

Who should be referred?

1. Any seriously ill patient who needs expert advice or tests to find the cause of the illness.
2. Any patient needing treatment or surgery which cannot be done in the health centre.
3. Anyone demanding a 'second opinion'.

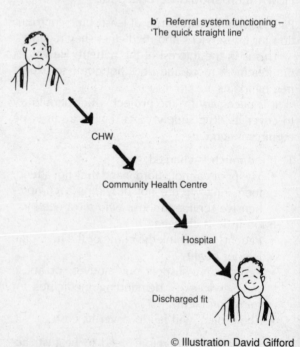

a No referral system functioning – 'The endless cycle'

Health worker/Doctor No.1

PATIENT

Health worker/Doctor No.4

Health worker/Doctor No.2

Health worker/Doctor No.3

b Referral system functioning – 'The quick straight line'

CHW

Community Health Centre

Hospital

Discharged fit

© Illustration David Gifford

Figure 8.21   Recycling illness

HOSPITAL REFERRAL LETTER

Dear Doctor,

    Thank you for seeing this patient and if necessary admitting him/her to hospital.

Patient's Name .... Age .... Sex ....

Patient's Village .... Number ....

Reason for referral:

Relevant History and Clinical Findings:

Current Drug Therapy:

Known sensitivities

Financial status

Other relevant details

    We would be glad if you could give the patient a discharge letter and tell him/her to report to the health centre bringing the letter.

                                  With thanks for your help.

                                        Yours sincerely,

I .... (patient's name) agree to pay ....
direct to the Hospital.
The remainder will be paid by the project direct to the Hospital.

                    Signature   (a) Project Medical officer..

                                (b) Patient or patient's relative ....

Figure 8.22   Example of a referral letter used by one project

All health workers must be trained to recognise the patients they are unable to treat or diagnose themselves. Unless they learn to refer such patients, the community will lose confidence in the project and use other health facilities.

How should patients be referred?

1. They should be given a **referral letter** (see Figure 8.22).

   One copy should be given to the patient, the other kept in a clinic file. Alternatively a note can be written on the self-retained card.

   In the case of patients unable to afford the cost of hospital referral and where subsidy may be available, this system can be used:

   Discover the **maximum** amount the patient is able to afford, **agree** this amount with the patient, **record** it at the foot of the referral letter, **ask** the patient to sign and a health worker to countersign.

2. They should be given a careful **explanation**.

For the poor, sick or timid, going to a crowded hospital can be a terrifying experience. They will be wondering: Can I afford it? What will they do to me? Will I need an operation? Supposing I die? Are the stories I have heard about this place really true?

The health worker must take time to meet the patient's fears and to answer his questions.

3. When necessary they should be **accompanied** to hospital.

   Many patients need someone to go with them who **knows** the **system** and can **show solidarity** with them. This might be a project member, an experienced CHW, or a member of a health committee, who will help to guide the patient through the frightening world of white coats, queues and demands for illicit payment.

   Projects with their own referral hospitals still need to ensure that the poor are treated with dignity and respect.

   Seriously ill patients should be transported in a

Figure 8.23   Partnership between the community and project in referring a patient to hospital

© Illustration David Gifford

Figure 8.24   Cured patients make effective teachers

project vehicle or accompanied on public transport by a project member.

> Patients discharged from a hospital or health centre should be **referred back** to the CHW or other appropriate health worker.

Who should patients be referred to?

Many projects will have their own hospital to which most patients will be referred.

If this is not the case the project director needs to set up links with suitable doctors, clinics and hospitals to which patients can be referred.

In practice the success of such a referral system will depend on making a network of social contacts and friendships outside the project.

Concentrate on teaching

Clinics give great opportunities for teaching. Patients who are either worried or unwell are often open to new ideas.

When clinics are busy, health teaching is the first activity to get squeezed out, unless everyone knows that teaching is a priority and that a particular health worker, CHW or community member has been appointed to carry it out.

The following teaching methods are appropriate for clinics:

1. Person to person.
   This occurs at each station and 'Health drills' can increase its effectiveness.
2. Health talks, dialogues and demonstrations.
3. Learning through 'overhearing' see page 29.
4. Patient support groups.
   TB, leprosy, AIDS patients or those wanting to stop drinking or drugs can be formed into self-help groups, with a health worker working as facilitator.
5. Demonstrations using patients.
   A health worker can use a patient (with their permission) to underline a health message.
   For example: If an interesting or important case is seen by a health worker from which others would benefit by learning, clinic staff can be summoned and a teaching session held, similar to a hospital ward round.
6. Patients teach other patients.
   Cured TB patients can teach those newly diagnosed. Mothers of children once malnourished, now on the road to health, can share their experiences of how they successfully fed their children.
7. CHWs can teach health songs.

See also Chapter 3.

Summary

Most projects will be asked to set up clinics. This should always be carried out in partnership with the community with the aim that the community should eventually manage it.

Buildings can be built or rented. They should be as simple as possible, well-designed, with careful patient-flow plans, and sufficient waiting area.

Clinics comprise various stations which patients visit in turn – registration, weighing, consulting, nursing, field laboratory and pharmacy. At each point patients are treated with respect and compassion. As well as offering curative care health workers also discover and treat the real needs of patients and their families, in an attempt to cure causes of ill health and to promote health-affirming practices in the community.

Careful records are kept but registers should be few in number and easy to use. A fair method of payment needs to be set up so that the poor are not excluded. An effective referral system has to be established with close links between the project and its referral hospitals. Finally, clinics provide an excellent opportunity for both teaching and sensitising the community.

Further Reading

1. *Paediatric Priorities in the Developing World*. D. Morley. English Language Book Society, London, 1977.
   A classic. Most parts are still relevant.
   Available from: TALC. See Appendix E.
2. *Primary Child Care Books 1 and 2*. M. and F. King. Oxford, 1981.

Another classic text packed with useful and relevant information.
Available from: TALC. See Appendix E.
3. *Where There is No Doctor*. D. Werner. Macmillan. Editions in various languages and specific for different regions.
   Available from: TALC. See Appendix E.
4. *Common Medical Problems in the Tropics*. C. R. Schull. Macmillan, 1987.
   A clear and useful guide especially written in simple language for those without formal medical training. A copy of this should be found in all community health clinics.
   Available from: TALC. See Appendix E.
5. *Health Centre Management*. Medex Primary Health Care Series. Books Nos. 27, 28 and 30. J. Burns School of Medicine University of Honolulu, Hawaii, 1983.
   The whole series is good, these books especially useful.
   Available from: Publisher as above.
6. *On Being in Charge*. R. McMahon, E. Barton, M. Piot. WHO, Geneva, 1980 (reprinted 1986).
   Several sections relevant to health centre management.
   Available from: WHO Regional Office. See Appendix E.
7. Medical Laboratory Manual for Tropical Countries Volume 1 (revised reprint) 1991, *Volume 2* (revised reprint) 1990. M. Cheesborough. Tropical Health Technology/Butterworths.
   A practical and comprehensive manual designed for hospital laboratories but also of value to community based health programmes. A manual specifically designed for primary health workers is in preparation.
   Available from: THT. See Appendix A.
8. '10 Questions to ask about Revolving Drug Funds.' C. Waddington, A. Panza. *Tropical Doctor* 21: 50–54, 1991.
   Available from: Tropical Doctor. See Appendix D.

9
Improving Childhood Nutrition

In this chapter we shall consider:

1. What we need to **know**
   - Why good nutrition is important
   - The different types of malnutrition
   - The root causes of malnutrition
   - The common ages for malnutrition
2. What we need to **do**
   - Measure malnutrition
   - Record malnutrition
   - Set targets
   - Prevent and cure malnutrition
   - Evaluate the programme

What we need to know

Why good nutrition is important

'No loud emergency, no famine, no drought, no flood has ever killed 280,000 children in a week. Yet that is what a silent emergency is doing now – every week.'

Each year almost 15 million under-5 children die and many millions more suffer permanent disability. **Most of these deaths and disabilities can be easily prevented**.

It does **not** need a large number of doctors, huge sums of money or expensive equipment. What it **does** need is an enthusiastic health team and good management.

> The greatest health problem of our time – childhood malnutrition and its associated illnesses – can **best be prevented and cured through community based health programmes**.

Good nutrition is important in order to prevent death and increase survival and also to prevent disability and so increase the quality of life.

Prevention of death and increased survival

Well-fed children get ill – sometimes – but usually recover on their own.

Malnourished children get ill – frequently – and die more often.

For example: Diarrhoea, measles and chest infections are not dangerous for most well-nourished children, but those with severe malnutrition **are many times more likely to die in childhood** from these diseases than those on the Road to Health.

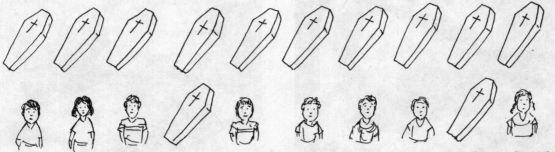

© Illustration David Gifford

Figure 9.1 In poor communities 8 out of every 10 under-5 deaths can be prevented by simple community-based health improvements

> The key to good under 5 health is good under 5 nutrition.

Prevention of disability and increased quality of life

Malnourished children under the age of 2 have **smaller brains** than normal children. This means they grow up to become less intelligent adults, less likely to get good jobs and so less able to provide for their own children. If there is also iodine deficiency, this effect is multiplied.

A child with **vitamin** A **deficiency** may become blind. A girl with **vitamin** D or **calcium deficiency** may develop rickets, leading to a malformed pelvis and extra dangers in giving birth.

Children receiving insufficient food over a long period of time may become **stunted**. They will grow up shorter and less strong than those who are well fed in childhood. They will become less productive farmers and less able workers.

> This means that the malnourished children of today will not only have a lower quality of life themselves: they will pass this on to the children of tomorrow. By correcting malnutrition in **this** generation **we are also helping future generations**.

The different types of malnutrition

Before planning a nutrition programme we must first understand the common forms of malnutrition. These include:

Protein-energy malnutrition (PEM)

This is the correct name for the commonest form of malnutrition. There is a lack both of energy foods (carbohydrates and fats) and of body-building foods (proteins).

Usually both these types of food are in short supply. However where there is a particular lack of energy foods children may suffer from **marasmus**;

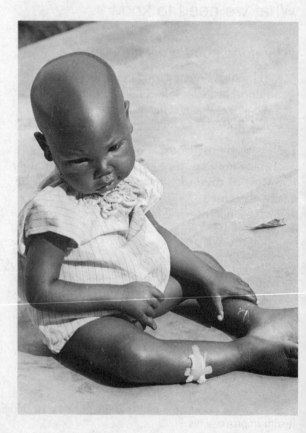

Figure 9.2   Marasmus (**a**) and kwashiorkor (**b**)

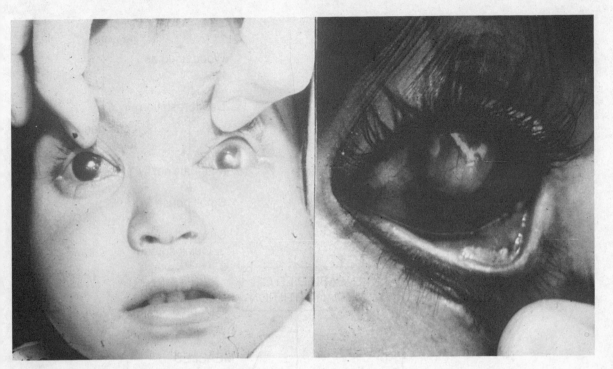

Figure 9.3 Eye symptoms of vitamin A deficiency

where there is a lack of body building foods children may get **kwashiorkor**.

Marasmus is classical starvation where children look 'all skin and bones' or resemble 'wizened old men'. They feel very hungry meaning that feeding them is usually easy.

Kwashiorkor is less common. Children tend to develop swollen legs or bodies, flaking skin and thin, reddish hair. They are usually lethargic, have poor appetites and can be difficult to feed.

Marasmus and kwashiorkor are severe forms of PEM.

> Most cases of mild or moderate malnutrition are not obvious to the mother or even to the health worker. They often look like ordinary children. This 'hidden' group of malnourished children have higher than average health risks.

Anaemia or iron deficiency

This is nearly always present in PEM, and is often present in apparently well nourished children.

Children with anaemia have pale mucous membranes but may **otherwise look quite normal**. However they will often be tired, may perform less well at work, school and play and will get infections more easily.

Anaemia is usually caused by insufficient iron in the diet but malaria, bilharzia and hookworm can make it worse.

Vitamin A deficiency or blinding malnutrition

This may lead to blindness, the eyes of affected children going through these stages: nightblindness, dislike of sunlight, dryness of the cornea with bubbly ('Bitot') spots, ulceration and bursting of the cornea.

Lack of vitamin A also increases the dangers of diarrhoea and respiratory infections, and measles.

> **Nearly half a million children per year in Asia alone** become blind through lack of vitamin A. Nearly all these cases could be avoided if mothers **simply knew that feeding their children green vegetables and yellow fruits available in their communities** would fully prevent it.

Iodine deficiency

Nearly 400 million people live in areas, usually mountainous, where there is lack of iodine.

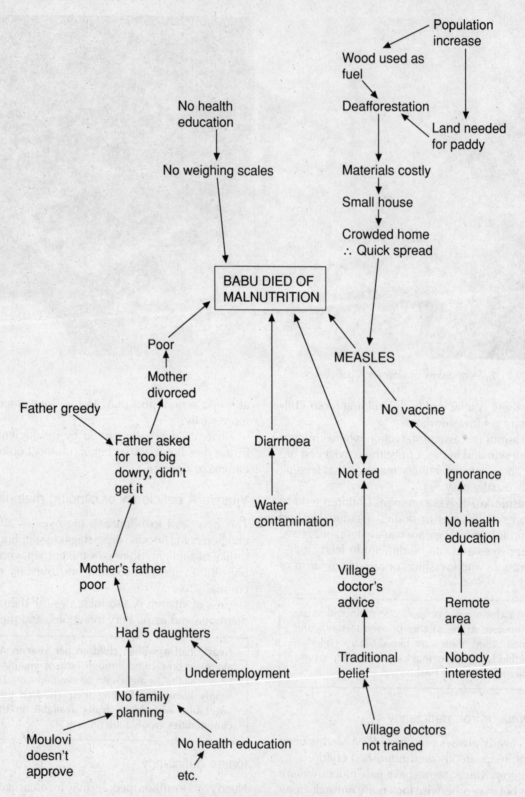

Figure 9.4   Some causes of malnutrition (from a workshop held in Bangladesh)

The most obvious **sign** of iodine deficiency is a swelling (goitre) in the lower neck, most commonly in women. The most dangerous **effect** is in children born to iodine-deficient mothers. Known as cretins these children will sometimes be deaf, dumb, slow, puffy and constipated.

Most iodine-deficient children however may **show very few signs**, but may still grow up to become less intelligent adults.

Other deficiency diseases

These include:

- Lack of vitamin B leading to pellagra and beri-beri.
- Lack of vitamin C leading to scurvy often found in refugee camps.
- Lack of vitamin D or calcium leading to rickets.

The root causes of malnutrition

The root causes of malnutrition are:

1. **Poverty** – where insufficient food is available.
2. **Lack of appropriate knowledge** – where food is available but incorrectly used.

Community health programmes are **ideally placed to deal with such causes**.It is also helpful to consider causes in more detail.

Causes in the child

- Low birth weight.
- Frequent infections such as diarrhoea, coughs and malaria leading to loss of weight, appetite and decreased resistance to further infection.
- Roundworms.
- Poor relationship with mother.
- Bottle feeding.
- AIDS – now the commonest cause in parts of Africa.

Causes in the mother

- Mother herself tired, ill or malnourished.
- Overwork in home, and through demands of other children.
- The daily need to collect fuel and water.
- Work outside home to help family income.
- Mother illiterate and uneducated, thus following incorrect practices, such as withholding food from an ill child and fluids in diarrhoea.
- Mother divorced, separated or widowed.

Causes in the family

- Husband uncaring, absent, drunk, addicted, unemployed, overworked, violent.
- Too many children to feed and care for; no family planning, no child spacing; twins.

Figure 9.5 The circle of infection and malnutrition

- Tensions with mother-in-law.
- Cash crops replacing food crops, meaning less food for children. Extra money wrongly spent on cigarettes and tonics rather than better food.
- Daughters not wanted.
- One or both parents with AIDS.
- Child orphaned.

Causes in the community

- Insufficient land or employment.
- Poor farming practices, soil erosion and deforestation; no irrigation, unproductive land, no land at all.
- Remote area with poor transport and little access to markets.
- Debt, bonded labour. Threats by landlords and moneylenders.
- Money by tradition, spent (and wasted) on weddings, religious ceremonies and dowries.
- 'Guns and drugs' culture.
- Tribal, class and religious conflicts.

Causes in the country

- War, civil unrest, famine, seasonal floods or drought.
- Depressed economy, national debt, lack of foreign exchange.
- Previous food aid leading now to attitude of dependence. Depressed local prices for food and so no incentive to grow. Seed grain used up.
- Corrupt, inefficient or right-wing political system causing the poor to suffer the most.
- Unjust trading laws which favour wealthy countries.

The common ages for malnutrition

This partly depends on local customs, the season of the year and the types of food available in the community. The greatest risks usually occur at the following times.

1. At birth.
   In poor communities the child will usually be of low birth weight, and therefore at greatest risk in the first week (perinatal) period, and the first month (neonatal period).
2. At 8 to 10 months.
   In many communities breast milk alone is given for the first year. A child fed only on breast milk will start falling off the Road to Health at about 8 months.
3. Between 12 and 24 months.
   Weaning problems occur at this age:
   - **Breast** feeding is often stopped. This may happen either gradually, or suddenly if the mother becomes pregnant or gives birth to another child.
   - **Mixed** feeding is started or continued. The dangers here are several. The food itself may be contaminated with germs, the child may place objects in his mouth and bottle feeding may be started. All these can lead to diarrhoea and weight loss.
4. Whenever a new child is born.
   The mother will give her time, attention and breast milk to the newborn meaning that the next youngest child receives less of each. This effect is most important when the birth interval is less than 3 years.
5. Any time of family crisis.

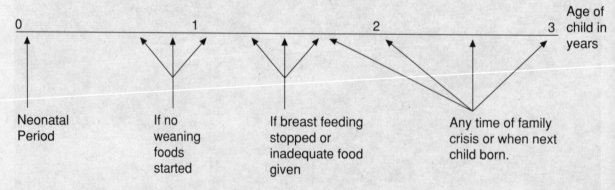

Figure 9.6 Common ages of nutritional risk in a young child

What we need to do

Measure malnutrition

> Remember: **we cannot depend on observation alone**. A malnourished child may look much the same as all the other children. A stunted 5 year old may look like a normal 3 year old. **Malnutrition** can **only be discovered by accurate measurement**.

There are two ways of measuring malnutrition: by using a weighing scale and by using an arm measurer.

Weighing scale

Advantages of weighing: It is accurate, and relatively easy to do.

Disadvantages of weighing: Scales are expensive and may be hard to obtain. Also clock face scales are heavy to carry around, meaning each community and clinic will need to have its own.

The TALC direct recording scale is recommended.

How often should weighing be done?
- Usually once per month.
- With serious cases once per week.
- With life-threatening marasmus once per day.

Where should it be done?
- At first probably in the health centre or clinic.
- As soon as possible in the community for example on the CHW's verandah, or in the child's own home.

Who should do it?
- At first probably a nurse or MPW. She will teach
- the CHW who will teach
- the mother, father or older sibling.
- Members of women's clubs or health committees can weigh children either from house to house or as a community activity.

All those involved in weighing will need **careful teaching** and **supervision** until they can do it without making mistakes.

How is it done?
- This is described in Chapter 8.

Figure 9.7 Community weighing session in Zimbabwe

AN ARM-CIRCUMFERENCE-FOR-AGE GRAPH

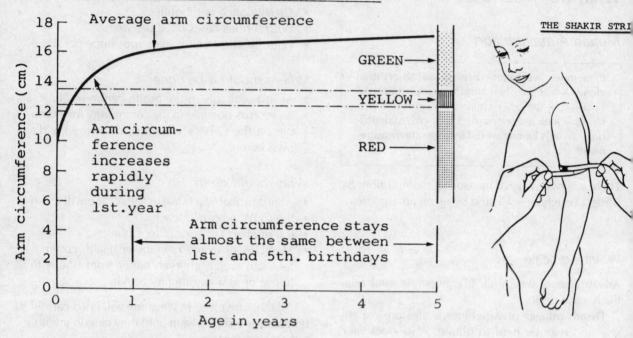

Figure 9.8 Measuring mid-upper arm circumference

Arm measurer

How does it work?

In children the Mid-upper Arm Circumference (MAC) hardly changes at all between the ages of 1 year and 5 years (see Figure 9.8).

Measurements are as follows:

- Well-nourished child: MAC 13.5 cm or more
- Malnourished child:
  moderate: MAC 12.5–13.5 cm
  severe: MAC 12.5 cm or less

In practice a measuring tape with coloured zones is usually used, for example red for severe malnutrition, yellow for moderate and green for normal. Locally appropriate colours can be used instead. Tapes can either be bought, or made from strips of X-ray plate.

How is it used?

- The child should be sitting or standing with his arm hanging unsupported from the shoulder.
- The tape should be wrapped firmly but not too tightly around the **left mid-upper arm**.
- The CHW, mother or older siblings are the best

people to carry it out, but again will need supervised practice.

Advantages of MAC measuring:

- The strip is cheap and easy to carry.
- It is ideal for remote or scattered communities, or to use at the start of a project before weighing scales can be obtained.
- It can be used by those who are unable to read, write or understand numbers.

Disadvantages

- It is slightly less accurate than weighing. Growth charts cannot be used.
- Mistakes can easily be made especially if the person measuring is in a hurry or if the child is fretful.
- It is not valid under one year of age, an important time to know a child's nutritional state.

Further use of the MAC

MAC measurements can be used at birth to assess if the newborn is malnourished.

An MAC of 8.7 cm at the time of birth is approximately equivalent to a birth weight of 2500 grams. If a tape is marked at 8.7 cm any measurement below that is considered low birth weight.

> Measuring the MAC enables illiterate Traditional Birth Attendants (TBAs) or CHWs to discover low weight children **at the time of birth** and target care towards them.

Record malnutrition

MAC measurements can be recorded on an MAC Record Card (see Figure 9.9).

The best way of recording **weights** is on a growth chart. These are used in almost all countries of the world and are available in different languages and layouts. The basic design is the same.

We will need to follow these stages:

1. **Obtain** and if necessary **adapt** growth charts so they are suitable for our target population. We must ensure that the feeding advice on the card is relevant to the mothers in our community, and is written in the local language.
2. **Teach** all team members (and CHWs where literate) how to use them.

> Many growth charts are completed incorrectly. No one should start teaching others until he no longer makes mistakes himself.

When using a growth chart we should:
a) Fill in the **month** and **year** of birth in the long box in the lower left corner.
b) Fill in the **month** and **year** each time the child is weighed.
c) Put a dot and a ring, or a (×) for the measurement, checking and rechecking that it is in the right place, and linking it up with previous measurements using a pencil.
3. Learn to **interpret** our findings, and **explain these to the parents**.
The **direction** of the weight curve is the most crucial.
a) If it is rising – good – reinforce teaching.
b) If it is flat – this is a warning – find the cause, take action and give suitable teaching to the parents.
c) If it is falling – there is a serious problem which must be discovered and treated as soon as possible.

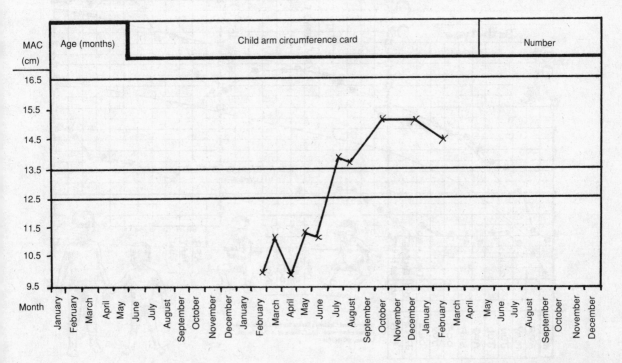

© Illustration David Gifford

Figure 9.9   Mid-upper arm circumference record card

The actual **weight** itself is also important. We should not be satisfied until all weights are regularly on the Road to Health.

The most common causes of poor weight gain are:

- The child is not getting enough food.
- The child has an infection.

In some parts of the world AIDS is becoming the commonest cause.

4. Remember the **value** of the chart.
   a) It is **an early warning system**.

> The Road to Health Chart tells us if things are going wrong before we (or the mother) would otherwise notice them. This means we can find and treat the cause at an early stage so preventing illness and disability later.

   b) It helps us to **evaluate** whether parents have understood the nutrition teaching they have been given.

5. Identify **mistakes** commonly made.

These occur very frequently especially when the child is crying. Examples include:

a) **Mother forgets** the date of birth – often the month, sometimes the year.
   - Buy or make a local events calendar. This has festivals, seasons etc. marked on it which serve as a reminder.
   - Take time to work out the date with the mother. Always consider: does the child **appear** and **behave** the age the mother says?

b) **Health worker gets confused**.
   - Health workers need **plenty of supervised practice**.
   - A ruler or straight edge helps in reading off the correct weight.

c) **Mother doesn't understand the chart**. It looks complicated and she thinks it must belong to the health worker.

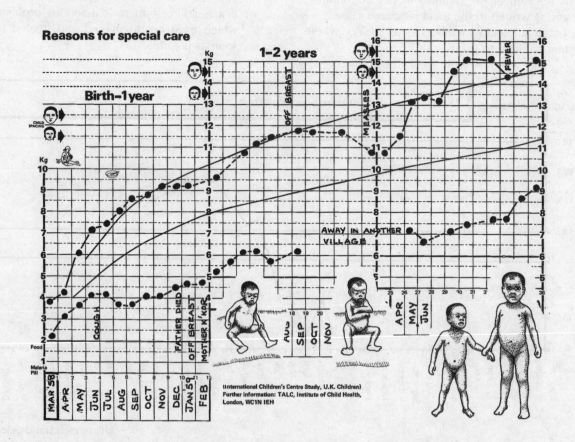

Figure 9.10 Growth chart for two children born in the same month in the same village

Figure 9.11 Mother **says**, 'Yes, Sir, I'm sorry – I will bring my child for weighing next week', but **thinks**, 'I'm never going to that clinic again'

Include the mother at **every stage in weighing** and **recording**, taking time to explain how the card works and how it shows the progress of her baby. She will soon start taking a pride not only in the card but in the **weight gain of the child**.

Nearly all mothers, even those who are illiterate will be able to learn how to use a growth chart. Many will be able to weigh children themselves.

d) **Mother forgets the card** or has spoiled it.
- A mother who takes pride in her child and his card will usually remember to bring it.
- Try and provide a protective plastic envelope.

e) **Health worker gets angry: mother gets discouraged** and stops coming.
- Teach the team to be **patient** and to make sure that weighing is enjoyable.
- Make sure that the mother is always commended for something she has done well.

6. Ensure the **mother keeps** the card.
She should bring it whenever she visits the CHW, the clinic or the hospital.

Set targets

These will depend largely on how **serious** malnutrition is and on **how difficult** it is to solve the causes.

We could **aim** for 90 per cent of children to be on the Road to Health within 3 to 5 years, and any other specific form of malnutrition e.g. vitamin A deficiency to be largely eradicated.

Prevent and cure malnutrition

Before doing this we will need to understand both the **general** causes in the community and the **special** causes in the family we are caring for (see page 125).

Having discovered these we will need to target our teaching both in the clinic, the community and the home.

For example (1). There is a well-known health programme in North India where many children attend local clinics and where their parents attend health talks. Yet studies here have shown that children who attend these clinics continue to have levels of malnutrition **little different from those who do not attend**.

For example (2). In a small Himalayan health project working among seven scattered villages 32 per cent of the children aged between 1 and 5 years were found to be severely malnourished by MAC measurement when the project first started. By training CHWs to give nutritional advice from **house to house**, using foods grown by each family, only two severely malnourished children remained 2 years later (Table 9.1).

Table 9.1 Children with mid-upper arm circumference of 12.5 cm or less

Village Name	April 1985		January 1988	
Parogi	4/16	25%	0/17	0%
Bell	7/21	33%	0/17	0%
U. Sarab	1/17	6%	0/17	0%
L. Sarab	13/30	43%	0/30	0%
U. Kandi	10/19	53%	2/19	11%
L. Kandi	6/24	25%	0/24	0%
Total	41/127	32%	2/128	2%

From these examples we can learn this lesson:

Where food supplies are adequate the key method of **curing** and **preventing** malnutrition is to train community health workers to make regular visits to each home. Here they give practical advice according to the exact needs of the family, and **make sure this advice is put into practice**.

There are **six rules of good nutrition**:

1. Ensure good nutrition for the pregnant mother.
2. Promote breastfeeding.
3. Introduce mixed feeding between 4 and 6 months.
4. Continue to feed ill children.
5. Prepare, cook and store food correctly.
6. Avoid harmful and inappropriate foods.

Rule 1. Ensure good nutrition for the pregnant mother

The baby's weight at birth and during the first few weeks of life depends mainly on the **health** of the **mother**.

One-quarter of all under-one deaths occur in the first week of life, and one-half occur in the first month. These deaths usually happen because the **mother herself is ill**, **malnourished** or **poorly prepared**.

In our prenatal care we should aim for birth weights of 2500 grams or more, or MACs of 8.7 cm or more.

In order to achieve this:

1. Encourage adequate weight gain in pregnancy. Mothers should ideally gain about 5–8 kg during pregnancy.
   Adequate maternal nutrition depends on:
   - Eating **enough food** and eating **well-balanced** food throughout pregnancy (and during lactation).
   - Taking enough **rest** especially in the month before the baby is due.
2. Prevent and treat anaemia.
   Mothers should have a haemoglobin level of

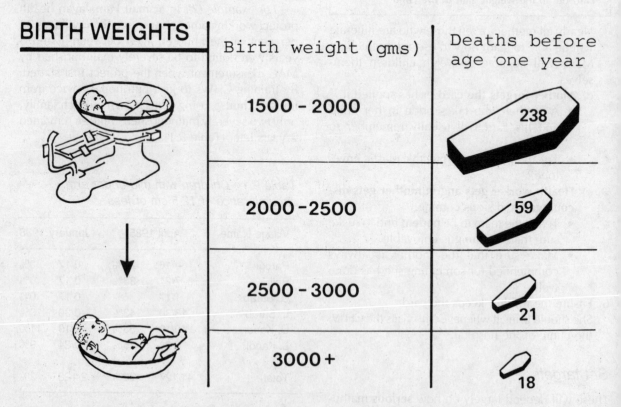

BIRTH WEIGHTS

	Birth weight (gms)	Deaths before age one year
	1500 - 2000	238
	2000 - 2500	59
	2500 - 3000	21
	3000 +	18

Figure 9.12   Smaller infants die more often and if they survive are more likely to grow up short and undernourished. A major cause of low birth weight is short undernourished mothers

12 g/dl or more at the time of the delivery. This will depend on:

- Eating enough iron-rich foods such as green leafy vegetables, eggs and meat where locally available.
- Taking iron–folate tablets daily.
- Treating and preventing malaria, hookworm and bilharzia.

3. Prevent and treat vitamin A deficiency.
This will depend on:

- Eating vitamin A rich foods such as green leafy vegetables, yellow fruit, fish oil or palm oil.
- During lactation taking supplements as follows where vitamin A deficiency occurs: Vitamin A 200 000 units by mouth 4 weeks or more **after** the delivery, but **not** during the pregnancy.

4. Prevent and treat iodine deficiency.
Carry out the following where goitre is known to occur:

- Use only iodised salt.
- Give a supplement as follows: **Iodised oil** 1 ml (480 mg iodine) **either** as an oral dose every 12–18 months, **or** as an injection every 3–4 years.

5. Discourage smoking, alcohol and drug-taking.
If the mother smokes, or drinks heavily, the baby is born **smaller** and **weaker** and is **more likely to die** in the first months of life.

6. Treat and prevent serious illness.
Tuberculosis, sexually transmitted diseases in-

Figure 9.14 More than 7000 families live on this rubbish dump in Manila

cluding AIDS, and other chronic illnesses can all seriously affect the baby's health.

7. Ensure regular prenatal care (see Chapter 2).

> There is little value in teaching pregnant woman about correct nutrition and regular prenatal care **unless the husband** and **other family members** are willing to make available the food and support which the mother needs.

Rule 2. Promote breastfeeding

Many mothers today are being wrongly persuaded to use the bottle instead of the breast. They may listen to the advertising of big companies who sell artificial milk, or think that wealthy and fashionable women use bottled milk. They may start thinking that breastfeeding is dirty or old-fashioned.

Figure 9.13 Iodine deficiency affecting three generations in the Bolivian Andes

Bottle-fed babies are three times more likely to die than breast-fed babies. Our job is to make sure that our teaching in favour of breastfeeding is more powerful than the pressures on mothers to adopt bottle feeding.

Breast is best because:

1. It is the natural food for babies, having the perfect balance of nutrients and providing natural protection against illness.
2. It is free and easily available.
3. It is clean meaning the baby is less likely to get diarrhoea.
4. Breastfeeding strengthens the bond between mother and child.
5. Breastfeeding, if regular and frequent, acts as a contraceptive and so helps child spacing.

For example: The Kung tribe in Southern Africa are famous for their natural child spacing – the gap between children commonly being between 2.5 and 3 years. The reason is because Kung mothers breastfeed **long** enough and **often** enough to prevent pregnancies.

Help mothers to understand:

1. The reasons listed above why breast is best.
   Be imaginative: *for example*, help mothers work out how much money they would save if they used breast milk instead of bottle milk. Families sometimes spend up to one-quarter of their income on dried milk for their baby.
2. Colostrum is good!
   The watery milk produced in the first one or two days is not 'bad milk', but full of nutrients and antibodies which the child really needs.

In many communities children are only put to the breast on the 2nd or 3rd day. Patiently encourage mothers to start breastfeeding within hours of birth.

3. Breastfeeding should be continued where possible for 2 or 3 years.
4. Breastfeeding is usually possible.
   Mothers often incorrectly believe they cannot make enough milk. Where this is the case encourage them:
   • To drink more fluids.

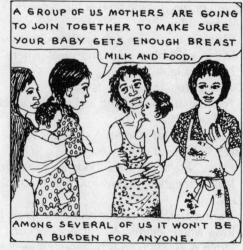

Figure 9.15   Members of a women's club help a recently widowed mother

• To eat more green leafy vegetables if available.
• To allow the baby to **suckle often**, both day and night.

The more the baby suckles, the more milk is produced. This is especially important in the few days after birth when milk may not flow easily.

If the mother is really not able to breastfeed it may be possible to find a 'wet nurse' in the community (both Moses and Mohammed were reputedly fed in this way). Other family women with children, and even grandmothers may be able to provide breast milk.

Finally:

Encourage women's clubs and other social groups to promote breastfeeding and where necessary to take joint action against those trying to sell artificial milks.

Rule 3. Introduce mixed feeding between 4 and 6 months

If mixed feeding is started **too early** the child may refuse or find it hard to digest. This may worry the parents who then wait until it is too late to restart.

If started **too late** the child will start falling off the Road to Health. This usually happens at about 8 months.

Follow these guidelines:

© Illustration David Gifford

Figure 9.16 Make sure that health workers only encourage the use of foods that are locally available and affordable by the poor

1. Find out local customs and beliefs.

   Make sure that health workers only encourage the use of foods which are locally available and which the poor can afford.

   For example: This mistake is commonly made: health workers who come from a city or from a different part of the country will promote foods

they are used to eating. These foods may be very expensive in the project area or not be used at all.

2. Encourage appropriate foods:
   Such foods should be:
   - Easy to prepare and store.
   - Nutritious and well-balanced.
   - High in energy content, especially natural oils.
   - Easy to digest and not too thick or viscous.
   - Grown within the community if possible.

3. Use correct foods for different ages.

   Some general principles to follow.
   From 4 to 6 months:

   - Feed a little at a time, twice a day.
   - Foods should be soft and easy to digest.
   - Include soft fruits and a cereal.
   - Introduce new foods one at a time. Wait till the baby is used to one food before offering it another. A good rule is to start a new food about every 2 weeks.

   From 6 to 12 months:

   - Feed the child gently, never using force.
   - Feed 3 or 4 times daily, but **more often and with extra oil if the child is recovering from illness**, or is below the Road to Health.
   - Suitable foods might include vegetables, legumes, potatoes, roots such as cassava and yam, eggs, finely chopped meat or fish, as well as cereals and fruit. These can be prepared according to local custom.

"Until nutrition workers have tried to deal with the problem of the cranky child who refuses to eat whatever the mother prepares, they have not come to grips with the most essential element of applied nutrition."

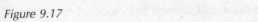

Figure 9.17

For example: In Nepal children are fed with what is known as 'super-porridge'. This is highly nutritious, is easy to make, is popular with the children and is made from local foods. It contains lentils, two different grains, and a little oil. The food is roasted and ground into a flour. Boiling water is then added to make a porridge.

The exact make-up of the porridge can be varied according to the lentils or grains available locally.

Alternatively traditional ways of preparing cereals can be encouraged, especially those involving fermentation which reduces the number of germs present.

From one year upwards:

- The child can eat 'from the family pot'.
  Although the child can eat the same foods as the adult he should have his own plate and care should be taken that he receives enough. By the age of 1 year a child will eat about half the amount his mother eats.
- Feed 4 to 6 times a day.
  Children will not be able to manage on the one or two main meals a day that adults eat. They have small stomachs and 'like chickens should often be pecking'.

A final point:

> Make sure all health workers and CHWs give identical advice on nutrition so as to avoid confusion within the community.

Rule 4. Continue to feed ill children

The belief that food should not be given to sick children is dangerous and many children die as a result. Illness leads to malnutrition and malnutrition to illness. This means that unless a child is vomiting or refusing to eat he should still be fed.

Ill children will have small appetites; they should therefore eat what they wish and in small amounts at a time.

> Even if a child does eat while he is sick there will still be plenty of catching up to do. After the illness he will need to eat **more** than usual and **more often** than usual until he is back on the Road to Health.

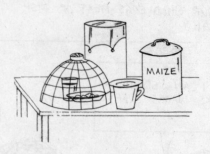

Figure 9.18   How to keep your food clean

Children with diarrhoea should also be fed. Oral rehydration using home-prepared liquid foods such as rice water can be used instead of simple salt–sugar solution (see Chapter 11, page 156).

Rule 5. Prepare, cook and store food correctly

Mothers or those preparing the food should be taught these basic rules:

1. To **clean** their hands before preparing food or feeding. Finger nails should be kept clean and short.
2. To use **clean utensils** and vessels.
3. To use the **cleanest water** available to wash fruit and vegetables, or for mixing with food.
4. To cook foods the **correct length of time**.
   Overcooked foods, especially vegetables, may loose their vitamins. **Undercooked** foods e.g. fish, pork or beef may still contain tapeworm eggs, or other germs.
5. To **cover** and **protect** food **after** it is cooked. Any food kept longer than 2 hours should be thoroughly recooked.

Rule 6. Avoid harmful and unnecessary foods

Harmful foods include spoiled or mouldy grains, beans and groundnuts and any food which has been inadequately reheated or allowed to spoil.

The use of **unnecessary** foods is becoming common in developing countries. This leads to the overweight child who is fed on 'junk foods' such as artificial milk, tinned baby foods, tonics, bottled drinks including beer and cola and excessive sweets and biscuits.

Money saved can be used to buy nutritious foods to improve the family's diet.

Beware the 'Curse of Malinche' – Malinche was a Mexican who helped the foreign soldier Cortes invade Mexico and conquer the country. The Curse of Malinche is the belief that anything foreign or western is good and must be better than things made in our own country.

The Curse of Malinche makes poor people want to buy the latest drink, food, cigarette, or drug from the nearest 'smart' country. Parents may spend all their savings on fancy foods from abroad. This in turn leads them deeper into poverty.

Mothers need to be taught to use foods **from their own communities**.

Other ways of improving nutrition

Sometimes more serious causes for malnutrition are present in a community meaning that 'The 6 Rules' on their own are inadequate. Where this is the case joint community initiatives can be taken including:

Setting up a community feeding programme

Often known as a 'nutrition programme' this refers to the communal feeding of regular meals to malnourished children.

When is this needed?

The community may ask for a feeding programme,

Figure 9.19

either because it is necessary, or more commonly because they hope for free food subsidies.

We should only start a feeding programme if these conditions exist in the target area:

1. Serious malnutrition which is both **widespread** and **severe**.
2. Good community organisation.
   This can be a health committee, or a church, temple, mosque, school or social committee. It can be a single motivated CHW with a band of community volunteers.
3. The existence of sufficient food.
   Where possible use food **from within** the community. (Famine, war and refugee situations are obvious exceptions where outside food may be needed to save lives.)

How is it done?

We can help the community, CHW or committee carry out the following:

1. To select a suitable time and place for feeding.
   Examples might be: midday or evening in the CHW's house, morning outside the clinic.
2. To collect and prepare suitable food.
   This must be well-balanced and high in calories, proteins and vitamins. A 'super-porridge' may be appropriate.
   Wherever possible food should be supplied by the community itself. Wealthier members can be encouraged to contribute supplies for the programme.
3. To organise cooking stoves and utensils.
4. To gather the children, feed them and keep order.
5. To teach and motivate the parents.
   This is an excellent time to teach the rules of good nutrition, weigh the children with the parents' help and distribute vitamin A and worm medicine if needed.

In practice the CHW will usually be the organiser and the motivator. To be successful she will need effective back-up both from the **project** and from the **community**.

For example: In Jamkhed, India, a feeding programme was needed when villagers first joined the project. Young Farmer's Clubs were formed whose members would help to collect the food, gather the children and motivate the community. They were careful always to support the CHW by giving

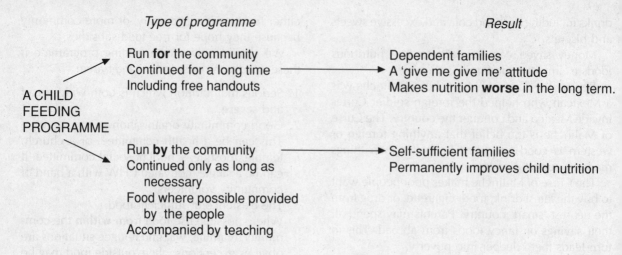

Figure 9.20   Feeding programmes can either prolong or cure malnutrition

the same advice and teaching as she herself gave. With clubs and CHWs working together the programme achieved quick results and could soon be discontinued.

Some Dos and Do nots:

1. **Do** run the programme for a short time only.

> As soon as children are gaining weight and mothers understand the rules of good nutrition **stop the programme**, and shift feeding back to community homes. Unless this is done the community becomes dependent.

2. **Do** include only severely malnourished children.
   Choose a cut-off point on the Road to Health chart and **only include children below that point**. Children should not be included simply because their parents request it or because they come from influential families.
   Where malnutrition is very widespread and severe, an alternative is to include **all** under 5 children at the start.
3. **Do** follow up each child at home.

> When the feeding programme has been stopped make sure that each child **receives the right food at home and continues to gain weight**.

4. **Do not** run the programme **for** the people. They themselves should do it with our help.
5. **Do not** give out free supplies.

> We should never give **free handouts, supplies or rations through clinics** except in famine conditions. Where this is done it creates dependence and in the long term may even worsen nutritional problems.

Setting up an income generating project

Poverty is often **the** root cause of malnutrition. This means that helping a community to generate their own income may be more helpful than running a feeding programme.

When starting an income generating programme make sure that teaching is given about the correct use of extra income, and also about the dangers of extra income when it is not used constructively and for the benefit of the family. Try and encourage women to control the means of production and the way the money is spent. Women's clubs or co-operatives can help to make this possible (see Chapter 2, pages 20–22).

Female literacy

Improvements in this **alone** reduce infant mortality and improve nutrition.

Kitchen gardens

Vegetables and fruit can be grown near the home, be tended by mothers and be fed to the children (see page 22).

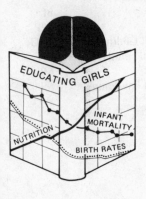

THE EDUCATION OF GIRLS
IS CLOSELY ASSOCIATED
WITH A FALLING INFANT
MORTALITY AND BIRTH RATE
AND IMPROVED NUTRITION

Figure 9.21 Improvements in schooling of mothers lead to reduced infant mortality and improved nutrition

'Bulk-buying clubs'

Mothers can set up 'bulk-buying clubs' to reduce the cost of foods which have to be bought.

Evaluate the programme

This is most simply done by seeing how the nutritional status of children changes over a period of time. The percentage of children on the Road to Health, or of 1–5s with MACs of 13.5 cm or more, are compared between the start of the programme and a resurvey 3 or 5 years later. However nutritional status varies with seasons and repeat surveys should therefore be done at the same time of year.

All stages of the evaluation should be done in partnership with the community. Results should be explained carefully as changes in child nutrition may not be obvious and the community may not realise that improvements have occurred unless this is clearly presented to them (see Chapter 2, page 14).

Summary

Child deaths in a community can be halved by ensuring that children are adequately nourished. Community health programmes are ideally placed to bring this about.

For each community and family the causes of malnutrition must first be discovered. Practical advice can then be targeted from house to house, the CHWs taking a leading role. If sufficient food is available the 'Six Rules of Good Nutrition' may be sufficient, but where causes are deeper-rooted further community action may be needed such as feeding programmes and income generating schemes.

Regular evaluations should be carried out with the community, by resurveying after 3 or 5 year periods.

Further Reading

1. *Guidelines for Training Community Health Workers in Nutrition.* 2nd edn. WHO Offset publication No. 59, Geneva, 1986, reprinted 1991.
   Available from: regional WHO office. See Appendix E.
2. *Primary Health Care Technologies at the Family and Community Levels.* Aga Kha Foundation, Geneva. UNICEF, New York, 1986.
   Section 4: Nutrition-related Technologies by Dr A. Tomkins is especially helpful.
   Available from: AKF, PO 435, 1211 Geneva 6, Switzerland.
3. 'Breastfeeding for life.' *Contact* No. 111, October, 1989.
   Good, practical overview and list of further resources.
   Available from: CMC. See Appendix E.
4. *Manual on Feeding Infants and Young Children.* M. Cameron and Y. Hofvander. Oxford, 1983.
   Simple and effective book for use at clinic and community levels.
   Available from: TALC. See Appendix E.
5. *Maternal and Child Health in Practice.* G. J. Ebrahim, A. M. Ahmed, A. A. Khan. Macmillan, 1988.
   A useful book for middle level workers.
   Available from: TALC. See Appendix E.
6. *Preventing and Controlling Iron Deficiency Anaemia through Primary Health Care.* E. M. DeMaeyer *et al.* WHO, 1989.
   Available from: WHO. See Appendix E.
7. *Vitamin A Supplements: a Guide to Their Use in the Treatment and Prevention of Vitamin A Deficiency and Xerophthalmia.* WHO/UNICEF, 1988.
   Available from: WHO. See Appendix E.
8. *The Growth Chart.* WHO, 1986.
   Available from: WHO. See Appendix E.
9. *Practical Guide to Selective Feeding Programmes.* Oxfam, 1984.
   Available from: Oxfam. See Appendix E.
10. *Growth monitoring and promotion in young children: guidelines for the selection of methods and training techniques.* N. B. and E. F. Jelliffe. Oxford, 1991.

An excellent and valuable practical manual.
Available from: Oxford University Press. See Appendix E.

Slides

The following slide sets are available from TALC. See Appendix E.

- Breastfeeding   Bf
- Breastfeeding Problems   BFP
- Charting Growth in Small Children   ChG
- Xerophthalmia (Vit A Deficiency)   EyX
- Malnutrition   MI
- Malnutrition in an Urban Environment   MUE
- Weaning Foods and Energy   WFE

10

Setting up a Childhood Immunisation Programme

In this chapter we shall consider:

1. What we need to **know**
   - Why childhood immunisation is important
   - Facts about the vaccines that are used
   - Immunisation schedules
   - Equipment needed
   - How to maintain the cold chain
2. What we need to **do**

- Assess needs for immunisation in the programme area
- Set targets
- Train the team
- Prepare the community
- Carry out immunisation in the field
- Carry out immunisation in the clinic
- Keep records
- Evaluate the programme

What we need to know

Why childhood immunisation is important

> Every year nearly 4 million children die from diseases which **could easily be prevented** by immunisation. Many million more suffer serious illness or become disabled for life from these same diseases.

Measles kills one child every 20 seconds.

Every year 50 million children suffer from **pertussis** (whooping cough) of which 500 000 die.

Tetanus kills approximately 800 000 newborn babies each year.

Apart from death and disability many more people suffer grief and loss of earnings because of diseases which immunisation can prevent.

Much progress has been made by the World Health Organization's Expanded Programme on Immunization (EPI), but much remains to be done.

Facts about the vaccines that are used

Table 10.1 gives details about the commonest immunisations used: DPT (triple vaccine), OPV (oral polio vaccine), measles vaccine and BCG.

The following vaccines are sometimes used

Figure 10.1 WHO plans to eradicate polio by the year 2000

Table 10.1 Details of common immunisations*

Type of vaccine	Who should have it?	How is it given?	How many are needed?	Side-effects	Contraindications	Storage	Comments
1. DPT (Triple) against: Diphtheria Pertussis Tetanus	Children from 6 weeks to 5 years	0.5 ml subcutaneously into thigh	3 doses at intervals of 4 weeks or more	Pain, swelling and redness at site of injection. Fever for 24 hours Very occasionally fits	Any child with high fever or seriously ill	Between 2 and 8°C It is destroyed by freezing	To check if spoiled: shake bottle. If uniformly cloudy use – if white flecks appear throw away.
2. OPV (or TOPV) (oral polio vaccine)	Children from birth to 5 years or more*	2 drops by mouth	3 or 4 doses at intervals of 4 weeks or more	Usually none	None	Under 8°C. Unharmed by freezing	* Common cut-off points 5 years or 12 years
3. Measles	Children from 6–9 months to 5 years or more*	Add diluent to powder and shake. 0.5 ml subcutaneously into upper arm or thigh	1 only if given at 9 months or later. Where very prevalent: 1 dose at 6 months, 2nd at 9 months	Fever and sometimes mild rash at 7–10 days	Any child with high fever or seriously ill	Under 8°C. Unharmed by freezing. Any unused reconstituted vaccine should be discarded	* Variable cut-off points between 5 and 12 years. Follow national guidelines or local advice
4. BCG against Tuberculosis (see also Chapter 14)	Children from birth upwards Upper age limit varies: follow national guidelines	Add diluent to dried vaccine. Give intradermally into upper arm (or forearm, Africa) Below 1 year 0.05 ml Over 1 year 0.1 ml using BCG syringe	Usually one only. Some programmes give 2nd at school entry	0–2 weeks: red, tender nodule 2–4 weeks: small ulcer 4–6 weeks: scar appears and persists	Any child known to have active TB or AIDS, or seriously ill with high fever	Under 8°C. Unharmed by freezing. Any unused, reconstituted vaccine should be discarded	If no nodule, ulcer or scar develops **repeat**. If nodule appears at once, ulcer is 2 cm or more or glands develop in axilla, report to health centre

*Manufacturer's instructions and local EPI guidelines should be followed depending on national policies and which diseases are locally prevalent.

1. IPV (inactivated polio virus) instead of OPV. This is given by injection in a similar way and at the same time as DPT.
2. Hepatitis B (HBV)
   Where this disease is common (e.g. where carrier rates in the population are greater than 2 per cent) and national governments are able to afford it, HBV is being built into EPI schedules (see page 152).
3. DT (diphtheria and tetanus)
   This is used in some countries for children between 6 and 12 who have not been immunised with DPT when under 5.
4. Tetanus vaccine is given to women of childbearing age to prevent tetanus in the new-born (see Chapter 12, page 184).
5. Other immunisations are sometimes included such as meningitis, Japanese encephalitis, yellow fever and typhoid. Cholera vaccine is weakly effective, plays no part in controlling epidemics and should not be used.

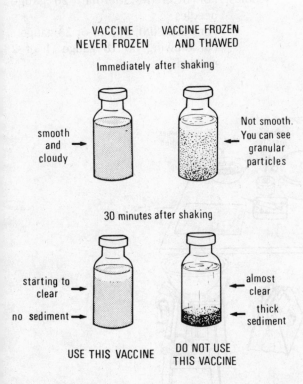

VACCINE NEVER FROZEN   VACCINE FROZEN AND THAWED

Immediately after shaking

smooth and cloudy →

Not smooth. You can see granular particles

30 minutes after shaking

starting to clear →

no sediment →

almost clear

thick sediment

USE THIS VACCINE   DO NOT USE THIS VACCINE

Figure 10.2 Testing DPT or TT vaccine for damage caused by heat

Vaccines against other diseases are currently being tested.

Immunisation schedules

Although WHO recommends certain schedules for world-wide use there is considerable variation from country to country. Recommendations also change from time to time.

> In order to avoid confusion we should generally follow the schedule laid down by the National Ministry of Health or our District Medical Officer. Having decided on one schedule we should be slow to change to another.

From the practical viewpoint it is helpful to consider schedules in two phases: the **catch-up** phase and the **regular** phase.

The catch-up phase

This should only be used when we start an immunisation programme in areas with little previous coverage. Our aim is to complete immunisations as quickly as possible.

Here is a suggested 'catch-up schedule':

- First visit (any time under 5 years)
  - Give BCG
  - Give first DPT and OPV
- Subsequent visits (4 weeks or more apart)
  - Give measles as soon as the child is 9 months or more
  - Give DPT up to a total of 3
  - Give OPV up to a total of 4

The regular phase

Here we aim to immunise all children born into the target population as they grow up, at the ages recommended by our national or district immunisation plan.

Here is the **regular schedule**, appropriate for most developing countries as recommended by the EPI:

- 1st visit   Birth   BCG
                                              1st OPV
                                              (1st HBV)
- 2nd visit   6 weeks   1st DPT
                                              2nd OPV
                                              (2nd HBV)

- 3rd visit   10 weeks   2nd DPT
                          3rd OPV
- 4th visit   14 weeks   3rd DPT
                          4th OPV
- 5th visit   9 months   Measles
                          (3rd HBV)

This schedule should be followed wherever immunisation at birth can conveniently be carried out. If not easily possible **an alternative schedule** can be used:

- 1st visit   3 months   BCG
                            1st DPT
                            1st OPV
- 2nd visit   4 months   2nd DPT
                            2nd OPV
- 3rd visit   5 months   3rd DPT
                            3rd OPV
- 4th visit   9 months   Measles
- 5th visit   After 2 years   4th OPV
                            (4th (booster) DPT)

1. **Notes**
   The time interval between successive doses of DPT/OPV is not important, providing it is a minimum of 4 weeks.
2. In countries where measles is a significant cause of death before the age of 9 months, and where high titre EZ vaccines are available, immunisation can be given at 6 months or as soon after as possible.

Equipment needed

> Much time and effort is saved if we always have the correct equipment in good working order.

In particular vaccines must remain **cold** and injectable supplies remain **sterile**. We will therefore need a refrigerator and steam steriliser at **the project base or hospital**.
   Equipment for **the field** and the **clinic**:
   The following will be needed:

1. Vaccines.
   Ensure that sufficient supplies have been ordered **well in advance**.
2. Needles and syringes.

> It is essential that we use a **separate**, **sterile** needle and syringe for each person that is immunised and for each immunisation that is given.

Needles: For BCG (intradermal) 26 gauge needles
           For others (IM, SC) 22 or 23 gauge
           For drawing up 18 gauge (1 or 2 needed)

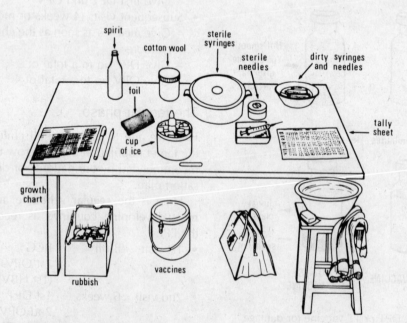

Figure 10.3   Equipment needed for immunisation

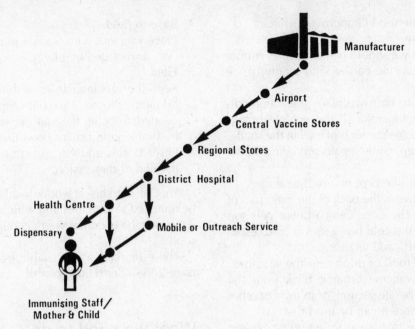

Manufacturer

Airport

Central Vaccine Stores

Regional Stores

District Hospital

Health Centre

Dispensary

Mobile or Outreach Service

Immunising Staff/
Mother & Child

Figure 10.4 Maintaining the cold chain is vital

Syringes: For BCG 0.05 ml or 0.1 ml BCG
syringes
For others 0.5 ml, 1 ml or 2 ml
syringes
For adding diluent 5 ml or 10 ml
syringes
Where possible disposable needles and
syringes should be used (and then discarded).
Needles and syringes designed for reuse must
be taken apart, cleaned, and thoroughly steril-
ised (see Chapter 4, page 46). Blunt needles
can be sharpened.
3. Other field supplies needed:
• A tray for placing syringes ready for use.
• Forceps for fixing needles on to syringes.
• Spirit for cleaning skin, plus cotton wool and
spirit bowl.
• File for opening ampoules.
• Table cold box (or cup with ice) in which to
place vaccines which are currently being
used.
• Bowl with disinfectant for used syringes and
needles.
• Rubbish bag or bin.
• Equipment for washing hands.
• Supply of clean water.
• Adrenalin and an antihistamine for emergency
use.

4. A vaccine carrier with **plenty** of ice packs.
5. A kit bag in which to pack all supplies.
6. Records and registers.

How to maintain the cold chain

The cold chain refers to the set of cold containers
in which vaccines are stored and transported, from
the moment of manufacture to the time of injection. If the cold chain is broken even once a vaccine may become useless.

> Unless vaccines are kept at the right temperature
> they lose their effectiveness. **Millions of doses have
> been spoiled and lives lost because vaccines have
> been allowed to warm up**.

We can help to maintain the cold chain by
taking careful precautions at each link:

1. **The source**
Identify a reliable source as near as possible to
the point of manufacture or import. Only use
sources which are known to be kept cold.
If supplies are obtained from the District Medical Officer, from a government hospital or private pharmacy we should ensure that the fridge
is working when we collect supplies.

Where possible use EPI approved sources.

2. **Source to base**

   On collection we should place supplies immediately in a vaccine carrier with plenty of ice packs.

   On returning to base we place them immediately in the refrigerator. If the vehicle breaks down, the vaccine carrier is placed **in the shade**, **outside the jeep**, while repairs are being made.

3. **Base**

   Supplies should be kept in a refrigerator.

   - Place supplies in the back of the main part of the fridge. The door compartment gets too warm, and the cold box gets too cold, especially for DPT and tetanus.
   - Do not put food or drink near the vaccines.
   - Place any vaccine brought back from the field in a separate section, or in front of other supplies where it can be used first.
   - Any vaccine that has warmed up or expired should be thrown away and not stored.
   - Keep a thermometer with the vaccines so that the temperature can be readily checked. Keep a twice daily chart.
   - Maintain the fridge in good working order
   - If the fridge works on electricity set up an alternative store in case of power cuts, keeping a good supply of ice in the fridge in case this happens.
   - Defrost the fridge regularly and while doing so place the vaccines with ice in the vaccine carrier, or in a second fridge.
   - Do not open the fridge unnecessarily: check the rubber door seal regularly: seal the plug into the socket with tape to avoid accidental disconnection.

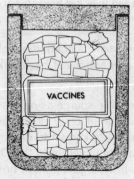

Figure 10.5 Vaccine carrier with ice bags packed around vaccine

4. **Base to field**

   Place vaccines within a box in the vaccine carrier, surrounded by plenty of ice packs.

5. **Field**

   Keep the vaccine carrier in the shade with the lid tightly closed. Take out supplies as they are needed, keeping the vial currently being used in a table cold box or bowl filled with ice.

   Discard any unused, reconstituted vaccine at the end of the session.

Special markers are now available which can be attached to vaccines and which change colour if the vaccine becomes warm enough to cause it to spoil.

These markers are available from 'PATH' (see page 288 under 'Directions').

What we need to do

Assess the need for immunisation in the programme area

Before starting a programme we will need to assess:

1. Past immunisation coverage in the target area. We will know this from the community survey; the immunisation status of each child is recorded on the front of the family folder.
2. Present programmes being carried out by other organisations, both government and voluntary. Some areas will already have effective programmes. In others there may be good plans on paper but little being done in practice. Sometimes there is a difference between the coverage claimed by the government and the immunisations which have actually been given.

As far as possible we should co-operate with other programmes in the area. We should establish close contact with the EPI manager and his team.

Set targets

Our overall aim might be to see 90 per cent or more of all under-5 children in our project area fully immunised within 3 to 5 years. To accom-

...not simply fault finders...   ...but part of a joint effort.

Figure 10.6 Supervisors must be fully involved in giving immunisations

plish this we will need to set yearly targets, appropriate for the area.

At this stage we can also work out the total number of children needing immunisations and hence the number of injections we will need to give each year. These figures can be obtained from the family folder. In most developing countries the number of children needing to start immunisations each year will be approximately 3 or 4 per cent of the total population.

Reaching targets may not be difficult where people are educated or where parents have been made aware through radio and television. In poor, backward areas or scattered communities it may be a major challenge.

> Often those who need vaccines the most want them the least. We will need to target extra time and energy to these individuals and communities.

Train the team

1. The team will need to be **motivated**.
   Encourage all those involved in the programme to help set targets and contribute to planning. Let them enjoy the results of successful programmes and make suggestions to help improve coverage.
   The more team and community members feel this is **their** programme the stronger will be their motivation.
   Any supervisor appointed must be fully involved in the giving of immunisations.
2. The team will need to be **informed**.
   All team members will need to know:
   • **Why** each immunisation is needed.
   • **How** each immunisation is given.

• **How** a clinic station and how an outreach session are organised. This will include knowing about:
  – equipment needed for a field trip,
  – how to keep supplies **sterile**,
  – how to keep supplies **cold**.

> An increasing number of immunisation programmes depend on informally trained health workers giving injections. It is especially important that such people receive clear, practical training, especially on the technique of injection.

Prepare the community

The whole immunisation programme should be carried out in full partnership with the community with responsible members being involved in planning and management. This will include helping to raise awareness among parents.

It is very common to see eager health workers forcing immunisations on unwilling people. Before giving any immunisation health workers will need to spend a great deal of time and patience in raising community awareness. Only when parents are ready should the programme be started.

> Perhaps the most important, and most difficult part of any programme is creating awareness. Parents may find it strange that we refuse to give penicillin injections when their children have colds, but that we plan to give a whole series of injections when their children seem completely healthy.

In raising awareness there are two distinct stages:

1. Discovering fears and objections.
   Each individual and each community will have

NO ONE HAS DIED FROM MEASLES IN MY SISTERS VILLAGE SINCE THEY WERE IMMUNISED LET'S GO TOMORROW TO OUR NEW MOTHER AND CHILD CLINIC

© Illustration David Gifford

Figure 10.7   Motivation is the key to high immunisation coverage

its own beliefs, and suspicions, about immunisation.

Here are some common examples of what people may be thinking:

- We don't understand why our children need these injections.
- The diseases you talk about don't occur in our area.
- Your centre is too far away for us to reach.
- We are worried about side-effects.
- We can't afford to lose half a day's wages each time we have to bring our children.
- We always have to wait such a long time at the clinic and there's not enough shade to sit in.
- The nurse shouted at us last time we came.
- Our husbands and mothers-in-law say our children shouldn't have these needles.
- We are afraid of making the spirits angry.
- We have heard that needles spread AIDS.

2. Giving appropriate teaching.

After discovering common objections we can now give appropriate teaching. In doing this we will use a variety of **methods**, **places** and **people**.

Useful **methods** include: drama, puppetry, question and answer, flash cards, billboards, radio. Suitable **places** include individual homes, the clinic, a convenient meeting place in the community, the CHWs home or verandah, a temple, church, mosque or school.

Appropriate **people** to give teaching are CHWs, health committee members, mothers who have completed immunisations, members of women's groups and young farmers clubs, priests, teachers and older children.

> Community members themselves are often more effective than health workers in motivating parents for immunisation.

Here are three examples of methods that have proved successful:

1. Special immunisation days.

   Many countries and districts set aside special days when people are encouraged to attend. Join in with these plans if they exist, spreading information and explaining details of radio and TV programmes that give further details.

   If such days are not set aside – consider trying to arrange special immunisation days in the project area.

2. 'High-uptake' families get special recognition.

   Some programmes give special status to mothers whose children have completed their immunisations. They may be given a flag to fly from their home, a badge to wear on their clothes, a reduction in fees at the clinic or hospital, or bonus points in the next baby competition.

3. House-to-house preparation.

   One successful programme taught each household about immunisations at the time of the first community survey, giving a time and place the following week where immunisations could be obtained. Many villages in that project reported 80 per cent of their under 5s completing immunisations within one year of the project starting.

Carry out immunisation in the field

Where should this be done?

> Any community programme must be at a place which is convenient for the mother and the child. The best site is within the community itself.

When should this be carried out?

At a time of day which is easy for the family. Depending on the community this may be an evening, a mid-day break from the fields, or a full day planned well ahead.

At a **time of year** convenient for the community. In rural communities it should **not** be during harvest, sowing or other busy times in the fields. It should not be just before major festivals when mothers are busy, or just after them when the community is recovering.

Who should carry this out?

A team of three is ideal for most immunisation sessions: two can manage small groups, four or five may be needed for larger ones.

The ideal team **leader** is a nurse, medical assistant or experienced health worker. She or another qualified person can give the injections and deal with other problems or illnesses which may need attention.

Other team **members** can include juniors in the health team, or Community Health Workers.

Motivated community members can make the best workers of all. They can organise the mothers and children, keep the records, and give the polio drops.

How should this be carried out?

This will be a joint venture with the community, who each year will take increasing responsibility

'Vaccinations in Yapad village today'

'I hope all the villagers turn up for their injections'

'Food or needle? The rice harvest won't wait. We can have the needle some other time'

'Stupid villagers! Why won't they cooperate?'

Figure 10.8   Immunisation sessions should be convenient for the community

for setting up the programme.

Before the programme:

1. The **community** must know in plenty of time:
   - When and where the session will be held.
   - What equipment they should provide (e.g. tables, chairs, a room etc).
   - What helpers will be needed.
   - Their responsibility in telling and gathering the children.
2. The **team** must have prepared their supplies (see above).

At the time of the programme:

1. The team should set up their equipment before the mothers arrive (see Figure 10.9).
2. Each team member should know his exact function.
3. Mothers and children should wait in an orderly way out of the sun and rain, coming forwards one at a time.
4. Health teaching should be given to waiting mothers. This is also a good chance for weighing children – 'Weights can be done during waits'.

After the programme:

1. Supplies are carefully gathered up including all syringes and needles.

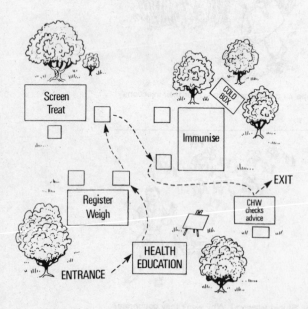

Figure 10.9 Plan for an outside immunisation session, making good use of available shade

2. The time and place of the next immunisation session is fixed. Community members are encouraged to make this known.
3. CHWs have supplies of paracetamol and are ready to visit and advise any parent worried about side-effects.

Carry out immunisation in the clinic

Most of the details just described also apply to clinic sessions.

Many parents are unwilling to come for immunisations alone, but may be willing if a visit to the clinic is needed for other reasons.

> **All** clinics should have **all** immunisations available on **all** occasions and offer them to **all** children who are eligible.

Many health centres will also arrange weekly or monthly immunisation days or have regular mother and child health clinics where immunisations are given.

Here are some ways of increasing **clinic immunisation uptake**:

1. Waiting times are kept as short as possible.
   Children who only require immunisations, go direct to the nurse, bypassing the doctor or other health worker seeing patients. A separate immunisation room or corner can be set up.
2. Immunisations are given free.
3. Health workers immunise **all** children who come to the clinic, unless there is a strong reason against doing it.
4. Health workers send for unimmunised family members.
   The health worker can check the record cards of other children in the family (through the family folder system) and ask the parent to bring any child still eligible. **Today** if convenient, next time if not.
5. Teaching is given on immunisations.
   This can be given, both to waiting **groups** of parents and children, and to each **individual** parent when seen by the health worker.
6. No eligible child leaves hospital or clinic without being offered immunisation.
7. The CHW or TBA gives first OPV ('OPV Zero') at birth.
8. No mother is scolded or made to look foolish.

Treating mothers with love and respect improves immunisation coverage.

---

12 Suggestions for giving immunisations to children

1. Children awaiting immunisations do not watch other children being injected.
2. The injection is prepared without the child seeing it.
3. The smallest needle possible is used: 26 gauge for intradermal, 23 for IM or SC. It is neither blunt nor barbed.
4. The parent is asked about serious reactions. If the child has ever collapsed or been severely ill after a previous injection the doctor is consulted.
5. The skin is carefully cleaned. Spirit is used in all cases, soap first if visible dirt is present.
6. Explanations are given to the mother. **Before** her child is injected, she is told what the immunisation is for, what side effects she should expect and when to bring the child back. She is given two or three paracetamol tablets in case of fever or pain and told the correct dose to give.
7. The mother is shown how to hold her child in a comfortable position.
8. Injections are given in the correct part of the body. This should be in the upper outer thigh or the upper outer arm, but not in the bottom. The reason (reducing the risk of nerve damage) may need to be explained.
9. The syringe is dismantled after the injection. Syringe, plunger and needle are put separately into the bowl.
10. Needles are **not recapped** but put straight into chlorine solution. This is especially important where HIV infection and hepatitis are common.
11. Procedures to be followed in case of severe reactions are known by all.
    Adrenalin is ready and all team members know how to use it.
12. Parent and child wait for 15 minutes after the immunisation.

Remember: the better our injection technique, the more efficiently we immunise and the more friendly our attitude, the more likely it is that parents will bring their children for further immunisations.

Keep records

The following records can be kept:

1. The child's own self-retained health card (Growth Chart).
   Immunisations are recorded as they are given.
2. The immunisation register.
   Here all under 5 children are recorded family by family. This can be drawn up as in Figure 10.10. All eligible children are written beforehand in the register, space being left under each family for new members to be added as they are born.
   The register is filled in at the time of immunisation, the correct entry quickly being found if each child has his code number written on his self-retained card.
   When this system is used the exact immunisation status of any child can be seen at a glance. Every 6 or 12 months the immunisation statistics can be copied into the Master Register.
   Some projects may prefer to use a tally sheet at the time immunisations are given, or record a simple list of names which can later be added to the register. Where family folder insert cards are used, immunisation status can be regularly updated on each child's insert card directly from the register.
3. A proforma for the District Medical Officer.
   Immunisation details should be sent **on time** and recorded according to the DMO's design. These details can be copied down from the register or tally sheet.

Evaluate the programme

This is done with the community, and results are explained to all community members.

1. Make yearly totals.
   Each year we can calculate the total numbers of each injection given, first, second, third, fourth etc. for each community.
   From this we can calculate the **percentage** of under 5 children who have completed each immunisation, the percentage who have partially completed and the percentage of children who remain unimmunised.
2. By occasional questionnaires.
   If coverage is poor we can design a question-

Code No.*	Name	Date of birth	DPT 1 2 3 4	Polio 1 3 4	Measles	BCG	Comments
02/01/06	RAJU	4/7/88	2/6/89 4/9/89 22/7/89	11/6/89 4/9/89 22/7/89	—	11/6/90	Had Clinical measles Nov. '88
02/01/08	ANANDI	10/3/89	11/6/89 4/9/89 22/9/89	11/6/89 4/9/89 22/7/89	3/10/89	11/6/90	
02/01/12	VALHAN	1/5/89	11/6/89 22/7/89	11/6/89 22/7/89.	1/2/90	11/6/90	child + mother away for 6 months
02/02/03	MANY	5/2/88	11/6/89 22/8/89	11/6/89 22/7/89	3/11/88	11/6/89	Parents unwilling
02/02/04	MISHI	9/3/89	11/6/89 22/7/89	11/6/89 22/7/89	3/12/89	11/6/89	to complete course

*First digits village code number.
 Second digits family code number.
 Third digits individual code number.

© Illustration David Gifford

Figure 10.10   Sample entries from immunisation register

naire to find out **why** parents are not bringing their children.

3. By regular assessment of target disease incidence.
   Every 3, 5 or 10 years we can work out whether the target diseases are becoming less common (see Chapter 17, page 239).

Summary

The lives of millions more children could be saved each year if immunisation against preventable diseases was universally carried out. With effective community partnership and good planning this is within reach of all health programmes.

Equipment needs to be prepared, vaccines obtained and a cold chain maintained. Schedules need to be calculated according to local and national guidelines. Immunisations should be given by teams of health workers who have been carefully trained, to communities whose awareness has been raised.

Immunisations should be offered at places and at times that are convenient to mothers and children. Such sessions are best carried out in the community itself and in the neighbouring clinic. Waiting times must be kept to the minimum and any child attending the clinic should be offered immunisation, unless seriously ill.

Accurate records should be kept and regular returns sent in to the District Medical Officer. Yearly evaluations of coverage should be made.

Further Reading

1. *Immunization in Practice. A Guide for Health Workers who Give Vaccines.* World Health Organization, Oxford University Press, 1989.
   This is an excellent manual for health workers, giving detailed and practical advice.
   Available from: regional WHO offices. See Appendix E.
2. *Expanded Programme on Immunization.* WHO.
   Regular 'Update' *available from*: Regional WHO offices along with Hepatitis B Information Strategies. See Appendix E.
3. *How to Choose and Make a Cold Box.* AHRTAG, 1984.
   Available from: AHRTAG. See Appendix A.
4. *How to Look After a Refrigerator.* AHRTAG, 1992.
   Available from: AHRTAG. See Appendix A.
5. *State of the World's Children.* UNICEF, Oxford University Press, 1991.
   A new edition of this is published each year.
   Available from: TALC. See Appendix E.
6. *Primary Health Care Technologies at the Family and Community Levels.* Aga Khan Foundation and UNICEF, New York, 1986.
   Section 3 has useful information.
   Available from: AKF, PO Box 435, 1211 Geneva 6, Switzerland.

Slides

The following slide sets are obtainable from TALC. See Appendix A.
• Cold-Chain – Target Diseases   CoTD
• Cold Chain   CoV

11

Dealing with Childhood Illnesses: Diarrhoea, Pneumonia and Malaria

Community Based Health Care (CBHC) is ideally suited to prevent and treat three of the greatest killing diseases of childhood – diarrhoea, acute respiratory infection (pneumonia) and malaria.

DIARRHOEA AND DEHYDRATION

In this section we shall consider:

1. What we need to **know**

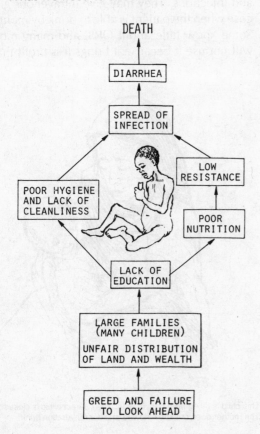

Figure 11.1 The chain of causes leading to death from diarrhoea

- Why treating diarrhoea is important
- The meaning of ORS and ORT
- How to recognise dehydration
- Understand dangers of diarrhoea

2. What we need to **do**
- Set aims and targets
- Choose a suitable method with the community
- Prepare ORS appropriately
- Feed ORS correctly
- Teach the use of ORS to all family members
- Evaluate the programme

What we need to know

Why treating diarrhoea is important

> Diarrhoea kills at least 3.5 million children each year. In some poor areas 1 child in 10 dies from diarrhoea.

Diarrhoea causes death through dehydration. In addition it leads to malnutrition which further weakens health, so that diseases such as malaria and measles may prove fatal.

The meaning of ORS and ORT

ORT stands for Oral Rehydration Therapy. This is a treatment for dehydration where Oral Rehydration Salts (ORS) – either packeted or home prepared – are mixed with water and given to those with diarrhoea.

This special solution which contains added sugar and salt is life-saving. The child needs the **fluid** and the **salt** to replace that lost in diarrhoea; he needs added **sugar** largely to help absorb the solution from his stomach.

The use of salt-sugar solution in treating diarrhoea has been described as one of the greatest medical discoveries of the 20th century. Nearly all cases of dehydration could be prevented and over 3 million lives saved per year if parents world-wide knew how to make it and give it. Probably one million lives are already being saved by those who do know.

It has been calculated that on average it takes a health worker about 30 minutes per community member to teach the effective use of ORS. This may seem a long time, but in terms of saving lives is there any more effective way of spending half an hour?

How to recognise dehydration

1. In **mild** dehydration there is:
   - thirst,
   - dry mouth and lips,
   - dark urine, small in amount.
   The child is usually alert and able to drink.
2. In **moderate** dehydration there is:
   - the signs of mild dehydration **plus**
   - sunken eyes, and a sunken soft spot in children under 18 months,
   - inelastic skin: skin pinched up between finger and thumb returns to normal **slowly**,
   - fast breathing.
   The child is often irritable or sleepy, but is usually able to take fluids by mouth.

3. In **severe** dehydration there are:
   - all the signs of moderate dehydration **plus**
   - the child is unconscious, floppy or having fits.
   He is unable to take fluids by mouth. He must be referred urgently for IV fluids.

Understand dangers of diarrhoea

1. **Diarrhoea** is dangerous, causing death by dehydration.
   In addition:
   - It leads to malnutrition if prolonged.
   - It is highly infectious, rapidly spreading in communities especially where there is poverty and overcrowding.
2. **The wrong treatment** of diarrhoea can be dangerous.
   Many doctors and health workers still believe that diarrhoea should be treated by medicines and injections. They may give intravenous glucose when the patient is able to drink by mouth. Some know little about ORS, and many more will not use it because it brings less profit than

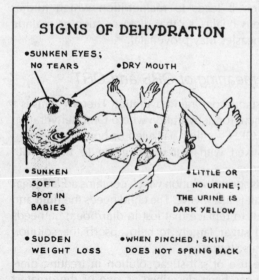

Figure 11.2   Signs of dehydration

This child is dying from dehydration. The nearest clinic is closed. The mother does not know how to make a rehydration drink.

© Illustration David Gifford

Figure 11.3

antibiotics or injections. On reason why medicine continues to be used is because it appears to cure diarrhoea. Usually however diarrhoea is self-limiting and would have stopped anyway.

> Medicines for diarrhoea may be dangerous in themselves, but the greatest danger is through the delay they may cause. Instead of starting home-based ORS at once, parents will delay treatment while they waste valuable hours seeking the wrong remedy from a clinic or pharmacy.

3. The **incorrect use of ORS** may be dangerous. Although ORS potentially saves more lives world-wide than any other treatment it does have occasional dangers.
   - Too much salt can be given which occasionally causes convulsions. For this reason ORS needs careful measurement and the solution must always be tasted before it is given.
   - Too little fluid may be given so failing to treat dehydration rapidly enough.
4. **Serious conditions** may be missed.
   Certain forms of diarrhoea such as cholera and typhoid are dangerous and need further treatment. Children unable to take fluid by mouth need intravenous fluids.
   Parents and health workers must therefore recognise when children need additional treatment or referral.

What we need to do

Set aims and targets

Our ultimate **aims** are these:

1. To make sure that every family member in our project area knows how to make and use ORS.
2. To make sure that every child with diarrhoea does actually receive ORS.

Our **targets** could be for 50 per cent of parents to understand and use ORS after 1 year, 90 per cent after 2 years.

These targets may be hard to reach in backward areas or where there is no support through TV and radio.

Choose a suitable method with the community

There are many different ways of preparing ORS. Before starting a programme we must work out carefully with the community which method is most suitable. We will never be successful if we use one method at the beginning and later change to another one.

We can follow these guidelines:

1. Decide which **overall method** is most suitable:
   - Consult with the **people**
     Discover which containers and measurers are commonly used at home. Find out if ORS packets are available locally. Discover what liquid foods are fed to children. Ask for the community's suggestions.
   - Follow **national guidelines**
     Many countries now have national programmes. Find out about these and follow them where possible.
   Even if there is no **national** programme, there may still be a method in use in our **district** or project area which we can discover by consulting with the DMO and any other programmes working nearby.
2. Decide whether to use **packeted** or **home-made** ORS.

> Unless packets are cheap, easy to obtain and always available, families should learn how to prepare their own ORS at home. They can still use packets when available, but **their children will not die when supplies of the packets run out**.

Home-made ORS can either be a **salt–sugar solution** or **traditional liquid food** such as rice water, soups, gruels, fruit juices, dilute tea, potato water, carrot juice or coconut milk.
Liquid foods have various advantages: they are easily available, children are familiar with them, they reduce the stool volume if some salt is added, and they provide food as well as fluid.

3. Decide on **containers** in which to make up the solution.
   Containers used should be **known** by everyone, be **available** in the homes and, be always the **same size**.
   Here are some *examples*:

- West Africa – a large beer bottle holding 1 litre.
- Zimbabwe – a soft-drink bottle holding 0.75 litre.
- India – a 'Lota' holding 0.5 litre.
- Most places – a medium-sized glass or cup holding 0.25 litre.

4. Decide on **measuring devices** for the salt–sugar. Again these must be widely known, easily available and of standard size. In addition they must be simple to use so that mistakes are not made in the amounts measured out. Here are some *examples*:
   - A 5 ml teaspoon
   - A human hand (a fistful and a finger pinch) Although less accurate this remains an important method in less developed communities.
   - A TALC or similar measuring device, either bought or home-made (see page 282).
   - A bottle top.

Prepare ORS appropriately

Having decided what is most appropriate in terms of container, measurers, packets or home-made preparations, we now prepare the solution.

Here are some examples of how ORS can be prepared:

1. Home prepared **sugar–salt solution**
   - To make a 1 **litre** solution (as currently recommended by WHO*):
     add **6** level teaspoons (6 × 5 ml) of sugar + 1 level teaspoon (5 ml) of salt to 1 litre of clean water.

   - To make a **half-litre** solution:
     add 1 fistful (4-finger scoop) of sugar + 1 pinch (thumb and 2 fingers) of salt to half a litre of clean water.

To each of the above we can squeeze in lime or lemon if available to give taste and provide potassium.

2. Home prepared **liquid foods**.
   To make 1 litre of rice water:
   - Grind any sort of ground rice into powder.
   - Take 2 to 3 large tablespoons (total 50–80 g) and pour on 1 litre of water.
   - Add 2 pinches of salt.
   - Boil and stir for 5 to 7 minutes.
   - Cool and feed.

Ground dried wheat, sorghum, millet, maize, or potato can be prepared in similar ways.

Coconut juice can be given with 2 pinches of salt added per litre.

Weak tea can be used to which is added salt and sugar in the same amounts as in preparing salt–sugar solution.

3. **Packeted** ORS.
   The standard WHO recommended packet should contain: (per litre of added water):
   3.5 g NaCl (common salt)
   2.5 g NaHCO$_3$ (sodium bicarbonate)
   1.5 g KCl (potassium chloride)
   20 g glucose (anhydrous)
   Instead of 2.5 g NaHCO$_3$, 2.9 g trisodium citrate dihydrate can be used.
   Any other substances added are **unnecessary** and **expensive**.
   If not available locally can be ordered from ECHO (see Appendix A).

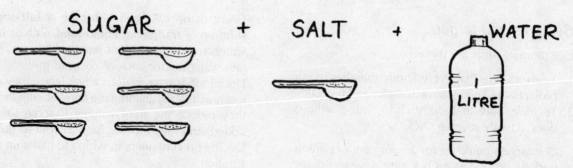

SUGAR + SALT + WATER

© Illustration David Gifford

Figure 11.4 Home prepared ORS kit

*Amounts follow WHO recommendation in leaflet *Safe food for travellers*, June, 1991.

Figure 11.5

We should make sure that any packets used or recommended contain the above substances in the correct proportions, are not overpriced, and have instructions which are easily understood by the local people. Those with written instructions alone, will be unsafe for use by illiterate members of the community.

Feed ORS correctly

ORS should be given to the child by the mother or other family member. We can first demonstrate this and then make sure **the mother does it herself**. Stages are as follows:

1. **Prepare** the solution (as above) by mixing and stirring.
2. **Taste** it.
   If should taste less salty than tears. If it is saltier it may be harmful to the child.
3. **Feed it** as detailed below.

When?

Start giving it at the **same time** as the diarrhoea starts. **Continue** giving it until **both** the diarrhoea stops **and** a normal amount of urine is being produced.

How much?

1. Diarrhoea without dehydration: After each loose stool:
   - Children under 2: half cup (100 ml). (If child is taking breast milk less ORS may be needed.)
   - Children 2–10 years: 1 cup (200 ml).
   - Older children and adults: 2 cups.
2. Diarrhoea with mild or moderate dehydration: in the first few hours the child will need to 'catch up' on fluid already lost. Give extra fluids – up to double the above amount – per stool.
3. Diarrhoea with severe dehydration and child unable to take by mouth: refer for intravenous fluids or feed by stomach tube.

How?

Young children can be fed from a spoon, **older** children and adults can sip from a cup.

Special situations

Child vomits or feels sick

Wait a few minutes then try again at a slower rate of one spoonful every 1 or 2 minutes. ORS taken at this rate **often helps to cure the nausea**.

Child malnourished: continue to feed

Soft, appropriate foods should be given in small amounts as soon as the child is able to take them. Spicy and acidic foods should be avoided. Identify local foods that are suitable and teach parents to feed them, e.g. bananas, lentils, cereals and coconut. Vegetable oils can be added as appropriate.

> Breast-fed children should continue to take as much breast milk as they want. Breastfeeding should **not** be stopped during an episode of diarrhoea.

After an episode of diarrhoea children should be fed extra until they have fully regained their weight.

Teach the use of ORS to all family members

Our aim is for every community member to know about ORS: for the use of ORS to enter **the folklore of the community**.

We will need to make sure that **every** member of **every** family:

- Knows how to **make** it.
- Knows how to **use** it.
- **Believes** in it so that when diarrhoea occurs ORS is **given at once and with confidence**.

Here are some ways of encouraging the community to use it:

1. **Understand** local beliefs about diarrhoea. Communities are often reluctant to use ORS. We must discover local beliefs about diarrhoea

Figure 11.6 A mother in Thailand feeding ORS by glass and spoon

© Illustration David Gifford

Figure 11.7 Test of a successful ORT programme: does the CHW trust in oral rehydration alone when her **own** child has diarrhoea?

and why people are suspicious of using ORS.
For example (1): In parts of Africa and South Asia many believe that giving fluid makes diarrhoea last longer; therefore children with diarrhoea should not be given fluids. This is quite logical when people believe that diarrhoea rather than dehydration is what kills the child.
Explain to parents that children die, not from the diarrhoea itself but because they dry out. Show them an orange dried out in the sun or a leaky gourd which only keeps holding water if it is continually filled up.
Explain also that giving fluid does not necessarily stop the diarrhoea. Mothers know this anyway. In fact ORS may seem to make diarrhoea worse and children will often pass a stool **shortly after receiving** ORS.
For example (2): People living in countries where private practitioners and drug companies have influence, believe that the only effective treatment for diarrhoea is a medicine, injection or intravenous drip given by doctors; that homemade remedies are useless. These wrong ideas

have to be discussed with the community until they are made aware of the situation. Unless objections are faced up to, people will listen politely, then go away and ignore our advice.
2. **Demonstrate** the use of ORS in **clinics**.
   Whenever a child comes to the clinic with diarrhoea a health worker should show the mother how to make and how to feed ORS. Then the mother herself gives it to her own child.

> Clinics can have special ORS or rehydration corners where equipment needed for making ORS is always available and ready for use.

3. **Demonstrate** the use of ORS in **homes**.
   This is usually the task of the CHW who should continue until family members are confident about using it.
   Make sure that CHWs **themselves use** ORS **in their own families**.
4. Help **community leaders** to know about ORS, to use it themselves and to encourage its use in the community. Teachers, religious leaders and shopkeepers must all be aware.
5. Teach **children** and pre-school children.
   Older siblings can give it to younger ones. Teaching on ORS should be a central part of school health programmes.
   Pre-school children can be taught in creches and balwadis.
6. Encourage the community to tune in to **radio** and TV **programmes** about ORS.
7. Explain how diarrhoea can be prevented.
   Alongside our teaching on ORS, explain to the community how diarrhoea can be **prevented** in the first place.
   Methods will include:
   • good personal hygiene (see Figure 11.9),
   • the correct preparation and storage of food (see Chapter 9, page 136),

Fresh fruit full of water. Fruit after it dries in the sun. It shrinks and wrinkles.

Figure 11.8 If the child with diarrhoea is not given water he will dry like a fruit in the sun

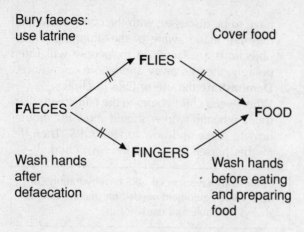

Bury faeces: use latrine

Cover food

Wash hands after defaecation

Wash hands before eating and preparing food

Figure 11.9   Diarrhoea prevention: breaking the '4 F' cycle

- the use of clean water (see Chapter 15, page 216),
- the use of latrines.

Evaluate the programme

After an agreed period of time the programme should be evaluated to see if targets are being met. We can discover:

1. Whether family members are using ORS in practice.
   Supervisors can find this out **informally** by keeping alert, enquiring from community members and CHWs, doing spot checks.
   We can find out more **formally** by preparing a questionnaire for use on a sample of homes. We would ask:
   - How, When and Why ORS is used.
   - How families have treated **actual cases of diarrhoea** in the past 3 or 6 months.
2. Whether deaths from diarrhoea are decreasing. We could use our own project statistics to calculate this as by comparing community surveys carried out before and after ORS was introduced, providing our sample is large and our methods are accurate. Alternatively we could total the various causes of under-5 deaths from CHWs' record books.
   If deaths from diarrhoea have become less common, other factors may be responsible, such as improved nutrition.

Summary

Diarrhoea and dehydration cause millions of unnecessary deaths each year. By the simple use of home-based ORS most of these deaths could be prevented.

In preparing a programme with the community decide which forms of ORS are most appropriate for the area, and which containers and measuring devices most suitable. Any method used must be acceptable to the community and follow national guidelines.

All community members should learn how to make and prepare ORS and be able to feed it to those with diarrhoea. Repeated and imaginative teaching methods are needed to raise community awareness and change incorrect beliefs. Unnecessary medicines should always be avoided.

The programme should be evaluated after an agreed length of time, to make sure ORS is actually being used in practice.

Further Reading

1. *Treatment and Prevention of Acute Diarrhoea, Practical Guidelines,* 2nd edn. WHO, 1989.
   An authoritative and practical handbook.
   Available from: WHO. See Appendix E.
2. *Dietary Management of Young Children with Diarrhoea.* D. B. and E. F. P. Jelliffe. WHO, 1989.
   Available from: WHO. See Appendix E.
3. *Management of Diarrhoea and Use of Oral Rehydration Therapy.* WHO/UNICEF, 1985.
   Available from: WHO. See Appendix E.
   The free quarterly newssheet *Dialogue on Diarrhoea* is extremely useful.
   Available from: AHRTAG. See Appendix E.

ACUTE RESPIRATORY INFECTION (ARI)

In this section we shall try and answer:

1. What is acute respiratory infection?
2. What is the importance of ARI?
3. What are the causes of ARI?
4. How can ARI be prevented?
5. How can ARI be treated?

6. What is the role of the CHW in ARI?

What is acute respiratory infection?

ARI includes several serious infections which affect the lungs and airways. The most important condition is **pneumonia**.

Pneumonia is an infection of the lungs which can rapidly cause the death of children (and adults), especially those who are weakened by other conditions or who are malnourished.

Symptoms of pneumonia include fever, cough, **a fast respiratory rate** (over 50 breaths per minute) often with flaring of the nostrils. Severe cases may show indrawing of the ribs, blue lips, vomiting, fits and coma.

Other forms of ARI are bronchiolitis found in children under the age of 2, laryngitis and diphtheria.

What is the importance of ARI?

ARI kills about 4 million children per year – about one child every 8 seconds. Of all under-5 deaths 25–30 per cent are caused by ARI.

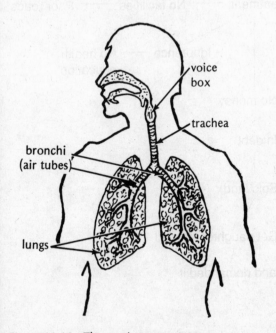

Figure 11.10   The respiratory system

voice box

trachea

bronchi (air tubes)

lungs

> Nearly all cases of ARI can be prevented and treated at community level without the need for a doctor.

What are the causes of ARI?

Most cases of ARI in developing countries are caused by bacteria, some by viruses.

One-quarter of all fatal cases follow measles or TB.

Some conditions increase the likelihood of getting ARI and make recovery more difficult. These include malnutrition, vitamin A deficiency, anaemia and household smoke – both from open fireplaces and from cigarette smoking.

> Deaths from ARI occur mainly in poor, remote, backward or crowded conditions. Fatal childhood pneumonia is largely a disease of **poverty**.

Some of the factors which can lead to pneumonia were recently recorded in a health workshop held in Bangladesh. They are shown in the 'spider chart' (see Figure 11.11). We can make a similar chart for our own area.

How can ARI be prevented?

Much can be done including:

1. Correcting malnutrition.
   Make sure that all children climb on to the road to health as soon as possible (see Chapter 9, page 130).
   Children who are malnourished can be given vitamin A (see Chapter 9, page 123) and those who are anaemic iron supplements (but not injections).
2. Immunisation.
   Check that all children are fully immunised against DPT, polio, TB and measles.
3. Reducing household smoke.
   If **cooking** is done inside with no ventilation the community can be encouraged to install chimneys or build outside cookhouses (see Chapter 18, pages 249–50).
   Tobacco smoking can be discouraged. We can

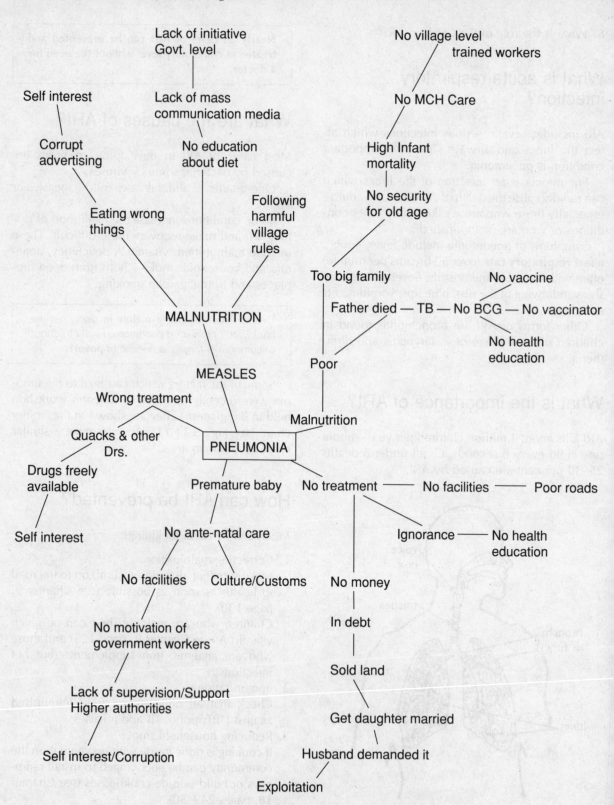

Figure 11.11   Some causes of pneumonia (from a workshop held in Bangladesh)

Figure 11.12 Smoking not only kills smokers, but affects children and others who breathe in their smoke

explain that smoke causes serious lung (and eye) disease in children.

How can ARI be treated?

> The treatment of ARI simply depends on having antibiotics available and using antibiotics correctly. Nearly all cases can be cured in the community by these simple measures alone.

Guidelines for treatment

- **Situation 1**: Simple cough and cold, with or without fever, breathing rate **less** than 50 per minute:
  Give supportive treatment only (see below): antibiotics are **not** needed. Check regularly to make sure the child does not become more seriously ill.
- **Situation 2**: Cough or cold with breathing rate **more** than 50 per minute:
  Give supportive treatment as above **plus** antibiotics (see below). Treat at home.
- **Situation 3**: Child seriously ill with breathing rate 50 or more **plus** either indrawing of ribs, or vomiting, or blue lips or coma: Give antibiotics and refer at once.

Type of antibiotic to be used

The choice will depend on **cost**, **availability** and which **antibiotic** is recommended in our country or district. A suitable regimen would be as follows:

1. **Co-trimoxazole**: twice daily tablets for 5 days in the correct dose for age or weight.
   Both CHWs and clinics can use these tablets which are suitable for all children able to swallow. See Appendix C (Antibacterials)
2. **Procaine benzylpenicillin**: once daily injection for 5 days in correct dose for age or weight.
   This can be used in clinics for children who are seriously ill or unable to take medicine by mouth. When using injectable penicillin:
   - Ask the parent if the child has ever had any reaction or rash following a previous injection or medicine. If they have, do not give it.
   - Make sure the child waits for 30 minutes after the injection in case a serious reaction occurs. If it does give adrenalin IM 1/1000 strength, as follows: 0.1 ml to child under 1: 0.2 ml to children between 1 and 2: 0.3 ml to children over 2.
3. **Ampicillin** or **amoxycillin** can be used instead of co-trimoxazole but they are usually more expensive. **Chloramphenicol** can be given to seriously ill children able to take medicine by mouth, before they are referred to hospital.

Remember:

> Antibiotics should not be used for ordinary coughs and colds.

Supportive treatment and feeding

Teach mothers to carry out the following in all cases of ARI:

1. To ensure plenty of fluids.
2. To reduce fever by removing extra clothes and giving paracetamol, but not aspirin, if necessary.
3. To give frequent energy rich drinks, such as fruit juices, soups etc. **Children being breast fed should continue**, even if their noses seem blocked.
4. To continue giving extra foods until the child is back on the road to health and has regained his original weight.

What is the role of the CHW in ARI?

CHWs have a key role in the treatment of ARI. They are usually available and can therefore start treatment early, before the disease has become too serious.

© Illustration David Gifford

Figure 11.13

Most of the 4 million deaths caused by ARI in the world today could be prevented if each community had an effective CHW or other primary health worker living in the community, with a supply of antibiotics.

The CHW will have the following roles:

Teaching

She will teach her community:

- How to prevent ARI
- The dangers of ARI
- The warning signs of ARI

She will demonstrate to parents and older siblings that fast breathing rates spell **danger** and that the child must be brought to her at once.

It is not necessary for the CHW or parent to be able to read a watch, or to count to 50. With practice nearly everyone can learn to recognise fast breathing by careful observation alone.

The CHW will make sure that all community members understand the two golden rules viz:

1. Children with simple coughs and colds need no medicines.
2. Children with fast breathing rates are brought to her at once.

Supplying antibiotics

She will keep a supply of antibiotics. Her supply must **never** run out.

Only when community members know that the CHW **always** has the correct medicines available will they trust her to care for serious illnesses.

If the CHW is not trusted children will continue to be taken on long and delaying journeys to distant health centres and doctors.

She will use the **right** antibiotic at the **right** dose for the **right** length of time, taking care that the parent knows how it should be used, and that the course is finished.

She will **record** details in her book.

Referring

She will **refer** seriously ill children. First the CHW

recognises a child who needs to be referred. Second she **starts** the child on antibiotics. Third she **sends** or **accompanies** the child and its parent to the nearest reliable referral centre.

Follow-up

She will **follow-up** all children with ARI until they have completely recovered, have regained their weight and are back on the road to health.

Any child who has a persistent cough for more than a month she will refer to the clinic or doctor (see Chapter 14 page 204).

Identifying risks

She will try and identify any preventable risk factors in the home. She will encourage immunisations and discourage **smoking**.

Summary

Acute respiratory infection (ARI), usually in the form of pneumonia, kills 4 million children per year. Nearly all these deaths could be prevented at community level.

The CHW plays a key role in this process. She teaches the community how to prevent ARI, working with them in reducing the risk factors. She keeps and uses antibiotics according to simple guidelines. She knows when and how to refer children who are seriously ill.

Further Reading

1. *ARI News*. AHRTAG Newsletter produced 3 times per year.
   This is the best way of keeping informed on the community management of ARI.
   Available from: AHRTAG. See Appendix E.
2. *Basic Principles for Control of Acute Respiratory Infections in Children in Developing Countries*. WHO/UNICEF, 1986.
   This give details of control measures at the primary health level.
   Available from: WHO. See Appendix E.

Slides

The following sets of teaching slides are available from TALC. See Appendix A.

- Management of Cough in Children (mainly for Africa)
  ARI
- Management of Cough in Asian Children
  ARIe

Available with cassette tapes to illustrate normal and abnormal breathing sounds.

MALARIA

In this section we shall consider:

1. Why malaria control is important.
2. Ways of controlling malaria at the community level.
3. Setting up a community control programme.
4. The role of the CHW in community malaria control.

Why malaria control is important

Over 2000 million people in over 100 countries (40 per cent of the world population) live in areas where malaria is present.

Most malarial deaths occur in children under 5 years of age. In Sub-saharan Africa about one in ten deaths under 1 year of age and one in four deaths between the ages of 1 and 4 years are caused by malaria. Where malaria is endemic (present all the year round) children are at greatest risk between the ages of 6 months (when immunity inherited from mother fades) and about 5 years (when their own immunity is increasing).

In many parts of the world malaria is becoming more common. Attempts at control appeared to be working during the 1970s but are now failing for various reasons. This is partly due to the resistance of mosquitoes to DDT, and of the malaria parasite to chloroquine. It is also a result of more widespread poverty, an increase in human migration because of war and famine, and the opening up of frontier regions to development as in the Amazon region of Brazil.

For areas where malaria is endemic The World Health Organization is now emphasising control

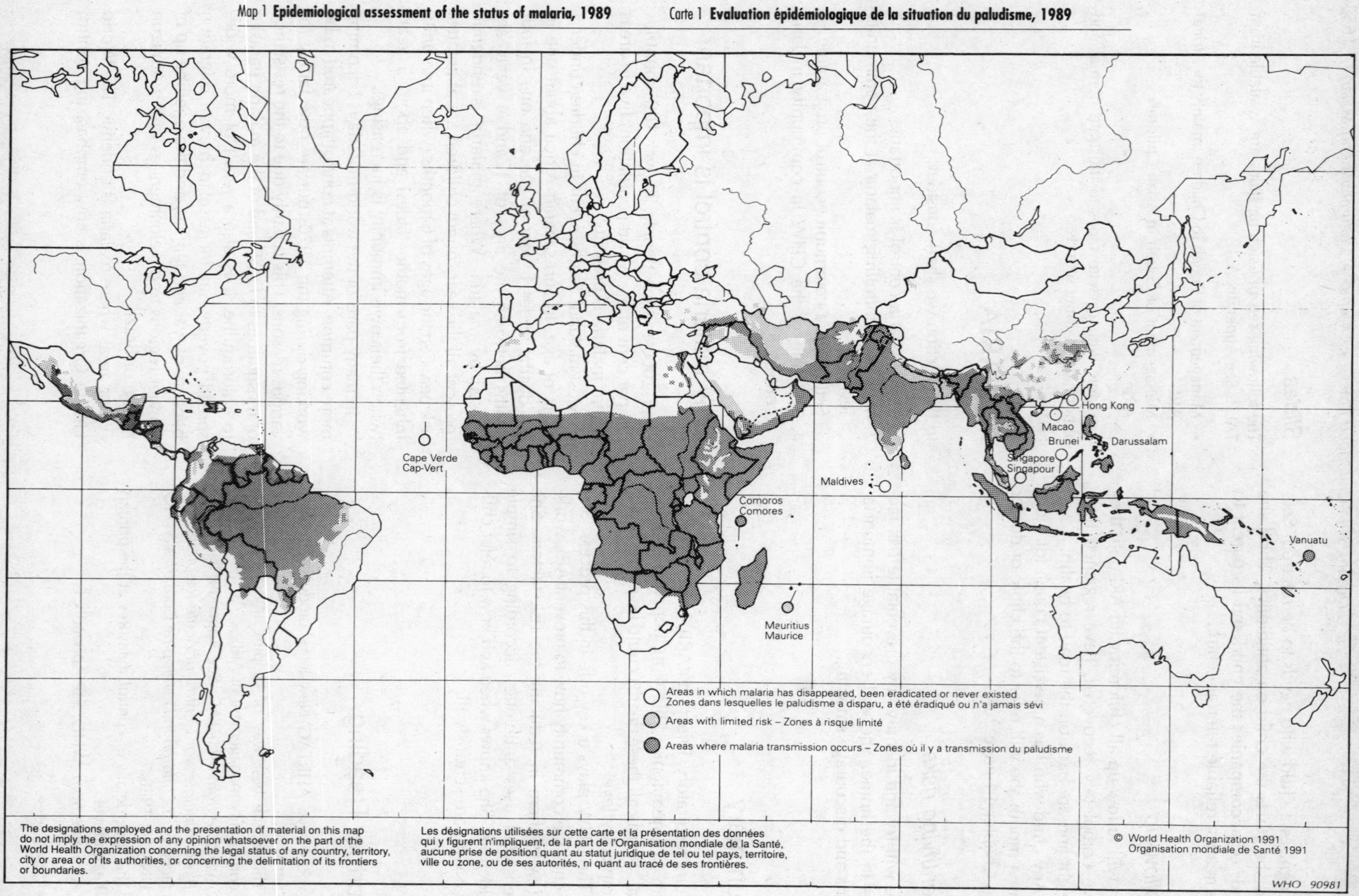

Map 1 Epidemiological assessment of the status of malaria, 1989   Carte 1 Evaluation épidémiologique de la situation du paludisme, 1989

Vanuatu

Hong Kong
Macao
Brunei Darussalam
Singapore
Singapour

Maldives

Mauritius
Maurice

Comoros
Comores

Cape Verde
Cap-Vert

○ Areas in which malaria has disappeared, been eradicated or never existed
   Zones dans lesquelles le paludisme a disparu, a été éradiqué ou n'a jamais sévi

⬚ Areas with limited risk – Zones à risque limité

⬛ Areas where malaria transmission occurs – Zones où il y a transmission du paludisme

The designations employed and the presentation of material on this map do not imply the expression of any opinion whatsoever on the part of the World Health Organization concerning the legal status of any country, territory, city or area or of its authorities, or concerning the delimitation of its frontiers or boundaries.

Les désignations utilisées sur cette carte et la présentation des données qui y figurent n'impliquent, de la part de l'Organisation mondiale de la Santé, aucune prise de position quant au statut juridique de tel ou tel pays, territoire, ville ou zone, ou de ses autorités, ni quant au tracé de ses frontières.

© World Health Organization 1991
  Organisation mondiale de Santé 1991

WHO 90981

Figure 11.14   Map showing the distribution of malaria

of malaria at the community level rather than eradication of malaria at the national level. This means that the focus of malaria control has shifted to the primary health care level.

> Within a national malaria programme, community based health care can greatly reduce the incidence of malaria within a target population.

Ways of controlling malaria at the community level

Malaria is caused by a mosquito (the vector) injecting *Plasmodium* (the parasite) into the human blood stream.

In order to reduce malaria both the vector and the parasite need to be controlled. In addition contact between the vector and humans needs to be prevented.

Figure 11.15 Health workers in Africa surveying a mosquito breeding site

Ways of controlling the vector

Reduce breeding sites

Mosquitoes can breed in very small amounts of water such as water-filled wheel ruts and hoof prints. All sources of standing water need to be identified and dealt with:

1. **Remove** or **fill** areas near houses where mosquitoes breed such as holes, ditches, the tops of bamboo canes, old cans and tyres.
2. **Drain** areas where water collects such as near bore-holes or around standpipes.
3. **Build** soakage pits to remove household waste.
4. **Cover** wells and drains.
5. **Plan** any new building or development programmes with care so that new breeding sites are not created.

Kill mosquito larvae

Introduce larva-eating fish (guppy). These are able to breed in shallow non-permanent water, though large numbers and careful management are needed.

Larva-killing bacteria can be used. The larvicide temephos can be added to water inappropriate for fish: petroleum oil can be poured on to the surface of water.

Kill adult mosquitoes

Spray DDT or malathion (known as residual insecticides) on the interior walls of houses twice yearly or before seasonal rains. This needs to be done by those carefully trained, following careful guidelines for personal protection and safety. Because spray teams may not be known to the community they should be accompanied by a health committee member.

Ways of destroying the parasite

1. **Treat** any case of suspected malaria as soon as possible. Follow local guidelines about which drug to use – usually either chloroquine or pyrimethamine + sulfadoxine (Fansidar). Any serious case or one failing to respond within 48 hours should be referred.
2. **Consider** giving malaria prophyllaxis to pregnant women. WHO recommends giving chloroquine to pregnant women in areas where there

is little or no chloroquine resistance.

Ways of preventing human–vector contact

At community level personal protection against mosquito bites is the most useful control measure.

1. Use **bed-nets**. These work most effectively when impregnated with permethrin every 6 months (see below). In Gambia and China there has been a considerable reduction in malaria among children where this has been carried out. CHWs can set up community programmes.
2. Hang **permethrin-impregnated** window and door **curtains** in houses where the house design is appropriate. This reduces malaria but is less effective than using impregnated bed-nets. Curtains and bed-nets can be treated at the same time.
3. Apply **insect repellent** (containing DEET). This is of greatest value for personal protection of individuals at special risk, rather than as a community wide approach.
4. **Screen** windows and doors.

For the most effective malaria control, each country (or district) selects a variety of measures from those listed above which are most appropriate for its circumstances. For example Indonesia combines case finding and treatment, indoor spraying with insecticide, use of larvicidal fish, tree-planting in marshy areas and the use of bed-nets.

Setting up a community control programme

Central to all programme stages is active partner-

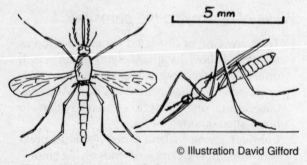

5 mm

© Illustration David Gifford

Figure 11.16   An *Anopheles* mosquito

ship with the community. These stages include the following:

Assessing the level of malaria in the project area

We can ask such questions as:

- How common is malaria?
- Which ages are most affected?
- What percentage of infants and children aged 1 to 4 years die from malaria?
- Is malaria seasonal or irregular (epidemic), or present the whole year round (endemic)?
- Where/what are the main malaria breeding sites?
- Is widespread chloroquine resistance present?

Assessing the resources of the community

- How much community understanding is there?
- How much community commitment to action is present?
- What control measures are already being carried out?

Such information – on level and resources – can be obtained from three chief sources: from the **community** through a survey or discussion with community leaders and CHWs; from the **District Medical Officer**, and from the clinical records of the **local referral hospital or health centre**.

Knowing answers to these questions will help us select control strategies which are both **effective** against malaria and **acceptable** to the community.

> The key to community-based malaria control is to select a combination of control measures which are most appropriate for our particular community. Depending on one form of control alone will usually be insufficient.

Following the recommendations of the District Medical Officer

Malaria control is most effective when government control measures are adopted by the district and carried out at the community level. It will therefore be necessary to plan in detail with the DMO.

Creating awareness

Even if malaria is a serious local problem there may be little understanding of how malaria is caused and how it can be prevented. It will therefore be necessary to **create awareness** before any useful joint planning can be carried out.

In past years malaria control depended largely on outside teams spraying DDT, and on hospitals and other health facilities providing medicine.

> Current control depends largely on the understanding and commitment of the entire community to carry out a number of strategies, which together will reduce the incidence of malaria.

Planning with community leaders or health committee

During these sessions we can match up the most effective control strategies with their acceptability to the community.

We can then draw up an action plan for each control measure to be adopted.

Carrying out malaria control

Central to this process will be the involvement of health committee members for any community action needed, and the CHW for providing cure and encouraging personal protection (see below).

For example: committee members can mobilise the community to clear malarial breeding sites, or plant trees in marshy areas to help drainage. They can work with the health team and development experts to set up fish-breeding ponds near health centres from which larva-eating fish can be distributed.

Evaluating the programme

Evaluation should in part be done by visits from government malaria control experts.

Community based evaluation can show how effective our programme is proving to be. It can answer such questions as:

- Is the community satisfied with the malaria control programme?
- Has the amount of standing water in the community been reduced?

- Does the community perceive any change in the number of mosquitoes or the number of mosquito bites?
- Is the number of patients with suspected malaria attending the CHW or health post declining?
- Is the number and percentage of children dying from malaria decreasing?

The role of the CHW in community malaria control

> With malaria control becoming an important part of primary health care the CHW can play a key role in the process. In order to do this effectively she will need adequate training, supervision and credibility.

Her tasks will include:

Recognising and treating suspected malaria as promptly as possible

If there is little chloroquine resistance she will treat suspected malaria with chloroquine (and aspirin/paracetamol where appropriate).

If there is **much** chloroquine resistance she will treat cases with other medicines as agreed with the programme/DMO. Pyrimethamine + sulfadoxine (Fansidar) is commonly used, where costs allow.

She will refer seriously ill patients or those not responding to antimalarials to a health centre or hospital.

Giving prophylactic treatment to pregnant women

The CHW will give prophylactic chloroquine to pregnant women providing this is being recommended by the DMO.

Organising a community bed-net programme

This should only be started if:

1. The community, after being sensitised, is eager to co-operate.
2. The use of bed-nets is appropriate in the community.

Figure 11.17   Villagers in Tanzania bring their bed nets for soaking in permethrin

3. Bed-nets and permethrin are reliably available at reasonable cost.
4. The health committee or community as a whole is prepared to give encouragement and practical support.

Bed-nets from all community members can be soaked 6-monthly as follows:

1. Previously cleaned 20–25 litre drums or tubs, preferably plastic or aluminium, are filled with permethrin solution, made up by adding 400 ml of 50 per cent effective permethrin concentration to 20 litres of water. This can treat about 20 nets.
2. Nets are thoroughly dipped into the solution, allowed to drip for about 1 minute, and then laid flat to dry (preferably on beds).

Note: Nets should ideally be made of synthetic material not cotton: they should not be washed until the next treatment is due: they should be soaked to coincide with the start of any seasonal rains: they should be allowed to dry before being used.

> Impregnated bed-nets not only protect against malaria but by being toxic to mosquitoes help to reduce the number of mosquitoes present. Children by having fewer bites sleep better and get fewer skin infections: in addition they are protected against bed bugs and headlice.

Bed-nets are most essential for those under 5, but should ideally be used by all community members as this reduces malaria within the community more effectively.

Permethrin-impregnated curtains can be used in addition if this is appropriate.

Liaison

Liaising with the health committee and health team on other community-based control activities.

Arranging teaching

Arranging community-wide health teaching on malaria. She should make sure that all, including preschool children understand that:

1. Community members, especially children, who develop a fever should receive treatment without delay.
2. Those with malaria should be given a **full** course of treatment.
3. Children with malaria should be kept cool but not cold.
4. Children recovering from malaria need plenty of fluids and extra nutritious food.

Summary

Malaria is one of the three greatest causes of death in children, and is found in over 100 countries.

Although many national control programmes have failed, it is still possible to control malaria at community level if a variety of measures are carefully implemented. These need to be adapted to each community and usually include: reducing breeding sites, killing vectors and parasites, reducing human to vector contact and having immediate treatment available for all cases of malaria.

The community is involved fully in all aspects of malaria control including planning. Health committee members can help to co-ordinate major community programmes, and the CHW can take a leading role in treating community members and encouraging personal protection.

Further Reading

1. *Malaria Control as Part of Primary Health Care.* WHO, 1984.
   The report that brought malaria control into the job description of community health programmes. Much of the contents is still very relevant.
   Available from: WHO. See Appendix E.
2. *The Use of Impregnated Bednets and Other Materials for Vector-borne Disease Control.* WHO, 1989.
   Useful background and practical suggestions on this important subject.
   Available from: WHO. See Appendix E.
   Information and guidelines on malaria are subject to change. WHO can arrange to send updated book lists on request.

12
Setting up a Pre-natal and Maternity Programme

This chapter will include details on prenatal (ante-natal) care, delivery care and postnatal care.

1. What we need to **know**
   - Why maternity care is important
   - Why mothers and newborn babies die
2. What we need to **do**
   - Prepare the community
   - Set aims and targets
   - Train traditional birth attendants
   - Set up pre-natal care
   - Set up delivery care
   - Set up postnatal care
   - Keep records
   - Evaluate the programme

What we need to know

Why maternity care is important

The **first** reason is to prevent the huge number of unnecessary deaths of **mothers** during pregnancy and childbirth.

> Half a million mothers die each year from causes related to pregnancy, most of which could be prevented. **99 per cent of these deaths occur in developing countries**.

According to recent figures, in parts of Africa one woman in 14 dies from the complications of pregnancy or childbirth. Large numbers of children are orphaned because of this.

A mother in the poorest parts of Asia is 150 times more likely to die during the births of her children than a mother in a developed country. In India there are as many maternal deaths in **one day** as there are in all developed countries in **one month**.

The **second** reason is to prevent the unnecessary death and disability of babies at the time of birth.

The World Health Organization has set up a 'Safe Motherhood Initiative' aimed at reducing maternal deaths. This plan, which includes a strong community emphasis is being supported by many governments.

Why mothers and newborn babies die

Mothers die from a variety of causes:

1. Haemorrhage (bleeding) usually during birth or shortly afterwards.
2. Abortion, because of infection and other complications due to lack of clean facilities and procedures.
3. Toxaemia. High blood pressure and swelling in late pregnancy can lead to fits and death.
4. Obstructed labour where the womb bursts or the mother dies from exhaustion.
5. Infection after the delivery.

In addition mothers suffering from **anaemia** are

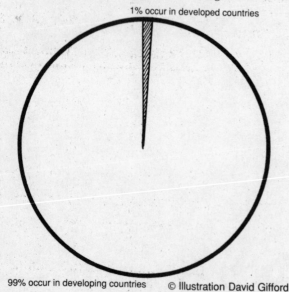

1% occur in developed countries

99% occur in developing countries   © Illustration David Gifford

Figure 12.1   Maternal deaths

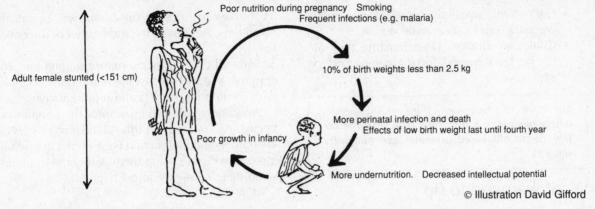

Poor nutrition during pregnancy   Smoking
Frequent infections (e.g. malaria)

10% of birth weights less than 2.5 kg

More perinatal infection and death
Effects of low birth weight last until fourth year

More undernutrition.   Decreased intellectual potential

Poor growth in infancy

Adult female stunted (<151 cm)

© Illustration David Gifford

Figure 12.2   Poor care in pregnancy: a key factor in the cycle of poverty and malnutrition

more likely to die from any of the above causes: malaria and iron deficiency are the commonest causes of anaemia in tropical Africa.

Newborn babies die for various reasons:

1. Maternal malnutrition and illness **during pregnancy** leading to low birth weight babies; twins increase the risk.
2. Complications **during delivery** including maternal haemorrhage, toxaemia and obstructed labour.
3. Inadequate care and nutrition **after birth**.

Underlying all these causes is poverty. This in turn means that:

1. Appropriate health care is **not available**.

> Facilities for the poor are not usually present either **when** they are needed or **where** they are needed.

There may be plenty of doctors working in private clinics and larger towns, but their services have very little effect on the overall death rates of mothers and babies. They are largely **out of reach** of the poor majority because they are too distant and too expensive.

2. Health care that is available **is not used**.

One recent study from a developing country has shown that 98 per cent of rural women and 85 per cent of urban women failed to use locally available maternity services. There are several possible reasons:

- Pregnancy is considered a natural process, which does not require the presence of doctors and clinics.
- Traditional birth attendants and local remedies usually exist.
- Women are busy, with jobs in home, field or factory, considered a greater priority than spending half a day visiting a clinic.

Her own priority

Health care:
for herself
for her baby

Other people's
priorities
for her

Mother of existing children
Preparer of food
Keeper of home
Worker in field
Wage-earner for family
Servant of all

© Illustration David Gifford

Figure 12.3   Few women from the poorest homes are free to attend pre-natal clinics

- Customs may not allow women to travel when pregnant, nor to see a male doctor.
- Clinics are disliked often because they are too far, too crowded, too frightening and too expensive.

> The most effective way of preventing deaths during pregnancy and delivery **is to set up effective community-based pre-natal and maternity services**.

What we need to do

Prepare the community

> Because care of the mother during pregnancy is not usually a felt need in poor communities, we must help the community understand that the good health of mothers and babies will benefit the **whole family**, including the husband.

The key to bringing this about will be raising awareness, not just of the mother but of the entire family.

Some of this will occur **before** starting the programme. We will discuss ideas and draw up plans with community leaders and representatives.

Awareness will also grow **after** the programme begins. As Traditional Birth Attendants (or CHWs) are trained and mother and baby clinics are set up, mothers will start using them and come to understand their value (see also Chapter 8).

Set aims and targets

Our overall **aim** will be to reduce the number of maternal and perinatal deaths in the target population. (A maternal death is a death from a pregnancy-related cause either during the pregnancy or within 42 days of the end of the pregnancy: a perinatal death comprises stillbirths and deaths of

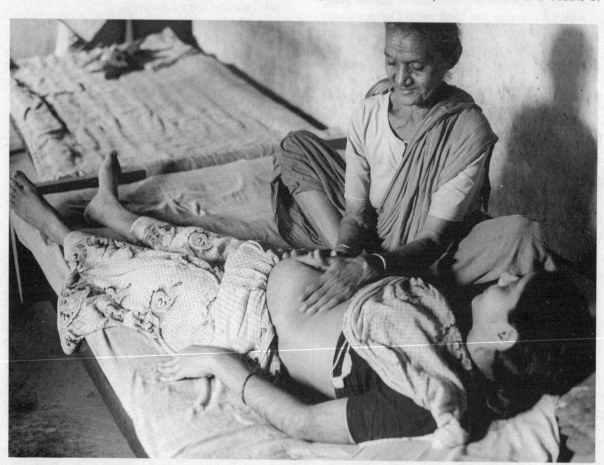

Figure 12.4   Pre-natal care at home

the newborn within 7 days of delivery.)
Our immediate **targets** will be as follows:

1. **Pre-natal care** (care during pregnancy).
   To increase the number of women receiving at least three check-ups during pregnancy.
2. **Delivery care** (or intrapartum care).
   To increase the number of deliveries being attended by a trained midwife (including trained TBAs, CHWs or other health workers) using a sterile delivery kit.
   To ensure facilities for emergency referral (including availability of emergency Caesarian section), as near as possible to target area with good transport system.
3. **Postnatal care**.
   To increase the number of women having two or more checks in the clinic or community.

Specific targets for each of the above must be realistic for the populations we are serving. An example might be for 50 per cent coverage after 3 years, 80 per cent after 5 years.

Train traditional birth attendants

Most communities have TBAs. With **careful training** and upgrading they can become excellent primary health midwives, assisting most births in the mothers' homes. They can also carry out the majority of pre-natal and postnatal care.
Some CHWs will also train as TBAs.

What are the characteristics of TBAs?

1. They live in or near the community and are usually available when needed.
2. They are usually older women, often of low social status, though in many communities highly respected.
3. Their skills are traditional, learnt from other TBAs – often their mothers or mothers-in-law.
4. Until trained they carry out little prenatal care and have poor understanding of hygiene.
5. They assist at births by advice, discipline and various interventions, some of which may not be appropriate.
6. In a crisis they save the mother rather than the child.
7. They are usually rewarded by gifts or small cash payments.

What should be the function of trained TBAs?

1. To carry out **pre-natal** examinations (see below).
2. To attend **deliveries** in order to:
   a) encourage and instruct the mother,
   b) monitor the progress of labour,
   c) recognise danger signs early and refer quickly,
   d) assist the delivery of the baby,
   e) assist the delivery of the placenta and check it is complete,
   f) cut the cord using a sterile blade,
   g) care for the **newborn** by:
      • drying him, keeping him warm and giving any necessary first aid,
      • putting him to the mother's breast to suck colostrum,
   h) care for the **mother** by:
      • making sure she is comfortable,
      • making sure the bleeding is controlled.
In carrying out these activities she will use the sterile delivery kit and ensure she has:
   a) clean **hands** – washed with soap and water after taking off all rings,
   b) clean **cutting** and tying of the umbilical cord,
   c) clean **surfaces** – she will place clean cloths under the mother and baby.
3. Carry out **postnatal** care (see below).

What should TBAs be taught?

Teaching should cover all the above functions as well as basic delivery techniques.
Training manuals are available in many countries and should be adapted and used.

How should TBAs be trained?

The **trainer** can be a nurse, professional midwife or any female member of the health team with practical experience in delivering babies. Doctors can be called in to teach selected lessons.
In practice TBAs will often be taught by the same person who teaches the CHWs.
The **timing** of training should be co-ordinated with the rest of the community health programme. Normally a CHW training programme is a higher priority than the training of TBAs.
The **location** should be the nearest place to the community which has sufficient deliveries to make

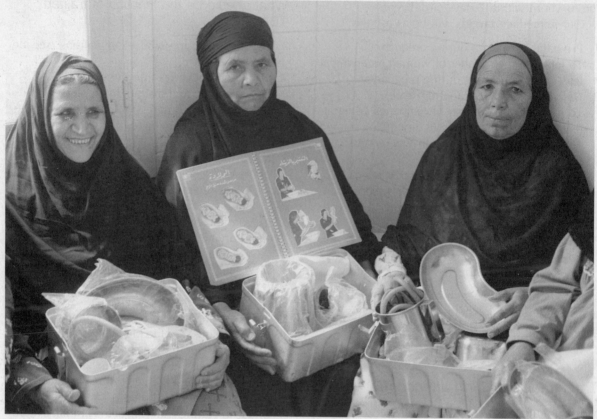

Figure 12.5   Egyptian traditional midwives with their new delivery kits

teaching worthwhile. Often this will be a health centre or small hospital. Alternatively basic teaching can be given in the community and extra practical sessions can be arranged. Community-based visits must **always** be part of any training programme.

If training is done in hospitals by nurses or doctors make sure that TBAs do not start adopting complicated methods or demanding special equipment.

> Remember that the purpose of training TBAs is to enable them to deliver babies as safely as possible in their communities using the simplest equipment.

The **duration** of training might total 30 days. This can either be given all at once, in several separate blocks, or 1 day per week over a period of time. An alternative is to give 7 days together, followed by a weekly training day, until the course is complete.

TBAs should be given thorough examinations especially in practical procedures and methods of referral and only then should they be 'accredited' by the project.

How should delivery kits be organised?

Why is a kit necessary?

Infection of the mother's birth canal and infection of the baby's umbilicus are common causes of death or illness. The purpose of the sterile delivery kit is to make these infections less likely.

What should the kit contain?

- Cord ties (three sterile pieces of cotton).
- Clean gauze to cover the stump.
- String to wrap around the cord dressing.
- Soap and a nail brush or nail sticks.
- Savlon and cotton wool.
- A small metal or plastic bowl.
- Two clean sheets or towels – one to place under the mother, another on which to place the de-

Figure 12.6 A traditional birth attendant in Senegal tends a newborn baby. Her training course has ensured that she knows the importance of hygiene

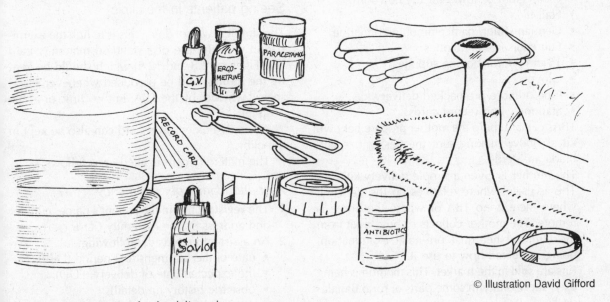

© Illustration David Gifford

Figure 12.7 Equipment for the delivery box

livery kit.
- A razor blade for cutting the cord.
- Gloves.

How should kits be used and replaced?

There are four ways this can be done:

1. The TBA is given a **separate pre-packed kit** for each delivery.
   This works well where the TBA/CHW does only a small number of deliveries e.g. fewer than 20 per year.
2. The TBA is equipped with a **delivery box** containing reusable items.
   This is a good system if the TBA has a larger workload e.g. more than 20 deliveries per year or where she covers several communities.
   Experienced TBAs can make up their own kits, cleaning reusable items, and obtaining expendable and sterile items from the health centre or project stores. Less-experienced TBAs can collect prepacked delivery kits from the project. The delivery box might contain the following:
   - Fetal stethoscope.
   - Fundal height measurer.
   - Tubular scales for weighing the newborn or a mid-upper arm circumference (MAC) measurer.
   - Bowls for swabbing perineum: Savlon.
   - Forceps and scissors.
   - Clean cloth or towel for the newborn.
   - Nail file.
   - Gentian violet, paracetamol, ergometrine.
   - Full course of antibiotics.
   - 15 cm pot for boiling supplies.
   - Gloves.
   - One or more pre-packed delivery kits.
   - Stationery and record cards.
   TBAs can also help the mother prepare her own kit as above making sure the ties, gauze and blade are sterile.
3. The **mother** is given a simple delivery kit.
   This is useful where relatives do the delivery, where there is no TBA or where the home is remote. The mother collects or buys a kit from the clinic at her final pre-natal examination, being instructed how to use it.
4. Kits are **sold** in the market. This method is being used successfully in some parts of rural Bangladesh.

Set up pre-natal care

Setting up a pre-natal clinic

General clinic or pre-natal clinic?

We shall consider a pre-natal clinic as **any** clinic in which pre-natal patients are seen. In most community health projects pre-natal care will be included in Mother and Child Clinic or in general clinics. In programmes serving larger populations or where patients live close by, it may be more convenient to run separate pre-natal clinics every week or every two weeks. There is limited value in setting up pre-natal care unless adequate referral for emergency treatment is available within a reasonable distance.

Mobile clinics travelling out from base should aim to provide pre-natal care whenever they visit a community, at least once per month.

How often should women attend?

Ideally pregnant women should have an examination every month from the fourth month onwards and weekly in the last month. **In practice** aim for each woman to have a minimum of 3 pre-natal examinations during each pregnancy, more if there are High Risk Factors present (see below page 181).

As TBAs become more experienced they can carry out routine pre-natals in the community.

Seeing patients in the clinic

The simplest way of doing this is to link the examination with the use of a standard maternity card (see Figures 12.8 and 12.9) which **should be kept by the mother** and be produced whenever she is seen – whether by the TBA, in the clinic or at the hospital.

A Family Folder Insert Card can also be kept in the clinic.

The maternity card is filled in as follows:

First attendance per pregnancy

1. The **registrar** fills in the patient's name, number and address on the Maternity Card.
2. An assistant records the following:
   - date of the last menstrual period (LMP),
   - the expected date of delivery (EDD),
   - obstetric history (in detail),
   - medical history and family history.

MATERNITY CARD

Name ....   Folder No. ....

Husband's Name ....   Village ....

Age ....

L.M.P. ....   E.D.D. [   ]

	Tet. Tox.	1	2	3	4	5
Height						

OBSTETRIC HISTORY

Pregnancy No.	Length of Pregnancy	Date of Birth M F	Outcome Ab SB LB	Complications	Name (if child alive)
1					
2					
3					
4					
5					

MEDICAL HISTORY
TB .... Diabetes ....
High B.P. .... Heart dis ....
Abdo surgery .... Disability ....
Blood transfusion ....
Other ....

PROBLEMS IN PRESENT PREGNANCY:

FAMILY HISTORY
TB ....
Diabetes ....
Twins ....
Other ....

DELIVERY NOTES
Type of delivery ....
Date ....
Conducted by ....
Complication ....

POSTNATAL NOTES
Involution ....
Lochia ....
Breast feeding ....
Any problems ....

BABY
Live: SB   M : F   Weight ....
Condition ....
Congenital abnormality ....

FAMILY PLANNING
Discussed (date) ....
Accepted (date) ....
Method ....

Figure 12.8   Maternity card used in SHARE project in north India (side A)

DETAILS OF PRESENT PREGNANCY

DATE	Height of uterus	Position & Presentation	Head High/Eng	Fetal Heart	BP	Oedema	Weight	Urine Alb	Sug	Hb	NOTES

Figure 12.9 Maternity card used in SHARE project in north India (side B)

She also:
- weighs the patient,
- takes the blood pressure,
- checks the urine for sugar and protein,
- sends her for routine blood tests.

These should always include haemoglobin (Hb), and may include a blood smear for malarial parasites, and tests for syphylis and HIV when appropriate.
3. The **nurse**, **doctor** or other **health worker**, examines the patient and records all the details. In particular she notes any High Risk Factors (HRFs).

She also gives teaching and reassurance to the patient which should include:
- advice about correct foods to eat (see Chapter 9, pages 132–3),
- how to keep healthy during pregnancy,
- how to prepare for the delivery,
- the need for regular check-ups,
- future ideas for family planning,
- answers to any special concerns of the mother.

Finally she arranges tetanus toxoid immunisation and gives iron and folate along with any other medicine prescribed. In some programmes this will include antimalarials.

> The correct treatment of anaemia and its causes is especially important where AIDS is common as it makes a blood transfusion (with its associated AIDS risk) less likely.

Other attendances in pregnancy

These are similar with the following changes:

1. The **assistant** will take routine measurements and discuss any problems.
2. The **health worker** examining the patient will note any new High Risk Factors and decide when and whether referral will be needed for a supervised delivery.

Planning for the delivery, breastfeeding and family planning will be discussed.

Blood tests will only be repeated if there is a specific reason. Tetanus immunisation will be completed.

A delivery kit will be given to the patient if this is project policy.

For time saving and convenience at all attendances ensure that:

1. Pregnant women are able to sit down at each clinic station and that waiting is kept to a minimum.
2. Weights, blood pressures, urine and blood tests, are taken **before** the woman sees the health worker.
3. Packets of iron and folic acid tablets are pre-counted and handed out by the health worker, not the dispenser.
4. Charges are kept as low as possible so that the poor can easily afford the services.
5. Health teaching is given to waiting patients.
6. Preparations are ready for unsuspected deliveries.

For further details see Chapter 8.

Caring for those with High Risk Factors (HRFs)

What is the importance of identifying HRFs?

Most health problems are found in a **small minority** of pregnant women. We can usually predict which women are likely to have problems by our observations at pre-natal checks. Features known to be connected with difficulties at the time of birth are known as HRFs.

> By targeting our care towards those with HRFs we will bring much quicker benefits. In addition we will save the time of patients and health workers and reduce expenses of the project.

How do we discover important HRFs for our area?

Some HRFs are found everywhere, others may be specific to our target population. We can discover important HRFs in two ways:

1. Before starting the project by learning from the experience of doctors and midwives working in nearby hospitals and health projects. We can also question local TBAs.
2. After the project starts by gathering our own information.

We should design our list of HRFs in such a way that approximately 20 per cent of pregnancies come into this category.

Antenatal Scoring Sheet
Northern Territory Department of Health

NAME: SETTLEMENT: E.D.D.:   U.S. DATE(S)S:

QUESTIONS		WRITE	IF MOTHER HAS:-	WRITE	EXAMINATION AT 1ST VISIT	WRITE	EXAMINATION AT 36 WEEKS	WRITE
AGE	Less than 16 years	1	Diabetes	3	Bleeding before 20 weeks	1	Bleeding after 20 weeks	3
	More than 35 years	2	Heart disease	3	Bleeding after 20 weeks	3	HB less than 10 grams	1
PARITY	Primiparous	2	Repeated UTI	2	HB less than 10 grams	1	BP more than 130/80	2
	Para 5 – 8	2	Kidney disease	2	BP more than 130/80	2	Premature rupture of membranes	2
	Para more than 8	3	Previous gynaecological surgery	1	Twins	3	Small for dates	3
PAST HISTORY	3 or more abortions or infertility	3	Bronchitis	1			Twins or breech	3
	P.P.H. or manual removal	1	Asthma	1				
	Previous baby less than 2500 grams	1	Other	1				
	Previous baby more than 4080 grams	1						
	High blood pressure or toxaemia	1						
	Previous Caesarian	3						
	Stillbirth or neonatal death	3						
	Difficult labour forceps/vacuum	2						
	TOTAL **A**		TOTAL **B**		TOTAL **C**		TOTAL **D**	

FIRST TOTAL
A, B & C

FINAL TOTAL
A, B, C & D

LOW RISK = 0 – 2
HIGH RISK = 3 – 6
VERY HIGH RISK – 7 OR MORE

Figure 12.10 One method of calculating high risk factors

This means we can target special care to the most needy fifth of pregnant women.

A scoring system can be used to identify them (see Figure 12.10).

What are common HRFs and when are they likely to be found?

1. HRFs discovered early in pregnancy.
   These will be discovered on the mother's first visit to the clinic. They usually include mothers who are:
   - primigravidae (pregnant the first time) and multigravidae (pregnant 4 or more times).
   - under 18, or over 35.
   - short – e.g., below about 140–150 cm (the height varies between communities) – a mark can be placed on the wall near the weighing scale.
   - known to have serious or chronic disease such as TB, malaria, AIDS, severe anaemia or heart disease.
   - heavy smokers or drinkers.
   - very poor or who do hard manual labour.
   - known to have had a stillbirth, a perinatal death, serious bleeding in a previous pregnancy, or a previous Caesarian section.
   - whose last baby weighed less than 2500 g.
   - whose previous children had birth intervals of less than 2 years.
2. HRFs discovered later in pregnancy.
   This group, discovered in the second half of the pregnancy will include:
   - Weight loss or poor weight gain during.
   - Twins, breech presentation (bottom first) after 34 weeks, or transverse lie (baby lies across mother).
   - Hydramnios (too much fluid in uterus).
   - Bleeding in last months of pregnancy.
   - Pre-eclampsia (swelling + high blood pressure + protein in urine).

How do we care for those with HRFs?

This group of women need the following **extra** care over and above routine pre-natal care described above:

1. Regular checks in the **clinic**, preferably once per month and more often in the last few weeks. This should include examination by a doctor or experienced nurse at least once in the pregnancy.

2. Regular visits in the **community** by the TBA or CHW who will keep a list in her book of all those known to have HRFs.
3. **Early** referral to a **hospital** or health centre for supervised delivery where indicated or when in doubt.
   Such mothers should ideally be admitted a good period of time **before** labour, either to have a supervised birth or, if really necessary a non-emergency Caesarian section.

For example (1): Cuba has been setting up a network of maternity waiting homes, located near hospitals. Here, women with HRFs from remote areas are referred a month before the delivery is due. As labour starts they are easily transferred to the nearby hospital.

For example (2): In Mnene Hospital, Zimbabwe, a maternity village has been in operation for a number of years. Women stay an average of 18 days, many consider this the best (and only) holiday of their lives.

It must be remembered however that some mothers will need emergency referral during labour itself and facilities for this will always need to be in readiness.

© Illustration David Gifford

Figure 12.11

Moving care from clinic to community

When a programme first starts most pre-natal care takes place **in the clinic**. Mothers may attend it, TBAs and CHWs may assist in it.

As TBAs (or CHWs) grow in experience they will be able to carry out more pre-natal care **in the community**.

As this shift takes place we will need to develop a different system for examining patients. The details of this will vary from project to project.

Here is one *example*:

1. All pregnant women still attend the clinic twice, once early in pregnancy and once late in pregnancy.
2. Those with HRFs attend more often according to instructions given by the clinic health worker and the TBA.
3. TBAs carry out a basic pre-natal check on all pregnant women each month in the community unless a clinic visit is due. In addition they identify and refer any new HRF patients or patients recently pregnant.

Prevent neonatal tetanus

What is neonatal tetanus (NNT)?

This is a disease which kills over half a million babies each year.

All forms of tetanus cause muscles to contract so that breathing becomes impossible. Germs enter the body through wounds and in newborn babies through the umbilical cord. **Traditional dressings often contain tetanus germs**.

An infected baby goes through these stages:

- He is healthy at birth.
- At 3–5 days after birth he stops sucking and closes his mouth.
- At 5–8 days he goes stiff, has fits and dies.

Preventing NNT by tetanus toxoid injections

1. The **best time** to do it:
   Pre-natal checks offer the best opportunity.

However **many mothers at greatest risk will not come to pre-natal clinics**. This means that Community Health Programmes should offer tetanus immunisations to girls and young women of childbearing age at every possible opportunity.

Such opportunities will include:
- during childhood – with DPT,
- during school years – with DT or TT,
- whenever a woman of childbearing age attends **any clinic or hospital for any reason**,
- during national or district immunisation days.

2. The **number** of injections needed:
   Follow this schedule:
   - two injections of 0.5 ml SC into the upper outer arm during the first pregnancy, the first as early as possible, the second at least 2 weeks before the delivery is due;
   - a booster dose during each further pregnancy up to a total of five injections;
   - if records prove three previous doses of DPT or DT have been given earlier, give one single dose of TT during each pregnancy.

3. Possible **side-effects**.
   There may be pain, firm swelling and redness for up to 3 days. This is not serious and needs no treatment. Later injections tend to give a greater reaction than earlier ones.

4. **Storage** of TT.
   As for DPT (see Chapter 10, page 142).

5. **Recording** of TT.
   This should be done:
   - on the Maternity Card if the woman is pregnant,
   - on a separate Tetanus Immunisation Card which the mother can keep with her all the time,
   - on her normal self-retained health card.

Preventing NNT **by other measures**

- By clean practices during delivery.
- By cutting the umbilical cord with a sterile blade.
- By placing a dry dressing on the stump.
- **By making sure that no traditional dressing, dung or ash is put on the stump**.

Set up delivery (or intrapartum) care

Birth is the most dangerous time of life both for mother and child. The purpose of good delivery care is to make birth as safe as possible for both.

Where should the birth take place?

1. In the mother's home.
   This is the best place unless there are known

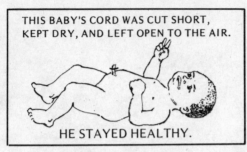

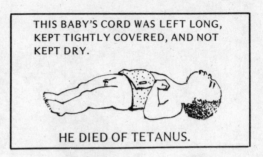

THIS BABY'S CORD WAS CUT SHORT, KEPT DRY, AND LEFT OPEN TO THE AIR.

HE STAYED HEALTHY.

THIS BABY'S CORD WAS LEFT LONG, KEPT TIGHTLY COVERED, AND NOT KEPT DRY.

HE DIED OF TETANUS.

Figure 12.12 Prevention of neonatal tetanus

complications. It is the only place which **most mothers in the world's poorest countries are able to afford**.

2. In the health centre or hospital.
Mothers with High Risk Factors may be referred for a hospital or health centre delivery.

> An essential part of any maternity programme is an emergency referral system, which both TBAs and CHWs know how to operate. Many deaths can be saved if emergencies are referred early to good maternity units.

Who should assist at the birth?

Deliveries should be carried out by **those who have been trained to do them**. Trained TBAs, CHWs or other midwives are the best people to do home deliveries. Doctors, nurse-midwives or Medical Assistants are the best choice for hospitals or health centres.

In some communities, mothers, mothers-in-law or relatives do deliveries. Where possible TBAs should be trained to replace them.

How should the delivery be carried out?

With skill and compassion. With good hygiene using a delivery kit and a partograph to give early warning of prolonged labour. For further details see Further Reading.

Set up postnatal care

Many **women** die after birth because of infection or blood loss. Many **children** die after birth because of poor feeding practice, ignorant or neglect.

In many traditional societies the mother is pre-vented by custom from leaving her home or community for several days or weeks. For this and other reasons postnatal care usually takes place **in the home** and **by the TBA, CHW** or equivalent health worker. Only where home visits cannot be made should clinics or hospitals be used.

Here is a suggested plan for postnatal care:

1. Immediately after the birth the TBA checks the mother and child as part of delivery duties (see opposite).
2. Within the first 24 hours.
The TBA sees the **newborn**:
   - She checks for obvious abnormalities such as breathing problems, swelling of the stomach, deformity or jaundice.
   - She weighs the baby or measures the mid-upper arm circumference (MAC).
   - She records details of the birth.
   - She gives the first polio drops (OPV Zero) if cold-chain facilities allow. See Chapter 10 page 143.
The TBA sees the **mother**:
   - She checks for any fever or continuing blood loss.
   - She checks for any feeding problems.
   - She discusses other any problems.
3. During the next 2 weeks the TBA visits daily for a few days, then gradually less often if mother and baby remain well.
During this time she pays special attention to fever and any vaginal loss in the mother, feeding problems, any sign of NNT or other infection in the baby, any other concern of the mother, and future family planning arrangements.
If the community has both a TBA and a CHW the TBA will now hand over care for the mother and child to the CHW.

Figure 12.13 CHW advises a mother on pre-natal care

Keep records

The following records can be kept:

1. Maternity Card (see Figures 12.8 and 12.9).
   This is the definitive card on which full details of the pregnancy are recorded. It is used not only during the pregnancy to help patient care, but also as the source for maternity statistics.
   The Maternity Card is best kept by the mother. A duplicate or summary can be kept in the family folder.
2. Record Card with symbols.
   This is for use by illiterate CHWs or TBAs. It needs to be purpose designed for each country and district.
   Symbols are used to represent both the factors which the TBA needs to check, and any HRFs which are present.
   This card is kept by the mother. It is usually used in addition to the Maternity Card, but in remote communities can replace it. Important details can later be copied on to the Maternity Card or straight into the Master Register.
3. The Master Register or Project Computer.
   Details from Maternity Cards can be copied in every 6 or 12 months.
4. Tallies and Report sheets.
   Some projects will use these to pass information from community to base.

Evaluate the programme

After an agreed time we will need to evaluate the project to see whether targets are being met.

Here are some useful annual **percentages** to measure:

1. Pre-natal coverage.
   The percentage of pregnant women who have attended for three or more pre-natal checks either in the clinic or with the TBA. All women who have given birth (whether live or still) over a one-year period are eligible (see Chapter 18).

2. Nutritional status of the newborn.
The percentage of newborn babies weighing more than 2500 g or having MACs of 8.7 cm or more.
3. Supervised deliveries.
The percentage of births attended by a **trained** TBA/CHW or other health worker using a sterile delivery kit.
4. Maternal tetanus coverage.
The percentage of women who have had two or more tetanus immunisations.

The figures needed for these measurements are obtained from Maternity cards or tallies or via the Master Register.
The results of any evaluation should be shared with the community as a basis for joint planning.

Summary

Large numbers of mothers and babies die each year from causes related to childbirth. Nearly all such deaths can be prevented through setting up effective, community-based maternity care backed up by a good referral centre.
The most ideal primary health workers are trained midwives, TBAs and CHWs. They will work in co-operation with clinics to provide pre-natal care, delivery care and postnatal care, targeted especially towards pregnant women with High Risk Factors.
As TBAs become more experienced they can take over much of the work originally carried out in the pre-natal clinic providing good referral facilities remain. Careful records need to be kept on all patients. These can form the database for yearly evaluations.

Further Reading

1. *Community Participation in Maternal and Child Health/Family Planning Programmes.* S. Rifkin. WHO, 1990.
A useful description and analysis of case histories.
Available from: WHO. See Appendix E.
2. *Training Manual for TBAs.* G. Gordon. Macmillan/TALC, 1990.
A useful and comprehensive guide.
Available from: TALC. See Appendix E.
3. *Guidelines for Introducing Simple Delivery Kits at the Community Level.* WHO, 1987.
Available from: WHO. See Appendix E.
4. *The Children Who Sleep by the River.* D. Taylor. WHO, 1991.
A novel set in rural Zimbabwe illustrating real-life situations relevant to most developing countries. Can be used to stimulate discussion.
Available from: WHO. See Appendix E.
5. *Maternal and Child Health in Practice.* G. J. Ebrahim et al. Macmillan, 1988.
Training modules for middle level workers.
Available from: TALC. See Appendix E.
6. *Management of Obstetric Emergencies in a Health Centre: A Handbook for Midwives.* B. Essex. Churchill Livingstone, 1981.
A useful guide for senior members of the health team involved in practical management of deliveries.
Available from: Churchill Livingstone. 1–3 Baxter's Place, Leith Walk, Edinburgh EH1 3AF, UK.
7. *Immunization in Practice.* WHO, 1989.
Section on prevention of neonatal tetanus.
Available from: WHO. See Appendix E.
8. *Preventing Maternal Deaths.* E. Royston, S. Armstrong (eds). WHO, 1989.
Available from: WHO. See Appendix E.
9. *Prevention of Neonatal Tetanus.* SEARO/WHO, 1984.
Available from: WHO. See Appendix E.
10. The partograph is a managerial tool for the prevention of long labour. WHO 1988/9.
Available free from: WHO. See Appendix E.
The WHO is organising a world-wide Safe Motherhood Initiative. In connection with this they publish a free newletter *Safe Motherhood*.
Available from: WHO. See Appendix E.
Safe Motherhood – an Information Kit is also available and includes guidelines for introducing simple delivery kits at the community level.

13

Setting up a Family Planning Programme

In this chapter we shall consider:

1. What we need to **know**
   - Why is family planning important?
   - What are the common objections to family planning?
   - What methods can be used?
2. What we need to **do**
   - Decide whether to start a programme
   - Set aims and targets
   - Prepare the community
   - Ensure supplies
   - Organise a family planning clinic
   - Set up family planning in the community
   - A summary of FP stages
   - Evaluate the programme

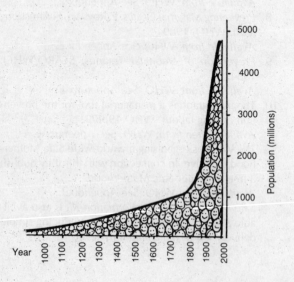

© Illustration David Gifford

Figure 13.1 The rise of the world population

What we need to know

Why is family planning important?

Family planning is important to reduce world population growth

Many areas of the world **already** have too many people. World population doubles every 25 to 30 years but most of this increase takes place in developing countries.

> In India alone 13 million people are added to the population each year meaning that 127 000 new primary schools are needed annually simply to educate the extra children.

When a population is either too large or increasing too fast the following problems get worse:

1. **Poverty**: there is less money, less food and less space for the poor. The rich remain largely unaffected.
2. **Disease**: overcrowding increases the spread of infection. Existing hospitals and clinics cannot cope with additional patients.
3. **Urbanisation**: cities grow in size rapidly. Overcrowding, squalor, drug abuse and prostitution become widespread. AIDS spreads more rapidly. In South America it is estimated that 20 million children live on the streets.
4. **Social breakdown**: overcrowding triggers off a chain reaction: exploitation, injustice and riots.

Family planning is important for each family

Poor families have only limited space, money, food and resources. The more children that are born to

Results of a 3% population growth rate on a village of 10 houses
The population will double every 20 years

Figure 13.2 Expanding villages

them the more likely are these children to become seriously ill or die.

Spacing between children is just as important as the total **number** of children born.

Child spacing leads to healthier **mothers**:

1. They have fewer children to look after at once, so having more time and energy.
2. They have an opportunity between pregnancies to regain strength and build up their iron stores.

Child spacing leads to healthier **children**:

1. They have more milk, more food, more love and more attention from their parents.
2. By the time the next child is born the next youngest has passed the most dangerous age for malnutrition.
3. Healthier children do better in school so becoming stronger, better educated adults who in turn will be able to provide more successfully for their children.

What are the common objections to family planning?

National objections

Some governments disapprove of family planning (FP) either because of low populations or for political or religious reasons. In addition AIDS will reduce population growth in parts of Africa.

Family objections

Help from children is needed to:

- assist on the farm and in the home,
- earn money,
- look after and provide for older parents and relatives,
- give the family status in the community, and
- carry on the family name, farm or business.

In many cultures boys are valued more than girls, meaning families will increase in size until at

© Illustration David Gifford

Figure 13.3   The poor man's question: 'How can I afford *not* to have a large family'

least 2 or 3 healthy boys are growing up.

Personal objections

Common worries include:

- What will people think?
- What happens if my children die?
- Will I lose my manhood or womanhood?
- Will my sex-life be affected?
- Will there be side-effects?
- Will my husband be suspicious?
- Will the government force me to use FP?
- Will it be difficult to get good advice and obtain regular supplies?

Each country, community and couple will have their own objections. Sometimes several minor fears, combined with a reluctance to discuss FP may prevent a couple seeking advice. We will need to discover and meet common objections.

For example: in Bangladesh family planning workers have discovered people's **real** objections by setting up 'Focus Groups'. These comprise 8 to 10 people of similar background, with a facilitator who encourages the people to share their ideas and fears. Objections are discovered and ways of overcoming them are suggested by the community.

What methods can be used?

There is a variety to choose from, and none is perfect. We should understand the merits and problems of each before deciding with the community, which to offer.

1. **Permanent methods** include vasectomy in the male and tubectomy (tubal ligation) in the

© Illustration David Gifford

Figure 13.4   Permanent FP methods are only appropriate if a couple have three or more children likely to survive into adult life

Table 13.1   Family planning chart

Method	How	Advantages	Disadvantages	Who for?
Natural (rhythm)	No SI from 4 days before to 4 days after ovulation	1. No supplies 2. No expense	1. High failure rate 2. Needs personal motivation 3. Difficult for those with irregular periods 4. Partner must be co-operative	1. Anyone well motivated 2. Useful for those unwilling to use other methods 3. Those with moral objections to other methods
Combined o/c pill (COC)	Take pill daily without missing	1. Very safe if regular 2. SI at any time 3. Regular periods 4. Comparatively few side-effects	1. Easy to forget 2. Reduces breast milk 3. Less safe in women who smoke	Any healthy women under 40 able to remember and not breastfeeding a baby 6 months or less
Minipill	Take pill daily without missing	As above but periods may be less regular and slightly less safe than COC	1. Easy to forget	Women breastfeeding a child 6 months of age or less
Injectable contraceptives	Injection every 2 or 3 months	1. Simple and safe 2. SI any time	1. P may be irregular 2. Some governments disapprove 3. May be harder to conceive after finishing	Any woman with 3 or more children
Condoms	Rubber sheath placed on erect penis	1. SI at any time 2. Some protection against AIDS and STD if used with care	1. Not reliable 2. Some couples dislike using them	1. Those who won't use more reliable methods 2. Those only having SI casually or occasionally e.g. couples living apart for employment reasons 3. Those in areas where AIDS is common
Vaginal foam	Foam placed in vagina which kills sperm	1. No side effects 2. Easy to use 3. SI at any time	1. Not very safe if used alone	Any woman not willing or able to use other more reliable methods Any woman uncertain if she is pregnant

continued

Table 13.1   continued

Method	How	Advantages	Disadvantages	Who for?
IUD, coil, Copper T, Copper 7	Loop or coil inserted into vagina and left for up to 5 years	1. SI at any time 2. Quite effective	1. P may be heavy and painful 2. May cause anaemia 3. Unsuitable for women who have not had children	Women with 1 to 4 children who want to delay having more.
Vasectomy	Cutting of male tubes (vas)	1. SI at any time 2. Effective, permanent	1. Occasional post-operative infection and psychological after-effects 2. Many men resistant	Stable couples with 3 or more children who don't want any more
Tubectomy or tubal ligation	Cutting of woman's tubes	1. SI any time 2. Effective, permanent	1. As 1. under vasectomy	Any woman with 3 or more children who doesn't want any more.

SI = sexual intercourse
P = periods (menses)
STD = sexually transmitted disease (VD)

female. These are used when no more children are wanted.

Couples will only accept these methods if there is a high chance that all their existing children will survive to adulthood.

2. **Temporary methods** include all other FP methods. They are used:
   - to delay starting a family,
   - for child spacing,
   - to prevent any further children if the parents are not willing or ready to use a permanent method.

Table 13.1 gives a summary of family planning methods.

What we need to do

Decide whether to start a programme

To help decide we must answer these questions:

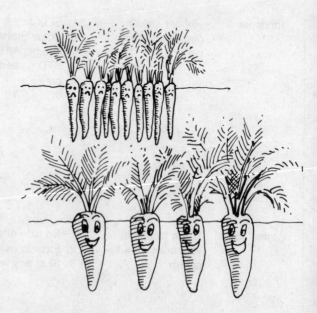

Figure 13.5   Well-spaced children, like well-spaced carrots, grow better

1. Is family planning a **government policy**?
   Usually this is encouraged. Where it is not we should act cautiously.
2. Is it a **felt** need in our target area?
   Do the people actually want it? Have they asked us to provide supplies or arrange operations?
3. Is it a **real** need in the area or in the family?
   We can work this out from the family folder:
   - If less than 50 per cent of couples are using family planning there is a definite need to extend the uptake of FP in the community.
   - Couples with three children or more have a need for family planning, ideally through use of permanent methods.
   In addition: all fertile couples have a real need to practise child spacing.
4. Can the programme be **sustained**?
   Trained staff, reliable supplies, good planning, long-term commitment and effective community partnership are needed if the programme is to continue.

Set aims and targets

These will vary and must be appropriate to the local area.

Here is one suggestion: an eventual **aim** if the community so wishes, might be to encourage a family norm of three children, spaced three or more years apart. This will take many years to achieve.

Specific **targets** might be:

1. Years 0 to 3:
   - To **create awareness** so that an increasing number of couples wish to use family planning services.
   - To **provide** family planning when requested.
   - To **set up** an effective mother and child programme, which will help to stimulate demand.
2. Year 3 onwards:
   - To **promote** family planning more actively.
   - To **set** an actual target for the project area: *For example*: 30 per cent of eligible couples to have used a permanent method or be regularly using a temporary method after 3 years, 60 per cent after 5 years.

Prepare the community

An interest in family planning will usually develop when families know that **children born to them are likely to survive**. Family planning tends to grow naturally as primary health care begins to take effect.

There will still be a need to create further awareness and above all to **explain details of methods available**.

Uptake and interest can be encouraged through:

- Meeting objections through Focus Groups, talking to mothers in clinics etc.
- Working through religious groups, priests or leaders.
- Teaching through women's clubs, youth clubs, co-operatives and schools.
- Training TBAs and CHWs to be FP motivators and suppliers.
- Using national publicity campaigns, in particular radio broadcasts, details of which can be passed on to the community.
- Including FP as a subject in literacy courses.

Methods used for teaching must be appropriate for the culture, remove fears, answer questions and underline the many **benefits** in using FP.

Benefits from family planning may include: more money, food and space for the family; no more worries about unwanted pregnancies; a better sex life; more peace and quiet at home; fewer dowries to pay.

Ensure supplies

It is better not to start a programme at all, than to start and run out of supplies. Community members must have confidence that repeat supplies are always available.

Nothing destroys a promising FP programme so successfully as apologies from the health team that supplies have run out.

To ensure supplies:

- Identify two or more sources for each type needed.
- Obtain adequate initial stocks.

SORRY, LAST YEAR THE CLINIC RAN OUT OF PILLS

© Illustration David Gifford

Figure 13.6 It is better not to start a programme at all, than to start and run out of supplies

- Order well ahead.
- Protect supplies, especially condoms, pills and injections from spoiling in storage.
- Set up a reliable system for moving supplies from central stores to clinics and other outlets.

Organise a family planning clinic

Although some activities take place in the community, the clinic usually remains the focal point of an FP programme.

Should the clinic be separate or combined?

Advantages of FP being part of a **general** clinic:

1. All health needs are met together, at the same time and the same place. This is especially convenient for patients travelling a long distance.
2. It reduces project time and resources if FP uptake is low.
3. It enables confidential advice to be given to women who may wish to keep their interest secret. (Generally couples, not individuals should be counselled.)

Advantages of running **separate** FP clinics:

1. Staff can concentrate on family planning rather than trying to provide a range of MCH services as well.
2. Equipment and supplies can be easily set up.
3. **Family planning** can be given the **priority** it needs. Without a separate clinic it can easily get squeezed out or forgotten because of more immediate needs.
4. Waiting time may be less.
5. Mutual support can be gained from fellow clients, so encouraging uptake.

When a health centre **first starts** one or two rooms can be set aside exclusively for family planning activities during an MCH or general clinic. As **clinics** develop and numbers increase, separate FP clinics can be considered.

Who is involved in an FP clinic?

1. The Family Planning Provider (FPP), often a nurse who except in large clinics will also be in charge.
2. Assistants such as TBAs, CHWs, or responsible community members.
3. The visiting doctor.
   His jobs can include doing tubectomies and vasectomies on prefixed days, advising on difficult cases and giving training and supervision. He can arrange a referral system for more difficult cases.

In Zaire guidelines have been drawn up about how a Family Planning Provider (FPP) should be selected, trained and used:

1. A member of the health team is selected and sent for special training in FP.
2. The person chosen is acceptable to the community she will be serving, both in terms of her sex, age and personality.
3. The training takes place mainly within a well-functioning family planning clinic, so that the trainee becomes familiar with all techniques used and advice given.
4. On her return the FPP carries out family planning sessions at set times each week, during which she is not diverted into other primary health activities. Times of FP sessions are posted

© Illustration David Gifford

Figure 13.7 Family planning services must be convenient for clients

outside the clinic and made known to the community.

5. As soon as possible the FPP starts training another member of the health team both to share her work and to substitute when she is absent.
6. She avoids being rushed, trying to allow about 10 minutes per patient.

What supplies and equipment are needed?

Supplies will depend on the types of family planning we will be offering, (see Table 13.1). Plenty of **reserve** stocks will be needed in case of heavy demand, and careful **storage** to ensure supplies do not spoil.

Equipment will be similar to that listed for a community health clinic in Appendix B. If IUDs are used additional instruments are needed including uterine sound, cervical tenaculum, sponge and artery forceps, curved, blunt and long-handled scissors.

Instruction sheets for the **provider** on each FP method to be used. Each sheet will include: indications for use; method of use; contra-indications; side-effects; instructions to patient; type of examination needed; follow-up; treatment of any minor disease or infection discovered.

Instruction sheets for the guidance of the **client** will also be needed, in the local language and with clear illustrations.

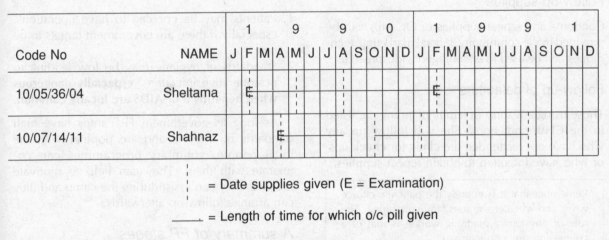

Code No	NAME	| 1	9				9					0	| 1	9				9					1
		J	F	M	A	M	J	J	A	S	O	N	D	J	F	M	A	M	J	J	A	S	O	N	D
10/05/36/04	Sheltama	E												E										
10/07/14/11	Shahnaz			E																				

| = Date supplies given (E = Examination)

_____ = Length of time for which o/c pill given

Figure 13.8 Sample page from oral contraceptive pill section of family planning register

What records should be kept?

These will include:

1. Person's own self-retained card.
   Record the method (and number if OC pill used).
2. Family folder insert card.
   Record type, amount and date to be seen again.
3. Family planning register.
   For a sample page see Figure 13.8.
4. Some projects with a strong FP emphasis can give each client a special family planning record card.
5. The Master Register.
   Figures of FP coverage can be copied into the Master Register or Project Computer at regular intervals.

Set up family planning in the community

Some FP activities are best carried out here:

Motivation for family planning

Many people can help to do this, for example:

* The CHW, TBA, FPP or other health team members.
* Satisfied community members already using family planning.

In addition the local women's club can arrange discussions and help to remove fear and suspicion.

Follow-up supplies

Condoms and repeat supplies of OC pills can be provided in the community. 'Social marketing' techniques can be used to encouraged widespread use.

Follow-up of defaulters

Those using any form of family planning are listed in the CHWs notebook. She will follow up any who have not reattended the clinic for check ups, or who have forgotten to obtain repeat supplies.

> Remember that it is entirely the patient's choice when and whether she uses family planning. The role of any family planning worker is that of a counsellor, not a policeman.

© Illustration David Gifford

Figure 13.9   Satisfied customers make effective family planning promoters

Family planning camps

In some countries special FP camps are organised by the government or by larger non-governmental organisations; vasectomies and tubectomies are carried out in the community, and supplies distributed.

This system can work well but may have dangers:

1. Patients may be coerced to have operations, especially if there are government targets to be met.
2. Standards of hygiene may be low leading to postoperative infections, **especially dangerous when hepatitis B or AIDS are locally common**.

As long as government FP camps have high standards of hygiene and are popular with the local people, voluntary programmes can co-operate with them. They can help to motivate couples, they can assist during the camp and they can arrange follow-up afterwards.

A summary of FP stages

FP provision includes these four stages.

1. **Motivation**
   - **What** is it?
     Helping the couple, or individual, to understand their **need** for FP so they actively **request** it.
   - **Where** does it happen?
     Anywhere e.g. the community, clinic, over the family radio.
   - **Who** does it?
     Friends, other family members, CHWs, TBAs, FPPs, other health workers, teachers, members of women's clubs, religious leaders, film stars.
2. **Counselling**
   - **What** is it?
     General explanation about different FP methods to help the **couple** choose.
     Detailed explanation about the method chosen, including the way to use it, its failure rate, side-effects and follow-up. The counsellor must be ready to answer questions.
   - **Where** does it happen?
     The clinic, the hospital, the community, the FP camp.
   - **Who** does it?
     A health worker, nurse or doctor – normally the same person who actually provides the service – the Family Planning Provider.
3. **Providing** the service.
   - **What** is it?
     The initial FP service after counselling is completed, including giving the first supplies.
   - **Where** does it happen?
     IUDs, injections and the first pack of pills in the clinic. Condoms and further pills in the clinic or community. Operations in the health centre or hospital.
   - **Who** does it?
     Doctors for operations. Family Planning Providers or nurses for IUDs, injections and the first pack of pills; other health workers or distributors for condoms and repeat supplies of pills.
4. **Follow-up**
   - **What** is it?
     For operations: checking for wound infections or other side-effects; answering questions.
     For IUDs: checking at least once after insertion and then every 3 or 5 years.
     For injections: repeats at the prescribed interval plus yearly check.
     For pills: yearly check. Community follow-up of defaulters.
   - **Where** does it happen?
     The clinic or community.
   - **Who** does it?
     The least qualified health worker able to do it well.

Evaluate the programme

At regular intervals we will need to evaluate the effectiveness of our FP programme. This will require baseline information **before starting** which should include:

- The total number of couples **eligible for family planning** in the target community (= all women of child bearing age 15–44 years and their partners). This information will be on the front of the family folders as recorded in the community survey (see Chapter 6).
- If the population is sufficient (e.g. 10 000 or more), and we have obtained accurate details about the number of births in the previous year, the crude birth rate or fertility rate can be estimated **before** starting an FP programme and then compared after 5 or 10 years. The **Crude Birth Rate** is:

$$\frac{\text{Number of live births in a year}}{\text{Population at middle of year}} \times 1000$$

Figure 13.10

Figure 13.11   The price of failure: a drift to the cities and urban poverty

The **Fertility Rate** is:

$$\frac{\text{Number of live births in a year}}{\text{No. of women aged } 15-44 \text{ in the population}} \times 1000$$

We can evaluate our FP programme as follows:

1. Every year:
   Record the total **number** of couples using each form of contraception and estimate the **percentage** of eligible couples (a) using regular temporary contraception or (b) who have had a permanent method carried out.
   The numbers using contraception will be recorded in the Family Planning Register and the number of eligible couples known from our most recent community survey.
2. Every 3 years:
   We can resurvey the target population and work out the numbers and percentages as above. This will act as a check for our yearly figures.

3. Every 5 or 10 years:
   We can estimate the fall in the crude birth rate or fertility rate.

Child spacing can be evaluated by averaging the gaps between successive births on our 3-yearly surveys.

As in all evaluations, the project and community should work in partnership. Findings should be explained and discussed with community members.

Summary

The world population is doubling every generation. Countries which are overcrowded develop serious social problems. In conditions of poverty the children of larger families are at higher risk, especially when the space between children averages less than 3 years.

Each programme must decide whether FP is a

current priority in its partner communities, and if so which methods are most suitable. These will include both permanent operations, and a variety of temporary methods which can increase child spacing.

Family planning is most successful when run as part of a primary health care programme because the guarantee of healthy children stimulates a wish to reduce family size.

A family planning clinic can act as the focal point of the programme and a health worker can be trained as a Family Planning Provider. Certain FP activities can also take place in the community, such as motivation, family planning camps, and the resupply of pills and condoms.

FP programmes should be regularly evaluated in partnership with the community.

Further Reading

1. *The Family Planning Clinic in Africa.* 2nd edn. R. and J. Brown. Macmillan, 1990.
   An extremely useful and practical manual relevant to all parts of the world.
   Available from: TALC. See Appendix E.
2. *The Church Health Educator.* I. H. Stober and B. Wecker. Macmillan, 1989.

A useful section on family planning, especially in the context of countries with high AIDS prevalence.
   Available from: Macmillan Education, Houndmills, Basingstoke, Hants, UK.
3. *Community Participation in Maternal and Child Health/Family Planning Programmes.* S. Rifkin. WHO, 1990.
   A useful description of case histories.
   Available from: WHO. See Appendix E.
4. *Traditional Birth Attendant in Seven Countries: Case Studies in Utilization and Training.* A. Mangay-Magiacas and H. Pizurki. WHO, 1981.
   Available from: WHO. See Appendix E.
5. *Injectable Contraceptives: Their Role in Family Planning Care.* WHO, 1990.
   A detailed description of this useful method of FP.
   Available from: WHO. See Appendix E.
6. *Natural Family Planning: A Guide to Provision of Services.* WHO, 1988.
   A practical guide for use in communities where other forms of FP are not acceptable.
   Available from: WHO. See Appendix E.

Slides

The following teaching slides are available from TALC. See Appendix A.

- Contraceptive Devices   Cd
- Physiology of Women   PhW

14

Setting up a Community TB Programme

In this chapter we shall consider:

1. What we need to **know**
   - What is TB?
   - How important is TB?
2. What we need to **do**
   - Decide whether to start a TB programme
   - Decide what type of TB programme to set up
   - Set aims and targets
   - Create awareness in the community
   - Identify TB cases
   - Manage TB cases
   - Immunise with BCG
   - Control TB in the community
   - Evaluate the programme

What we need to know

What is TB?

Tuberculosis is a life-threatening disease which

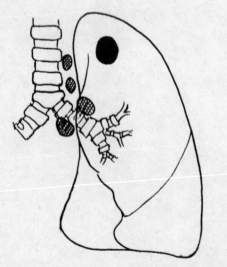

© Illustration David Gifford

Figure 14.1   The primary complex

normally affects the lungs but can involve almost any part of the body.

The **symptoms** of TB are weight loss, chronic ill health, and fever especially in the evening. Lung (pulmonary) TB also causes cough, often with sputum, sometimes with blood. Chest pain is commonly present. TB can mimic a wide variety of illnesses. Where AIDS is common the two diseases are often found together.

The **cause** of TB is a germ called *Mycobacterium tuberculosis* (also known as the acid-fast bacillus – AFB). Poverty, overcrowding, poor health and malnutrition makes infection with the AFB more likely and more serious.

TB **starts** as germs enter the lungs, commonly in childhood, and multiply to form a patch with nearby swollen lymph nodes, together known as a primary complex. At this stage germs may enter the blood and spread to other organs. If the person is in **weak health** at the time of infection the primary complex may enlarge at once to give active TB.

If the newly infected person is in **good health** the disease may spread no further, but there is always the danger that later in life, especially during a time of stress, illness, poor diet or AIDS the original infection will become active and lead on to fully developed (post-primary) TB.

Sometimes AFB lodge in the throat and tonsils, giving enlarged neck glands (gland TB).

TB is **spread** through the cough and sputum of a patient with active lung TB. A rarer form of TB (bovine TB) is spread through infected cows' milk.

> It has been estimated that on average each sputum positive case infects about 10 other people, and has been spreading infection for 6 months before detection.

How important is TB?

TB is one of the world's commonest and most

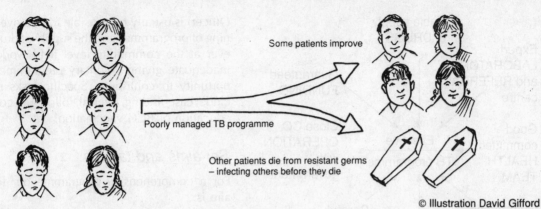

© Illustration David Gifford

Figure 14.2 A poorly managed TB programme spreads resistant germs through the community making eventual control even more difficult

serious diseases.

World-wide there are thought to be at least 25 million active cases. In India alone there are at least 10 million.

About 5 million new cases are found each year. On average an untreated patient with active TB will live about 2 years from the onset of his illness.

> TB is one of the commonest causes of death in developing countries. About 12 million people die from TB each year and many more suffer chronic ill-health. In addition poor families may spend their entire life's savings on treatment.

There is little evidence that TB is becoming any less common and where AIDS is prevalent TB is on the increase. *For example*: in a rural hospital in Malawi: TB admissions in 1987–88 were 2 times greater than in 1983–84 before AIDS was recognised locally.

What we need to do

Decide whether to start a TB programme

TB, though a serious disease, is both **difficult** and **expensive** to treat. This means we should only start a programme after careful consideration.

> Treating TB inadequately is probably worse than not treating it at all. A few patients may be cured but resistant germs will develop making TB **in the target area harder to cure in the future**.

We will need to ask:

1. Does the community wish to have a programme and will they work in partnership with us? Are they prepared to take on increasing responsibility for running the programme?
2. Is TB common or important in the target area? We should only start a programme if our community survey suggests a level of **possible** TB cases of at least 1 per cent.
3. Is TB already being adequately treated in the area?

   Although government TB programmes may be functioning and private doctors treating certain patients, effective programmes are rarely present in the neediest areas.

> As well as finding out **what** groups are working we will need to discover **how much** they are **actually** doing. Is there an effective and comprehensive programme which adequately includes the poor?

Part of our assessment will be through meeting the District Medical, or TB Officer and directors of any other programmes offering TB care in the area.

4. Have we the resources to set up a TB programme?
   - A **doctor** to plan, advise and give clinical care.
   - **Health workers** to find cases, organise treatment and ensure follow-up.
   - **Drugs**, often difficult to obtain, whose supplies must never run out.
   - **Money**, unless free supplies are available and

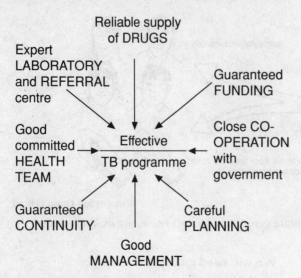

Figure 14.3 The essential ingredients in an effective TB programme

guaranteed from the government or an aid programme for 5–10 years.
• Effective **management**.
5. Is the project long-term or permanent?
Because it takes many years for a TB programme to be effective, we will need to make sure as far as possible that our programme will continue for a number of years.

Decide what type of TB programme to set up

There are two main choices:

A comprehensive TB programme

This is a programme where the project and community take full responsibility for case-finding, treatment, follow-up and BCG immunisation.

If this is decided upon, the community may wish to start TB control at the same time as setting up health centres. Alternatively they may wish to have a general community health programme first, and a TB component later.

A selective TB programme

If a local programme already exists we may be able to work in co-operation with the agency running it, or take over responsibility for certain parts of the programme.

For example: The government (District Medical

Officer) is usually responsible for the overall planning of programmes and the supply of drugs. However at the community level field work is often inadequate giving voluntary programmes an opportunity to contribute. Specific tasks might include: case-finding, referral, follow-up, community education or BCG vaccination.

Set aims and targets

For a comprehensive programme our **long-term aim** is:

• to **find** all infectious cases,
• to **treat** all infectious cases until they are cured,
• to **immunise** all infants with BCG,
• to **control** TB in the target community.

It will take **many** years to achieve this, and we will therefore need to define **short-term targets**.
For example: During the first 3-year period we could aim to:

• sensitise the community about the importance of TB,
• identify all those suspected of having infectious TB and arrange sputum tests,
• motivate 50 per cent to start treatment,
• ensure 80 per cent continue with their treatment regularly,
• immunise 50 per cent of the infants.

During the second 3-year period we could aim for 90 per cent of sputum-positive patients to be on regular treatment and for all children to be immunised with BCG.

In communities which are scattered, displaced, poorly educated or where AIDS is common, these targets are too high.

Create awareness in the community
(see Chapter 3)

Creating awareness is one of the key factors in eradicating TB. Once community members **recognise** their illness, **believe** it can be cured and **ask for** treatment an effective programme can be started.

We will need to understand local beliefs and customs and the difficulties faced by the poor in getting treatment.

TB is usually: curable for the rich
incurable for the **poor**

CLINIC

+ Money −
+ Contacts −
+ Time −

© Illustration David Gifford

Figure 14.4   TB in practice (1)

Local beliefs and customs

Though variable, patients may believe that:

- TB can't be cured (this may well be true in their experience).
- Only the poor, low caste or those under a curse get TB.
- TB is sent by God so has to be endured.
- TB patients are unclean and should be removed from their families or communities.

Difficulties faced by the poor

Imagine a poor villager or slum-dweller who starts to cough up blood. He will have to face a frightening sequence of problems:

1. Terror that he has a disease which usually kills the poor.
2. A realisation that he will have neither the en-

ergy nor the money to obtain a cure.
3. Mistrust of the doctor.

> More often that not the patient will leave the clinic, clutching a long list of expensive medicines, unable to understand what the doctor has told him, unsure of whether or not he has TB, or whether he will need further treatment.

4. Lack of money to pay for the drugs.
   He can hardly afford 1 week's treatment. How can he manage 6 months?
5. No one available, or affordable to give him the injection.
   He has collected streptomycin from the health centre but who will give the injection? Is it true that injections spread AIDS?

In the case of a woman with TB these problems

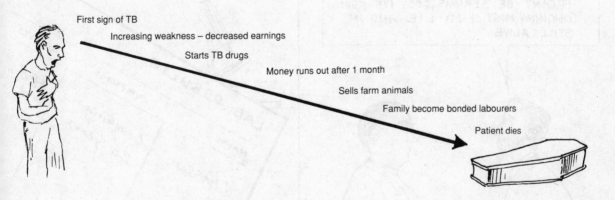

First sign of TB

Increasing weakness – decreased earnings

Starts TB drugs

Money runs out after 1 month

Sells farm animals

Family become bonded labourers

Patient dies

© Illustration David Gifford

Figure 14.5   TB in practice (2): within one year this TB patient died and his family lost their farm, their money, their independence, their dignity and their future

are multiplied. Often her family may be unwilling or unable to spend money on her treatment. They may prevent her from attending doctors and hospitals when she should be busy at home, collecting firewood, or earning income.

We must make sure that our teaching and our programme takes these problems into account and offers practical answers.

Identify TB cases

In this section we shall consider how to identify sputum-positive cases.

> Our aim in case-finding is to discover every sputum positive case in the target area. If we are successful, and all are fully treated, few new cases will arise and TB should gradually disappear. (In areas where AIDS is common these aims are not realistic.)

Most doctors and many programmes only test and treat patients **who come to them**. This is known as **passive** case finding and is an important part of TB control, but it **will never control TB in a community**. Our task is also to be **active** case finders. This means searching for and finding everyone in the community suspected of having active TB.

To identify sputum positive cases we should carry out the following: make a list of suggestive symptoms, make a list of possible TB cases and then test possible TB cases.

Make a list of suggestive symptoms

Anyone who has one or more of the following symptoms is a 'possible TB case'

Adults:
- Cough for more than a month.
- One or more episodes of blood in the sputum.
- Chest pain for more than a month.
- Increasing weakness, decreasing weight (there are many causes for this including AIDS but TB must be actively considered).
- Cases known to have had TB in the past, or **previously treated for cough**.

Children:
- Any of the above.
- Two or more fevers with no obvious cause such as malaria.
- Decrease in weight and falling off the Road to Health, where there is no other obvious cause.

Make a list of possible TB cases

We will discover patients with suggestive symptoms in the following ways:

From the house to house survey

This may be either the **general** community survey done at the beginning, or a **special** survey we do now.

In either case we ask the **right** questions, in the

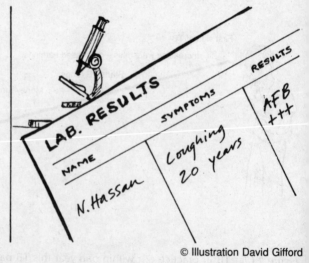

© Illustration David Gifford

Figure 14.6   A dangerous source of TB germs – the elderly villager with chronic cough

same way to every adult and older child, and about every younger child (see Chapter 6).

From reports in the community

The CHW can report any patients with suggestive symptoms especially those who have developed them since the survey was done.

Members of the **Health Committee**, women's club or young farmers' club can help to identify cases and put pressure on them to come forward for testing.

In remote areas, or with seriously ill patients the CHW can collect sputum specimens in the patient's home and bring them to the clinic or hospital for testing.

From clinic screening

All patients who come to the clinic or hospital for **whatever reason** are asked about the presence of any suggestive symptoms (see Chapter 8, page 106).

For example: One Himalayan project where dental problems are widespread, receives many requests for tooth extraction, especially from older men. This is the very group of patients most likely to have active TB. In the case of those with cough no teeth are pulled until a sputum test is first examined. Many infectious patients, otherwise unwilling to submit to tests, have been found and cured in this way.

All 'possible TB cases' are listed whether found through the survey, CHW reports or clinic, details being recorded on the family folder insert cards.

Test possible TB cases

This can be done by:

Sputum examination

This is the **correct** way of identifying active cases of lung TB. It is cheaper, easier and more effective than taking X-rays. Three negative sputums are necessary before a possible case can be labelled non-infectious.

Tests are best done **in the health centre** where a laboratory technician with basic training can identify active cases while the patients wait. If this is not possible sputums can be sent to the nearest laboratory or hospital which has reliable testing facilities.

The **method** of collection is important: sputum should be produced from a deep cough, ideally when the patient wakes in the morning. It should be produced away from other people, placed in a tightly-covered, labelled container and delivered to the laboratory as soon as possible.

The **accuracy** of the laboratory worker is important: he needs to be skilled, patient and honest. **False-negatives** result when the technician is too busy or insufficiently motivated to search thoroughly. **False-positives** occur where the laboratory worker records what he believes the doctor expects.

> No TB programme should be started unless reliable sputum testing is available.

© Illustration David Gifford

Figure 14.7 Results can be inaccurate if laboratory workers are over-worked

Chest X-ray

This is an inappropriate method for TB screening in developing countries.

The main value of X-rays is helping to assess possible cases who are persistently sputum negative and children unable to produce sputum. If an X-ray suggests TB in an ill patient with typical symptoms a trial of TB treatment can be considered.

> X-rays are expensive and usually unnecessary. Small projects can run adequate TB programmes on sputum testing alone.

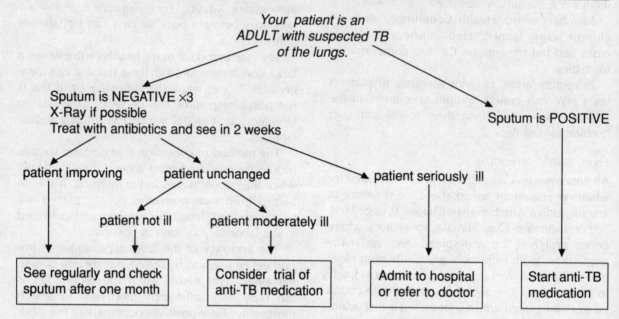

Figure 14.8 Suggested community health management of adult with suspected TB of the lungs

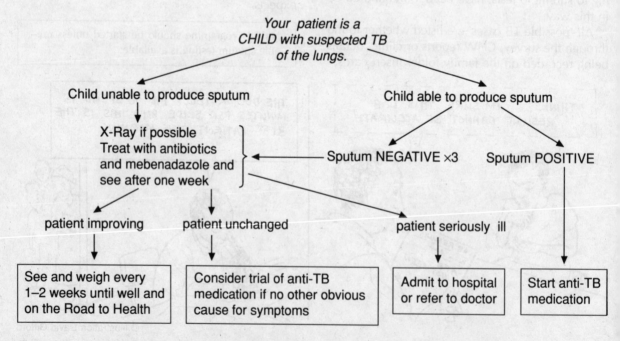

Figure 14.9 Suggested community health management of child with suspected TB of the lungs

Erythrocyte sedimentation rate (ESR) blood test

This is **not** an accurate way of **diagnosing** TB. Although usually raised in active cases, many other diseases also cause a high ESR. Although it may be of some value in assessing the effect of treatment,

the use of the ESR is no longer recommended in the management of TB.

Manage TB cases

In this section we shall consider:

A Message about Tuberculosis

Please read this very carefully or if you cannot read ask someone in the village to read it to you.

The tests we have done have shown that you have TB. This is a very serious illness.

If you do not take medicine regularly, the TB may kill you. You will also spread it to others including children.

But you can be cured of TB if you take your medicine every day for 8 months. You must not miss even a single day or a single dose.

After you have been taking medicine for about 3 months you may start to feel much better and think that you are cured. You must still go on taking medicine for the full 8 months. If you stop when you feel better then later the disease will come back much worse and it will be much harder to treat.

It is very important that you stop smoking all forms of tobacco. You should eat good nourishing food, including green vegetables, lentils, milk, eggs and meat if these are available. There are no foods that you should avoid.

You should avoid getting too tired but you can continue to work unless you are told not to.

When you cough put a hand or cloth over your mouth. This stops other people from catching your germs. Try not to spit in the house or when near other people. If you have to cough up sputum then put it into a cloth or small container and burn or bury it.

Also, if you are coughing a lot then you should sleep separately from other members of your family – if possible in a different room until your cough has stopped. This will stop them from catching your germs.

Make sure that you bring any other people in your family or village who have a bad cough, to the clinic. We can check them to see if they have TB.

If you are a married woman of child-bearing age try and avoid getting pregnant. If you do get pregnant then your TB will get worse and the baby may be born dead. We can give you special pills or insert a Copper T to stop you getting pregnant until you have finished your treatment.

You should come back to the clinic the week after starting treatment and then every month. If you feel ill or worried you can come back any time. BUT REMEMBER – You must take your treatment every day for 8 months – If you don't your TB will get worse and you may die. If you do your TB will get better.

Figure 14.10 TB advice sheet for patients used in a Himalayan health project. Adapt this for the programme area and add appropriate illustrations

1. When to start a possible case on treatment
2. What treatment to give
3. Advice and instruction for the patient
4. Records to keep
5. Follow-up
6. How to be sure the patient is cured
7. TB management in people with AIDS

When to start a possible case on treatment

Suggestions for adults and children are given in the flow charts in Figures 14.8 and 14.9.

What treatment to give

The project's drug regimes (drugs used plus length of course) should be decided by the doctor, the project director and the Government TB Officer or District Medical Officer. The treatment of TB is a national programme and wherever possible the drugs we use should be those suggested, and often supplied by, the Ministry of Health.

In the **past** TB patients were treated for **18 months** and were often brought into **hospital**.

The **modern** plan is usually to treat patients in the **community** for 6, 8 or 9 **months** using newer, stronger drugs.

Here are some **advantages** of this newer approach:

1. It is easier for the patient and the relatives which means **more** active cases actually receive treatment.
2. The period of supervised treatment is much shorter, meaning compliance is better.
3. All drugs used can be given together, in some cases twice per week instead of every day.
4. The newer drugs are more effective than the older ones.
5. Although newer drugs are more expensive, the programme is often more cost-effective.

   Examples of drug regimes:

1. Quicker but costlier regime.
   Rifampicin and isoniazid daily for 2 months, then twice weekly for 4 months,
   plus pyrazinamide and ethambutol daily for the first two months.
2. Longer but cheaper regime.
   Rifampicin, isoniazid, pyrazinamide and either streptomycin or ethambutol daily for 2 months.

Then **either** isoniazid and thiacetazone daily for 6 months,
or isoniazid and streptomycin twice a week for 6 months. See also Further Reading page 214.

A variety of other regimes are also in use.

NB1 **Streptomycin** should not be used in countries where AIDS is common, unless sterilised needles can be guaranteed. See also page 211.

NB2 **Supervision**. Ideally the taking of all doses of TB medicines should be supervised. However this is especially important in the first 2 months of the shorter regimes, when a health worker should check that the correct dose is taken on the correct day.

Make sure that twice weekly dosages are always supervised. If this is not possible, it is better to use daily dosages.

It has been estimated that 95 per cent of patients who take treatment regularly become non-infectious by the second month. The final cure rate for fully compliant patients, being treated for the first time may reach 95 per cent.

Such high success rates will in practice only be obtained by exceptional projects working with highly motivated patients, a combination rarely found in the poorest and neediest communities.

Advice and instruction for the patient

It is essential that patients who start treatment take it regularly without interruption.

This means that at the start of treatment each TB patient **plus** the members of his family, must understand basic facts about the disease and the necessity for **a full course of treatment**.

> The more time spent in explanation with each TB patient at the beginning of his treatment, the more time is saved later in tracking down defaulters.

Some projects ask those patients who can afford it to pay for the whole course of treatment at the start. This encourages patients to complete treatment, especially if a proportion is paid back to the patient on completion of the course.

Figure 14.10 is a suggested list of advice which can be given and explained to each patient. We can adapt this to our own area and project.

Records to keep

Why should records be kept?

These are needed in order to make sure that possible cases are thoroughly tested, and confirmed cases are fully treated. In addition the government expects to receive project records especially if they supply the drugs.

What information needs to be recorded?

1. Name and all contact addresses.
2. Type and duration of symptoms.
3. Findings on examination; general appearance, chest signs, weight.
4. Details of investigations: sputum test essential: Hb, ESR and chest X-ray if carried out.
5. Previous treatment if any – when, what and how long.
6. Current treatment.

Where should information be recorded?

1. On a record card kept by the patient: special designs are available in most countries.
2. In a clinic TB register: see Figure 14.11.
3. On a government record sheet, when the government supplies drugs or expects to see returns.
4. On the insert cards in the family folder.
   All possible cases will have an insert card which is regularly updated. Patients started on treatment can have this card marked 'see TB register' until treatment is complete (see Chapter 8, page 114).

In addition the CHW will keep a list in her notebook of all those currently on treatment.

Statistics of patients under treatment can be regularly copied into the Master Register or Project Computer (see pages 293–4).

Follow-up

Good follow-up is the key to successful TB programmes

> Patients who are irregular in treatment or who start treatment and then stop worsen the overall TB problem. Not only are **they** never cured themselves, but they pass on resistant germs to **others**.

Successful follow-up is based on:

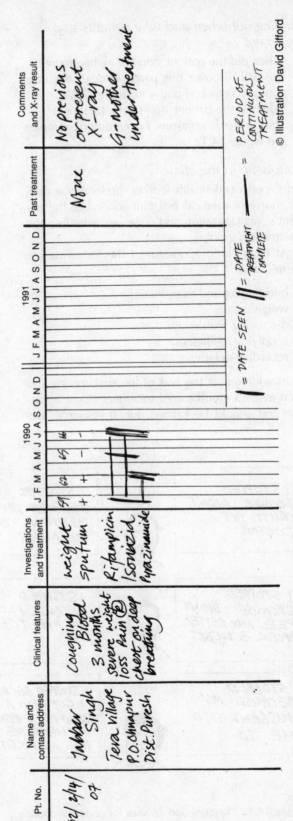

Figure 14.11 Entry in TB register of fully compliant TB patient

© Illustration David Gifford

Finding out when and why patients stop treatment

1. **When** did the patient stop taking treatment? We will discover this partly through accurate clinic records and partly from the CHW.
2. **Why** did the patient stop taking treatment? There are many reasons. For common examples see Figure 14.12.

Follow-up in the clinic

An experienced health worker, preferably a doctor, nurse or medical assistant supervises the patient's management and assesses whether the treatment is working.

At **each** clinic appointment the following are carried out:

- questioning and examination,
- **weighing**,
- discussing problems,
- supplying medicines,
- recording details.

In addition, at the end of the **first** month and then every **3 months** until treatment stops, a sputum test should be carried out. If resources are limited this is a lower priority than initial testing of possible cases.

Follow-up in the community

This is done by the CHW who keeps a list of all **confirmed** and all **possible** TB cases.

Her jobs can include:

1. A **regular visit** to each patient to ensure medicine is being taken regularly.
   This is important throughout the course of treatment and **absolutely essential** in the first 8 weeks of the shorter regimes.
   If patients are unreliable in taking medicines the CHW can hand them out personally, daily in the first 2 months, then twice weekly during the rest of the course.
2. **Collecting supplies** from the clinic either for all TB patients in the community or for those too ill to collect medicines themselves.
3. **Reporting** any patients refusing to take their treatment.
4. **Encouraging** known possible cases to have sputum tests. She can accompany them to the clinic or take a sputum specimen to the clinic for them.

© Illustration David Gifford

Figure 14.12   Reasons and excuses for poor compliance

In summary: it is the responsibility of the CHW to make sure that every TB patient in the community who starts treatment takes medicine regularly until the course is complete.

From time to time a supervisor or MPW should visit TB patients in their homes along with the CHW.

---

12 practical suggestions to help compliance

1. Explain about TB both by mouth and through written instructions. Even if the patient is unable to read someone in the family probably can.
2. Understand local beliefs about TB so advice will be appropriate.
3. Make sure the patient knows **how** he will be able to pay for the whole course of treatment.
4. Explain about common side effects of treatment so the patient will not be worried if they occur.
5. Spend extra time making sure that older men and women with chronic coughs get tested and fully treated. They are often the most infectious cases in the community and the least willing to complete treatment.
6. Make sure members of the patient's **family** understand about treatment so they can support the advice given.
7. Make sure the whole **community** understands about TB. They can then exert pressure on known TB cases to complete their course.
8. Use a cured TB patient to encourage defaulters or start a 'TB support group'.
9. Learn to spot 'Hidden Defaulters'. These are those who claim to be regular but who forget or are untruthful about treatment. Ask them to bring their medicine bottles, then count the number of tablets which remain unused.
10. Have a system of graded sanctions for repeated offenders. Start with a visit, then write a letter. Next report to a community leader, priest or health committee. Finally inform the DMO.
11. Make sure health workers are both kind and firm.
12. Make sure **supplies never run out**.
    Have a standby supply of medicines **in the community** in case bad weather, floods or civil chaos prevent further supplies arriving.

How to make sure the patient is cured

Most patients who have taken treatment without interruption will be permanently cured after a full course. A few however will not be. They may have resistant germs from previous half-completed courses; they may be hidden defaulters; they may be so poor and malnourished that their resistance is low; they may have AIDS.

All patients will need:

1. A medical assessment at the end of treatment. Those who are sputum negative and show signs of improvement e.g. increase in weight, decrease in cough, falling ESR, can have their treatment stopped.
2. Follow-up for 2 years after treatment is completed.

Patients who have completed treatment should report any return of symptoms and receive a regular visit from the CHW. Resources allowing they should have repeat sputum tests every 6 months for at least 2 years.

One so-called 'cured' TB patient who continues to cough resistant germs can undo the value of an entire programme.

TB management in people with AIDS

Where TB is present in a community, the spread of HIV infection causes a large increase in the number of TB patients. For this reason HIV infection and TB are commonly seen together.

In communities where HIV infection is common, TB patients should be offered HIV screening and counselling.

People with AIDS frequently have sputum negative TB or TB in parts of the body other than the lungs. Greater care therefore needs to be taken in diagnosis.

The aim of treatment in those with HIV infection is both to relieve symptoms and to render the patient sputum negative, so reducing the number of germs being spread in the community. For this reason TB patients with AIDS or who are HIV positive should be thoroughly treated, even though they may shortly die from AIDS or its complications.

People with AIDS often respond well when first treated with antituberculous drugs, though side-

effects especially with thiacetazone are sometimes more severe.

Because of the overwhelming number of TB
patients in some areas of tropical Africa, there is
often a serious lack of resources – both of health
personnel and drugs. Partly because of this, TB
treatment regimes in HIV positive patients are
subject to change. Follow updated guidelines.

Immunise with BCG

BCG vaccine should be offered to all children in
their first year of life unless they are seriously ill or
have AIDS. It is safe any time from birth onwards.

BCG helps to prevent TB and makes serious
infection less likely. It is part of the WHO Expanded Programme on Immunization (EPI). We
must co-operate with the government who will
often supply both guidelines, training and vaccine.
Full details are given in Chapter 10.

Control TB in the community

*'The best method of ridding TB from a com-
munity is to cure patients who have it.'*

In practice TB will only be **eradicated** from a
community if over a prolonged period all sputum-
positive cases are recognised and treated, and overall living conditions improve. In addition a high
incidence of AIDS makes eradication impossible.

TB can however be **controlled** so that the prevalence of TB starts to decline.

As soon as all community members are sputum
negative there will be no **source** for infecting new

contacts even though reactivated cases may continue to occur for many years.

The **keys** to community-wide control are:

1. To **identify** and **treat** all resident members of
   the community who are sputum positive.
2. To **identify** and **treat** any new TB patients moving into the community who may come at marriage, for seasonal labour etc. This may be
   extremely difficult in slum colonies.
   This means that all those moving into a community for the first time or rejoining after time
   away will need to be carefully questioned about
   symptoms, and sputum tested if they have suggestive features.
3. To **improve** basic living conditions.

> TB is a disease of poverty. The poor are the worst
> affected and the poor are the hardest to cure.
> Dealing with malnutrition, reducing overcrowd-
> ing, improving hygiene and raising community
> income will reduce the number of reactivated
> cases.

4. To give **BCG immunisation** to all infants.
5. To **continue** the programme sufficiently long for
   TB to decline or die out; 10–15 years is a minimum; a generation is an ideal.

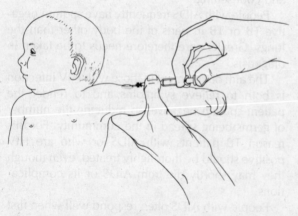

PATIENT   HEALTH WORKER

© Illustration David Gifford

Figure 14.13 Giving BCG vaccine

Figure 14.14 Health workers can get TB too

Community Based Health Programmes working in co-operation with the government offer the best promise of bringing this about. As the number of target groups covered by programmes increases so 'TB-free islands' develop and overlap.

Evaluate the programme

As with any community health activity we will need to evaluate our programme at regular intervals to see whether we are reaching the targets we set.

Each year we should record:

1. The **number** and **percentage** of sputum positive cases known to be present in each community.
2. The **number** and **percentage** of those patients known to be taking treatment regularly.
3. $\dfrac{\text{The number of } \textbf{new patients} \text{ put on treatment}}{\text{The number of } \textbf{patients completing} \text{ treatment}}$

This ratio should get smaller each year.

All these figures can simply be obtained from the TB Register or Family Folder and Insert Cards. Every 3 years on our resurvey of the community we can recalculate and confirm these categories.

From these figures we can calculate how compliance improves and incidence decreases over a period of time.

Other evaluations could include:

1. BCG vaccination.
   The proportion of children under 1 or under 5 who have a BCG scar.
2. Spot testing on the sputum of community members with chronic cough.
3. Community satisfaction with our service.
   This might include comments on the side-effects of drugs, ease of collecting medicines, whether drugs are affordable, and health workers' attitudes.

Figure 14.15 Part of TB programme evaluation: is the number of cigarettes being smoked in the community increasing or decreasing?

health and livelihood because of the difficulties in obtaining treatment.

TB can be cured, although treatment is both expensive and long term. At least three drugs need to be used together, and careful supervision of patients is essential.

Before deciding whether to start a programme we must liaise with the District Medical Officer and enter into an informed partnership with the community. TB control should only be started if a number of conditions can be met.

If we do decide to set up a comprehensive programme, our aim will eventually be to control TB in the community. The best way of doing this is to identify all sputum-positive cases, including new arrivals in the community, making sure that each completes a full course of treatment. Health education, improvements in living conditions and BCG vaccination of infants should also be carried out.

In order to be effective, TB programmes need to run for many years with a high degree of patient supervision both in the clinic and in the community. This involves careful case-finding and rigorous follow-up.

Regular evaluations should be carried out to make sure the incidence of TB in each project community is declining.

Summary

Tuberculosis is one of the world's most serious diseases: the poor are affected most, losing lives,

Further Reading

1. Tuberculosis. *Directions* Vol **6** (1) Programme for Appropriate Technology in Health, 1986.

A good practical overview.
Available from: PATH. See Appendix E.

2. 'TB: A 6 month cure.' P. Chaulet. *World Health Forum* **10**: pages 116–22, 1989.
A summary of commonly used shorter regimes.
Available from: regional WHO offices. See Appendix E.

3. *Tuberculosis Control as an Integral Part of Primary Health Care.* WHO, Geneva, 1988.

4. *Clinical Tuberculosis.* J. Crofton, N. Horne and F. Miller. Macmillan, 1992.
This practical and comprehensive book written by leading experts is especially designed for doctors and

senior health assistants in developing countries.
Available from: TALC. See Appendix E.

5. *Guidelines for Tuberculosis Treatment in Adults and Children in National Tuberculosis Programmes.* WHO TB Unit, 1991.

Slides

The following slide set is available from TALC. See Appendix A.

- Pathology of Tuberculosis in Childhood TbP

15
Setting up Public Health Improvements

In this chapter we shall consider

1. What we need to **know**
   - Why public health improvements are important
   - Water supplies
   - Effective waste disposal
2. What we need to **do**
   - Help the community to recognise its needs
   - Understand the cultural beliefs of the people
   - Estimate resources
   - Choose what improvements to make
   - Set up management committees
   - Task analysis
   - Ensure maintenance
   - Evaluate the programme

What we need to know

Why public health improvements are important

Many diseases are caused by water that has been contaminated by human faeces. Most public health measures are directed towards keeping human and animal faeces totally separate from water used for drinking and washing.

> It has been estimated that between 15 and 25 million people die each year by diseases which are caused in part by lack of clean water.

These include diarrhoea, dysentery, typhoid, cholera, hepatitis, polio and bilharzia among others. Quite apart from those who die, many million more, especially children are weakened by repeated infections.

Even though large-scale changes may be beyond the scope of smaller projects, a few well-planned improvements, if carefully adopted can make an important difference.

Water supplies

Why clean water is needed

Water is needed for two main reasons: to **drink** and to **wash**. Many diseases are caused through drinking contaminated water or eating food contaminated by dirty water; others such as scabies, trachoma and roundworm are caused by having insufficient water for washing bodies and clothes.

This means that each community will need a

Figure 15.1   A clean water source in Senegal

small supply of very clean water for drinking and a much larger supply of adequately clean water for washing.

Some health experts believe that the number of water points per 1000 population is a better guide to the level of health care than the number of hospital beds.

As an approximate guide communities should aim to have available 20–30 litres per person per day within half a kilometre of the home or settlement.

> Women traditionally do most of the fetching and carrying of water. The further away the water source, the greater the time and energy spent in carrying. This in turn means less time is available for looking after children, caring for the home and fields, and earning money. A reliable water source near the home therefore has multiple benefits for the family.

Water sources – improving those that already exist

This is well within reach of most community health programmes.

Springs

Spring water is usually clean when it emerges from

Figure 15.2   A properly protected spring

the ground but may quickly become contaminated. It can be made **safer** in the following ways:

1. By **erecting** a **fence** with a gate around the spring area to keep out animals.
2. By **building** a **ditch** to allow water to drain away.
3. By **building** a **stone wall** or 'box' around the spring itself, through which a pipe is led.

Wells and boreholes

Wells come in a variety of forms, including step wells, open wells from which water is collected by rope and bucket, and tubewells from which water is raised by a handpump. Open wells may be covered and fitted with hand or mechanical pumps.

Well water can be made **safer**:

1. By **fixing** a removable **cover**.
2. By **building** an outward sloping apron wall around the well, 0.5–1 metre high. The wall prevents dirty water from running into the well and acts as a shelf where water pots can be placed. The **slope** helps water to drain and discourages people from standing on it.
3. By **building** a concrete **drainage channel** around the outside of the wall.
4. By **providing one container** to draw water.
   This container with its fixed rope is allowed to rest only on the apron wall, never on the ground. Those using the container clean their hands before use and touch only the outside of the container and handle, never the inside.
5. By **ensuring** that no one uses the well for washing.
6. By **encouraging** the **community** to set up their own system for keeping the surrounds clean, repairing the well each year, keeping the hand pump in good repair, and chlorinating the well at regular intervals.

Ponds and watering holes

Although widely used, water from these sources is dangerous and can spread a variety of diseases, including bilharzia.

Pondwater should **not** be used for drinking unless there is no other supply available. If there is no other drinking source it should be boiled or sterilised before drinking. The pond should **not be used** for washing or for watering animals. Small ponds can be protected by a surrounding fence.

Figure 15.3   River water. 1. Draw water from above village. 2. Bathe and wash down-river from the village. 3. Exclude animals where possible

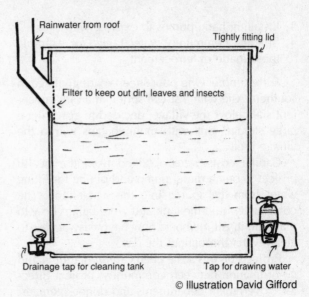

© Illustration David Gifford

Figure 15.4   A well-constructed rain water tank

Rivers

Water from most rivers is contaminated. If river water has to be used we should ensure that:

1. Water is collected from the river **above** the village, preferably through a sand filter or infiltration gallery.
2. Bathing, washing and the watering of animals only takes place **below** the village.

Tap water

Water from a tap is not always clean. It may come from a dirty source or become contaminated in the pipes.

Tap water can be made **safer** in the following ways:

1. By **checking** the **source** (see above).
2. By **checking** the **pipes** to make sure there are no leaks or joins where germs can enter.
3. By **keeping** the **surrounds** of a stand pipe clean and well drained.
4. By **building** a concrete or wooden **platform** to rest buckets on.
5. By **constructing** a **fence** to keep away animals.
6. By **encouraging** the **community** to set up a system for checking source, pipes, tap and surrounds and keeping them clean and in good repair (see page 224 'Setting up management committees').

Rainwater tanks

Water, though clean at first, may quickly become dirty on storage. It can be made **safer** in the following ways:

1. By **cleaning** the tank and entrance pipe before the rainy season.
2. By **placing** a **filter** or screen where the water enters the tank to keep out insects, leaves and other dirt.
3. By **placing** a sealed **cover** over the tank to keep the water clean and to prevent mosquitoes from breeding.
4. By **ensuring** that **taps** alone are used for withdrawing water.
5. By **allowing** the first heavy rainfall of the season to run through without being used.
6. By **chlorination** see page 218 below.

Water sources – developing new ones

Larger projects or those working in areas where improved water is a strongly felt need, can help their communities develop new sources or make major improvements in storage or transport.

Examples might include:

1. Running pipes from water sources to suitable sites in the community or into each house.
2. Drilling tube wells or building new 'open' wells.

3. Installing hand pumps to existing wells.
4. Building community water tanks, for example those made of ferrocement.

For example: One poor sheep-rearing village in southern Asia with a single spring at an inconvenient site below the village, decided to construct a large storage tank with multiple taps within the village itself.

Capital costs were obtained from the health project to buy a diesel pump and piping for lifting water from the source into the water tank. The community built the tank and were taught how to maintain it. All members now have easy access to clean water throughout the day.

Projects on this scale need careful planning and co-ordination between community, project director, government departments and donor agencies.

Water storage

Water may be dirty when collected, or become contaminated in transit or storage, especially in hot climates, crowded conditions or with distant sources.

Containers can be made of almost any suitable material. Earthenware or clay pots are suitable but should not be placed on dirty surfaces where germs can 'leach in'. No storage container should be used which has ever contained pesticide.

Storage can be improved if containers are: kept **off** the floor and **away** from animals and children, **covered**, and **cleaned** regularly e.g. with bleaching powder.

Water sterilisation

There are various ways of making dirty water cleaner. They include the following:

1. The three pot method (see Figure 15.5).
2. Filtration – there are various methods such as that shown in Figure 15.6.
3. Disinfection with chlorine or bleach. Although the best place for this to be done is at community level, for example in the storage tank or well, it can also be done in each household.
   One cup (about 250 ml) of household or laundry bleach is mixed with 3 cups of water to make 1 litre. Three drops of this solution is then added to 1 litre of water and allowed to stand. If the water is badly contaminated 6 drops can be used.
4. Boiling. Boiling for 2–3 minutes will kill most germs, 5 minutes almost all. Boiling is the most effective method but is costly on fuel and human energy.

This simple system will provide cleaner water. It will not provide pure water but will remove some of the diseases.
Day 1: Collect 1 pot of water and leave it to settle for 1 day.
Day 2: Pour off the clear top water into a clean pot and use this for drinking water. Use the remainder for washing. Collect another pot and leave it to settle for 1 day.

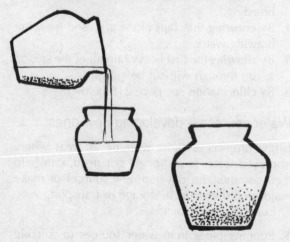

© Illustration David Gifford

Figure 15.5 The three pot system

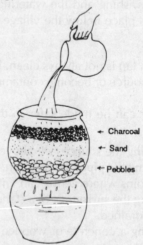

← Charcoal
← Sand
← Pebbles

Figure 15.6 Charcoal filter. 1. With a sharp instrument, punch holes in bottom of container. 2. Place pebbles, sand and charcoal in container to make a filter, which is set on top of a second receptacle. 3. Pour water into top filter and collect drinking water from bottom filter (PATH adaptation from *Peace Corps Times*)

The advice to boil drinking water should be made by the community itself with guidance from the project. Boiling is only appropriate if there is an adequate supply of fuel nearby, a water source which is highly contaminated, and time and energy available for fuel collection.

Water usage

Even if water is clean at the time of storage it can become contaminated at the actual point of use, usually by dirty hands or implements being put into the container.

Water usage can be made **safer** if we can teach the community to:

1. Use a container with a **tap** or
2. **tip** into a cup or glass or
3. **dip** with a long-handled dipper which is touched only above the level of the container.

Effective waste disposal

Liquid waste disposal

Liquid waste includes all household waste water including that used for washing clothes and utensils.

Where washing takes place outside, run-off is usually less of a problem. Where washing takes place inside with use of an exit pipe, pools of stagnant water quickly develop by the house or in the street.

Figure 15.7   Sanitation: a key need in village and city

Community hygiene can be greatly improved when stagnant, waste water is removed. Diarrhoeal diseases and **malaria** become less common.

Wastewater can be disposed of in various ways:

1. Through a **kitchen garden** where it can be used to water vegetables.
2. In a **soakage pit**. This can be constructed below ground outside each house, by making a cubic hole with sides 1.5 metres, lined with brick or stone.
3. A **biogas** (gobargas) plant.
   Waste water can be piped into this or taken by bucket. However biogas works effectively in very few areas.
4. A common **sewerage** system – of covered drains or pipes. This is the best method if working correctly, but is more expensive.

Figure 15.8   A well-placed community pit at least 20 metres from nearest house, 100 metres from river, well or spring

Household solid waste disposal

This can be disposed of all together in a household or community tip, or in cities by putting pressure on the civic authorities to arrange refusal removal. In rural areas waste can be separated into:

1. Material suitable for **burning**, such as paper which can be incinerated well away from homes at appropriate times.
2. Solid matter for **burying** which can either be done by each household digging its own hole at least 1 metre deep, or by the community making a communal rubbish dump. This must be at least 20 metres from the nearest house and 100 metres from any river or water source.
   Any rubbish tip should be **covered** with several inches of earth to reduce flies, and **protected** by a fence or enclosure to keep out animals.
3. Organic (vegetable matter) for **composting**, which along with animal dung can be rotted down and used as fertiliser after 4–6 months. A shallow pit is dug and kept covered by a few inches of soil. Wooden posts can be inserted as 'chimneys' to help take air into the pile which speeds up the decay.

Human waste disposal

Each community will need guidance about the most appropriate way of disposing faeces. Methods include:

1. The traditional **open** system which can be **improved** if the community is not ready to build latrines.
   * The site should be **appropriate**. It should be a safe **distance** from any house, at least 10 metres from any water supply, and away from any tracks.
     For example: in many parts of the world paths are used as the public toilet. This is an effective way of spreading germs throughout the community. The health team, supported by the CHW and health committee can raise community awareness and help to set up alternative sites.
   * **Shoes** should be worn which reduces the risk of hookworm and other infections.
   * **A small hole** should be dug with a stick, or simple digging implement, and the faeces

placed inside and covered with earth. This will help to keep off flies and animals. Sunny areas should be used rather than shady ones.
   * **Young children** should not normally go alone.
   * The **open system** is only appropriate in rural areas with relatively low populations.
2. The simple **pit latrine** (Figure 15.9)
   This is most suitable where bulk materials such as paper, stones or corn-cobs rather than water, are used for anal cleansing, as in much of Africa.
   The most basic type of latrine consists of a **pit** in the ground 2–3 metres deep, lined by bricks, blocks, concrete rings or making use of an oil drum. The pit is covered by a concrete or wooden **slab** slightly larger than the pit to avoid collapse. The slab has a **hole**, large enough for faeces to fall through and small enough to prevent children from falling in. The hole is fitted with a tight-fitting **cover** with a handle. A **wall** can be built for privacy using, wattle, grass, mud or brick.
   The twin problems of flies and smells are reduced by ensuring the cover is always replaced

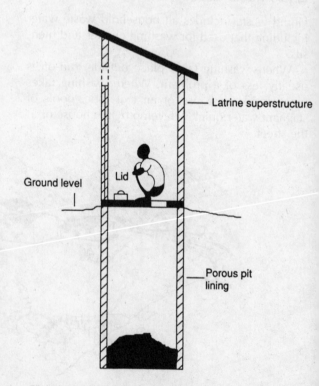

Figure 15.9 Simple pit latrine with sealed lid and single pit

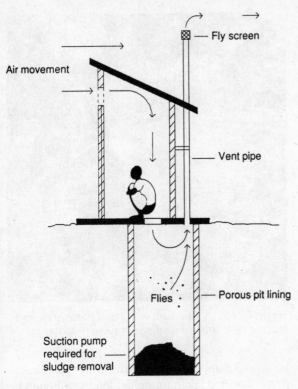

Figure 15.10 VIP latrine with single pit

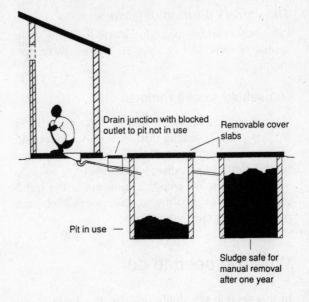

Figure 15.11 Pour-flush latrine with twin pit

and by regularly scrubbing the slab with soap and water. However the problems are more effectively solved by using VIP or water-seal latrines.

Children are often frightened to use latrines. Smaller versions can be built for them, with shallower pits (half a metre deep). In addition family members are encouraged to clean up the faeces of babies and toddlers as they are passed.

Remember that the faeces of young children are often more infectious than those of adults. Community sanitation programmes must therefore ensure that children's faeces are efficiently disposed of.

---

3. The **VIP latrine** (ventilated, improved pit) (Figure 15.10).
This is basically the same design but in addition contains a ventilating pipe with screened exit to reduce smells, flies and mosquito breeding.
The vent pipe must be high enough above the roof to ensure good air flow, and the screen should be made of fibreglass or stainless steel to

prevent corrosion, and placed on the sunniest side of the latrine.
A cover is not essential with a well-constructed VIP latrine.

4. The **pour–flush latrine** (Figure 15.11).
Pour–flush latrines are more expensive but also more hygienic. They are appropriate only in communities where water is used for anal cleansing, as in much of Asia.

Whichever type of latrine is chosen it must **be used** and **sited** correctly.

The *correct use* of latrines

Although the building of latrines should be encouraged they are of no value unless they are **well-used**, **well-maintained** and **well-cleaned**, and unless the population, including children have been **carefully taught how to use them**.

Soap and water should be kept near the latrine for handwashing, and leaves, paper or water kept in the latrine for anal cleansing according to local custom.

An effective way of spreading diarrhoeal diseases is to build public latrines, give no health teaching and arrange no maintenance. Such buildings quickly become the most serious health risk in the entire community.

The **correct position** of latrines

Latrines should be on ground lower than any water source or river and at least 20 metres away from them.

Household smoke removal

Household smoke arises mainly through tobacco smoking and cooking inside without adequate chimney or ventilation. Both are harmful and make lung, heart and eye diseases worse.

We can discuss with the community the building of smokeless hearths, and ways in which cigarette smoking can be reduced.

What we need to do

In this section we shall consider the stages in setting up community water and sanitation improvements.

Figure 15.12   A tube well with hand pump sunk in the low caste area of a village in western India

Help the community to recognise its needs

> In both water and sanitation projects we need to help the people identify their own needs and suggest their own solutions.

Water supplies

The community may identify problems such as:

1. Supplies too **distant**: in some communities women and children may spend up to 2–3 hours per day in collection.
2. Supplies **intermittent**: water sources may dry up completely at certain times of year meaning more distant sources have to be used. In the case of piped supplies water may only flow once or twice per day (or per week).
3. Supplies **contaminated**: the community may not always understand the need for clean water or may feel their existing supplies are sufficiently clean.
4. Supplies only **available** for the rich, the high caste or the dominant tribal group. The poor may have to use a more distant or more contaminated source.

The community, especially women, will already be aware of any need to improve water supplies, in particular time taken for collection. It will often be a strongly expressed need in our first meetings with the community.

Sanitation

In contrast to water supplies, the community may see no need at all to change existing patterns of waste disposal. Awareness raising is therefore an important part of any sanitation programme.

Where community members want their own latrine this is usually for one of two reasons: either they hope to improve the health of their family or they expect a latrine will give them extra status in the community.

> Whatever the motivation it is generally better to wait until a family is ready to build its own latrine and pay for it themselves, rather than providing the latrine and its construction free of charge.

Revolving loan funds will help to make this possible.

Understand the cultural beliefs of the people

Most communities have strong beliefs about waste

disposal and traditional rights over use of water. The knowledge, attitude and practice of the community must be understood before any plans are drawn up.

For example: In parts of Latin America it is sometimes believed that women who use the same latrines as men may become pregnant. In parts of east Africa daughters are forbidden to use the same latrine as their fathers.

In such situations building single-compartment family latrines is doomed to failure.

Estimate resources

We will need to ask the following questions of the community, project and any supporting government or voluntary agency:

- What is the level of **interest**?
- How much **time** will be available?
- What **skills** are present, including both technical and managerial skills?
- What **materials** are available?
- What sources of **funds** are available?
- What degree of **co-operation** is possible between the different groups who will need to work together?

We should encourage the community itself to contribute as many of its own resources as possible.

> The more a community contributes its own skills and depends on its own resources the more likely its water and sanitation programme will last into the future.

Choose what improvements to make

This should be done **by the community** with guidance from the health team. Any improvements chosen should be culturally **acceptable**, and **affordable** for most of the people.

In choosing what improvements to make, the following have to be 'matched up':

1. The **priority needs** of the people.
2. **Resources** available.
3. **Ability** of the community **to manage** the project and ensure upkeep afterwards.
4. **Methods** used successfully in nearby areas, either by government or other voluntary agencies.
5. **Government** or **national** guidelines. These should be followed where they exist. Funding may be available if they are.
6. In the case of **sanitation** – the type of system which ties in with the culture of the people.
7. In the case of **water** supplies – a method which does not interfere with traditional water rights or cause anger in a neighbouring community.

© Illustration David Gifford

Figure 15.13 Explanations and awareness raising are the keys to successful sanitation

In practice it is wise to start with small, simple schemes such as improving existing systems.

For example: Demonstrations should **first** be given on ways to improve water storage, simple systems of composting or, as appropriate, a better use of the open system for defaecation.

Later, larger scale improvements could be carried out such as the protection of an existing water source, e.g. a spring or a well, or the building of a latrine in the local primary school with teaching on how to use it.

Later still a new water source could be developed or a community latrine building programme be set up.

By progressing from smaller projects to larger ones several advantages occur:

1. Success is more likely. Without this the community will quickly lose its confidence and trust.
2. Experience is gained – both by the health team and by the community.
3. The community learns how to manage at levels within its ability.

For further details see Chapter 2 page 14.

Set up management committees

Some suggested guidelines:

Composition of the committee

Any existing health committees can be used or

Figure 15.14   In planning water projects traditional rights have to be understood and respected

Eleven guidelines for planning an improved sanitation programme*

1. Aim for a sustainable programme which makes long-term improvements. This will not happen quickly – it may take many years to be achieved.
2. Find an appropriate latrine design for the area. It should be technically able to provide adequate sanitation, affordable for most people and culturally and socially acceptable.
3. Discuss all you are doing and planning with the future users of the sanitation – especially the women and community representatives or leaders. Work **with** people. Don't aim to do the work **for** them.
4. Don't offer to give people latrines or to subsidise them. The desire to achieve rapid results often leads to serious problems. A credit scheme, or revolving loan fund, may help many people build a latrine while leaving them fully responsible.
5. Promote latrines so that people desire to have one – don't threaten people that they 'must get a latrine or else . . .'.
6. Use any means possible to promote improved sanitation. Convince community leaders, local officials, teachers, primary and village health workers and encourage them to assist in the promotion work.
7. Either encourage people to build the latrines themselves or privatise the construction of latrines, by training local builders.
8. Make sure all latrine construction is backed up with full health and hygiene education and help on how to use and clean the latrine properly.
9. Co-ordinate the work with those aiming to improve the water supplies or other forms of sanitation.
10. Keep the programme costs as low as possible and keep staff numbers low. This will help the programme keep running for a longer period.
11. Encourage and help schools, churches, clinics and other institutions to improve their sanitation. This has a good demonstration effect on everyone seeing them.

*Reproduced, with permission, from an article by Isobel Blackett in *Footsteps* December 1991, published by Tear Fund.

sub-committees can be appointed. In either case members must be committed to action.

Committees should mainly consist of community members, with one or two health workers seconded. Other involved agencies can appoint representatives. CHWs should be members and women should be strongly represented or dominant.

> It has often been shown that water and sanitation programmes work best when **women** are involved in planning them and carrying them out.

The reason for this is quite obvious: water projects bring greatest benefit to women who now spend much less time in fetching water than be-

Marakissa Latrine Plan

Things to be done	When	By whom
– Meet with village leader re Community Health Nurse working in village.	August	M.P.
– Meet with village leader re CHN to do survey of every compound. – Training for CHN to do survey work – population breakdown, latrines, health education (worm flip chart).	Sept	M.P. & F.C. M.P. & F.C.
– Survey of village.	Sept/Oct	CHN
– Meet village leader and heads of compounds re incentives for latrines & de-worming all compounds with latrines. – Analyse results of survey – how many interested in having new latrines?	Nov	F.C.
– Arrange for Health Dept. to make cement slabs for latrines. Give nos.	Dec	M.P.
– Organise transport of slabs from Banjul to Marakissa.	End Jan	M.P.
– Arrange for Mr Jobe, Health Inspector, to visit Marakissa. – Meet heads of compounds again to discuss details. – Mr Jobe to inspect siting of latrines with reference to well sites. – Arrange for Govt. Info. Office to show film 'How to Dig your Latrine' at the village Independence Celebrations. – Flip chart worm/latrine talk – Primary School, classes 4, 5 & 6. – Showing of film.	Early Feb Early Feb Mid Feb	M.P. M.P. Mr Jobe M.P. Fatou Film unit
– Latrine construction – holes to be checked before slabs issued. – Issuing of slabs.	Feb–May	I.S. & clinic compound man
– Deadline to finish.	May	
– All compounds to be visited. – Inform Mr Jobe of total no. new latrines.	June	F.C. M.P. I.S. Fatou
– Contact Mr Fal (Health Dept.) re no. of slabs still required after rice harvest for others wanting new latrines.	July	M.P.
– Photograph new latrines with owners. – De-worm compounds with new latrines.	June–Aug	M.P. F.C. & Fatou
M.P. = Marilyn Pidcock; F.C. = Fansainey Colley, I.S. = Ibrinia Sabally		

Figure 15.15 Marakissa latrine plan

fore. Also women usually take greater interest and responsibility than men in matters of family hygiene.

Education of the committee

Committee members will need education and training in order to know how to carry out the project and manage it in the future. This can be done through visits to other projects, seminars can be arranged with visiting experts and 'in house' teaching can be given from project or community members with appropriate skills.

Task analysis

Task analysis sheets are the detailed action plans for each stage of the project. They answer the questions What? Who? Where? and When? A task analysis must be worked out for each phase (see Chapter 18, page 250).

A common reason for projects failing or being delayed is through lack of communication. Task analysis sheets help all those involved to know their exact roles and responsibilities.

A simple, practical example is given in Figure 15.15.

Ensure maintenance

It has been estimated that in many poorer communities between 35 and 50 per cent of water and sanitation systems breakdown and become useless after 5 years. Many communities are littered with the wreckage of disused water tanks, broken pumps and abandoned equipment which now lie unrepaired and unusable while community members return to their traditional practices.

Sometimes this is because the community never wanted a new system in the first place. Often too it is because no one has been given either the training or responsibility for keeping equipment in working order.

> The upkeep of equipment should be the sole responsibility of the community. The key to this is a sense of ownership; we all know in experience that most people will only take care of things which belong to them.

Figure 15.16   £400 of unused well

In order to bring this about we should:

1. Ensure **responsibility** for upkeep is in the hands of the community **from the very beginning**. The management committee takes charge and in turn can select, arrange training for, supervise and pay an individual to carry out regular maintenance and cleaning.
2. Identify **suppliers** of spare parts and other materials needed for upkeep.
3. Ensure that **training** is given in how equipment can be maintained. This should be during an active project phase when interest is high. It is one of the most useful ways in which an outside agency can be of service.

Evaluate the programme

The simplest way to evaluate any improvements is by discovering whether:

1. The system is still **functioning** after a given length of time.

2. The community is still actually **using** the system.
3. The community **prefers** the new system to the old.
4. There are measurable **improvements** in health.

Evaluations can be carried out by the community, through inspection, questions and surveys. Often the answers will be obvious and visible.

Summary

Many serious diseases are spread through water that has been contaminated by human or animal waste. Many other conditions become worse by lack of water for adequate washing. Improvements in both water supply and waste disposal, if carried out successfully, can greatly improve community and individual health.

Water supplies can be made safer both at source, during transit, in storage and at the time of use. Health programmes can help to improve existing systems, and as needs dictate and resources allow, help communities to develop new ones.

Similarly help can be given to improve sanitation. This will cover all forms of household waste, and most important of all the effective disposal of human faeces through the building of latrines.

To ensure success communities themselves must identify their needs and suggest solutions. These need to be in line with cultural patterns, matched with resources available and guided by national health plans.

Health projects can act as facilitators in this process by creating awareness, co-ordinating personnel, and teaching management skills. Small-scale improvements can be made at first, and as experience and confidence grow the scale of programmes can be increased.

From the very beginning communities take full responsibility for maintaining equipment and carrying out necessary repairs.

Evaluation is necessary at regular intervals, especially as large sums of money can be wasted on programmes which bring little benefit.

Further Reading

1. *Rural Water Supplies and Sanitation: A Text from Zimbabwe's Blair Research Laboratory.* P. Morgan. Macmillan, 1990.
   An important book for Africa's health programmes.
   Available from Macmillan. See Appendix E.
2. *The Worth of Water: Technical Briefs on Health, Water and Sanitation.* J. Pickford (ed.) ITDG, 1991.
   This consists of 32 extremely practical briefs on various water and sanitation techniques.
   Available from: IT Publications Ltd., 103–105 Southampton Row, London WC1B 4HH, UK.
3. *Small Scale Sanitation.* S. Cairncross. Ross Institute London, 1988.
   An excellent guide with useful diagrams on latrines suitable for a variety of conditions.
   Available from: London School of Hygiene and Tropical Medicine, Keppel Street. London WC1E 7HT, UK.
4. 'Water for health: behaviour and technology.' *PATH* **9** (1): 1989.
   A useful 10 page summary.
   Available from: PATH. See Appendix E.
5. 'Safe water supply and sanitation: prerequisites for health for all.' *WHO Statistics Quarterly* **39** (1): 1986.
   Available from: WHO. See Appendix E.
6. *Achieving Success in Community Water Supply and Sanitation Projects.* WHO/SEARO, 1985.
   Available from: WHO. See Appendix E.
7. *Sanitation without Water.* Uno Winblad and Wen Kilama. Macmillan, Basingstoke, 1985.
   Available from: Macmillan. See Appendix E.

Filmstrip

A filmstrip entitled: 'How to Build, Use and Maintain a Simple Pit Latrine' is available from World Neighbors, 5116 North Portland Avenue, Oklahoma City, OK 73112, USA.

Part IV
APPROPRIATE MANAGEMENT

16
Using Medicines Correctly

In this chapter we shall consider:

1. What we need to **know**
   - The difference between medical care and health care
   - That medicines are often prescribed incorrectly
   - The shelf life and expiry date of medicines
2. What we need to **do**
   - Make an essential drug list
   - Train the health team
   - Create community awareness
   - Use the right medicines in the right way

What we need to know

The difference between medical care and health care

Most health workers enjoy prescribing medicines and many will expect to relieve symptoms and cure diseases simply through prescribing medi-

cines and giving injections. This is **medical care** as opposed to **health care**. It is summed up in the slogan: PPNN: a Pill for every Problem, a Needle for every Need.

Community Based Health Care follows a different model. It aims to **promote** good health and to **prevent** ill health mainly through raising awareness in the community. Medicines are still used but only when necessary. This is **health care** as opposed to medical care.

Those who are more interested in profit will wish to continue a **medical** model of care. In CBHC we will be actively opposing this.

One of our main tasks as community health workers is to educate the people about the correct and incorrect use of medicine. If we succeed communities will become healthy and self-reliant. If we fail communities will become poorer, more exploited and more dependent.

© Illustration David Gifford

Figure 16.1 PPNN – a pill for every problem, a needle for every need – an effective way of robbing the poor to pay the rich

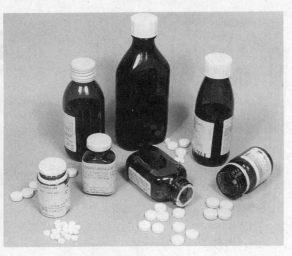

Figure 16.2 Avoid over prescribing

That medicines are often prescribed incorrectly

There are two main faults in prescribing:

1. Using too **much** of what is **not** needed – overprescribing.
2. Using too **little** of what is **most** needed – underprescribing.

Using too much of what is not needed

Here are some common **reasons** for overprescribing:

1. Health workers have been **wrongly** trained: they have learnt a medical model, not a health model. This is later reinforced by drug company representatives who encourage high prescribing.
2. They get a feeling of **satisfaction**, or a free handout from the drug company, the more they prescribe.
3. It is **easier to prescribe** for each symptom than to discover and treat the illness and its cause.
4. Those **poorly trained** or lacking in confidence will use several medicines in the hopes that at least one will work.

For example: Where malaria, typhoid and pneumonia are common many practitioners will prescribe chloroquine, chloramphenicol and co-trimoxazole to cover serious illness, then add a vitamin B injection, a tonic, and some red iron tablets for customer satisfaction.

However the commonest reason why doctors over-prescribe is this:
Patients expect lots of medicine: the more they receive the more satisfied they are and the more likely they are to return to the same doctor.

If patients fail to receive the medicine they want or expect, they will often try to obtain it from another source.

Here are some common **results** of over-prescribing:

1. Patients become **dependent** on drugs and doctors. This in turn means:
   - They spend more and more money.
   - They don't know what to do if no medicine is available.
   - They develop a demanding attitude.

For example: One project decided not to pay money to its CHWs but instead to provide free medicines both for the CHWs and their families. The heads of these families soon came to realise they could obtain a profit by reselling such medicines. Encouraged by their families the CHWs demanded ever increasing amounts, refusing to co-operate when medicines were refused. The project was forced to close down.

2. Patients fall into **debt** to pay for medicines.
3. People take no interest in disease **prevention**.
4. Patients pass on **consumerist thinking** to their children.
5. When essential medicines are really needed **supplies have run out**.

Figure 16.3 The vicious circle that leads to the overuse of medicine

© Illustration David Gifford

Figure 16.4   TB programmes must ensure regular supplies of medicines

Using too little of what is really needed

Here are some common **reasons** for under-prescribing:

1. **Medicines** are not **available**.
   They may be hard to obtain, be delayed in transit, or not ordered in advance. Stocks may have been used up because of overprescribing when supplies last arrived.
2. **Patients** may not be able to afford the full course of the medicine nor understand why they need to complete it.
3. **Health workers** may not follow the correct treatment schedules.

Here are some common **results** of under-prescribing:

1. People **die** from curable diseases such as malaria, pneumonia and TB.
2. People **lose faith** in the hospital, health centre or programme when they fail to get better.
3. People **waste money** and **endanger their health** by buying useless substitutes.

The shelf life and expiry date of medicines

What is the shelf life?

Medicines can only be kept a certain length of time before spoiling. This is known as the shelf life. Usually a printed expiry date shows when the shelf life has been reached.

What happens to a medicine after the expiry date?

1. It may become less **effective**: the case with many antibiotics.
2. It may become more **toxic**: sometimes the case with tetracyclines.
3. It may become more likely to **cause an allergy**: sometimes the case with **penicillin**.
4. It will often continue for a time to be both **safe** and **effective**. Drug companies may record early expiry dates to protect themselves from legal action if adverse effects occur.

How can we know if a medicine may be spoiled?

The normal way is to see if the expiry date is passed. However some medicines, under bad storage conditions may spoil **before** their expiry date.

Check **all** medicines to make sure they are not:

• damp or sticky,
• discoloured,
• broken.

In addition check **certain** drugs and supplies for specific problems, for example:

- tetracycline which turns brown when ineffective,
- aspirin which may smell unpleasant,
- condoms which may dry out,
- vaccines which must be kept cold (see Chapter 10, page 145).

How can medicine be prevented from spoiling?

We can help medicines last longer by:

1. Keeping them in a dry place at even temperature out of direct sunlight.
2. Making sure containers are air-tight and lids are firmly closed.
3. Using sugar-coated or foil-wrapped tablets where cost allows.
4. Packing medicine carefully to reduce breakages in transit.
5. Storing supplies in peripheral health centres for as short a time as possible.
6. Maintaining the 'cold chain' for all vaccines.

Should expired medicine still be used?

Reasons against using expired medicines:

1. Supplies may be less effective or unsafe.
2. If discovered it may anger the local people: we may be accused of dumping unwanted or expired foreign medicine on the local community which no one else is prepared to use.

Reasons in favour of using expired medicines:

1. There may be no other supplies available.
2. It may mean throwing away supplies which are desperately needed. Large sums of money may be wasted if supplies are discarded.
3. Many expired medicines still work and are still safe.

Some suggested **guidelines**:

1. Only use medicines past their expiry dates when **really necessary** i.e. when no alternatives are available.
2. Never use medicines which shown signs of having spoiled – see above.
3. Order the right amounts of medicines in plenty of time so as to have sufficient in-date supplies.
4. Check expiry dates on arrival, **using first** any with an early date.
5. Use a storage system in both stores and clinic to guarantee that old supplies are used up first (see Chapter 8, page 113).
6. Be sensitive to the community's beliefs about expired drugs. Some will be greatly concerned, others will not mind at all.

© Illustration David Gifford

Figure 16.5

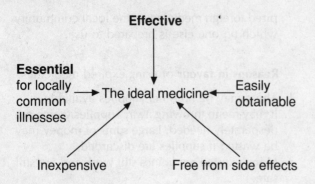

Figure 16.6 The ideal medicine

What we need to do

Make an essential drug list (EDL)

What is an EDL?

An EDL is a list of important drugs needed for the cure of serious diseases and the relief of major symptoms.

CHWs will need approximately 12 essential

Figure 16.7

© Illustration David Gifford

drugs (see Chapter 7). Clinics and hospitals will need more.

The EDL will be different for each country, each region and each project. For this reason each programme should draw up its own Essential Drug List.

What are the ideal features of an 'Essential Drug'?

See Figure 16.6.

Whom should we consult?

1. The project **doctor** or medical advisor.
   His suggestions, though valuable may include **more drugs than are actually needed**.
2. Other projects working in the area.
3. The District Medical Officer who will know which essential drugs should be used in local primary health centres.
4. The World Health Organization which publishes an essential drugs list for primary health care (see page 291).

> The final EDL should be worked out between the director of the project (who will know how much drugs cost) and the medical officer (who will know which drugs are necessary).

A suggested list is given in Appendix C.

Train the health team

All those who will be prescribing need careful instructions on the following subjects:

1. The dangers of **overprescribing**.
   We will need to correct any wrong knowledge, attitude or practice in the health workers and point out the extent and the dangers of overprescribing which is probably already taking place.
   For example: To show the extent of overprescribing we can arrange a simply survey. Sample homes are visited to find out what medicines have recently been used and where they have been obtained. Alternatively patients who come to the clinic are asked which medicines they have been prescribed in the last few months from other practitioners. Often wads of old prescriptions or bills will be produced.

Unless the whole health team understands and practises the right use of medicines at all times, community members will never be taught how to change their expectations.

2. The methods of **correct prescribing**, these include:

- **Understanding** and **using** the EDL.
- **Knowing** the right amount of the right medicine for each condition.
- **Writing** the prescription correctly.
- Being aware of possible **side-effects**.
- Knowing the approximate **cost** of each drug.
- Giving the right **advice** with each drug.
- Using **prescribing aids** such as the EDL, Standing Orders or Treatment Schedules.

Those learning to use drugs need **careful supervision** until they do it correctly. Although classroom and book teaching is important, the most valuable way of learning is on the job. At the beginning the **trainer** sees the patients while the trainee watches how the diagnosis is made and medicines are used. As soon as possible the **trainee** sees the patients under the trainer's guidance.

No health worker should prescribe without supervision until she has been well tested and is known to be accurate and reliable.

Create community awareness

The correct use of drugs is one of the most important subjects for the community to understand. Among health workers and practitioners there will often be a hidden struggle between followers of the **medical** model – those who want to prescribe as many medicines as they wish – and followers of the **health** model – those who want to prescribe medicines only when they are essential. Both sides will be trying to 'win the hearts' of the community.

It must be our aim to sensitise the people so successfully that when tempted by glossy advertisements promoting the latest health tonic they refuse to buy it.

In creating awareness we can use a variety of **methods** as listed in Chapter 3. Drama is one of the most effective.

For example: We can help our health workers or community members to write a play which contrasts two mothers: The **wise** mother who develops a healthier and wealthier family by following good health practices and using a few essential medicines: the **foolish** mother who sees many doctors, takes many medicines, falls into debt and whose children remain sick.

Overprescribing

Patient's demand

Figure 16.8 Spend time in correcting expectations

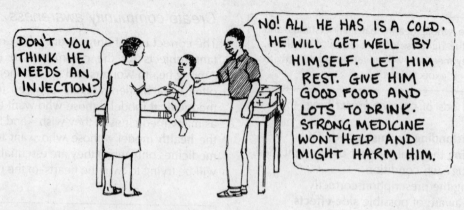

Figure 16.9 When medicines are not needed, take time to explain why

Use the right medicines in the right way

Here are some useful **DOs** and **DO NOTs**.
Some **DOs**:

1. **Do** use as few medicines as possible.
   Fight the belief that if one pill is good, more must be better. Some patients will need no medicine at all, few will need more than two or three varieties.
2. **Do** spend time explaining rather than prescribing.
   Explain why medicines are not always necessary. Simple advice may not only cure the problem but prevent it from recurring.
   For example: A doctor working in North Africa, frustrated by the large number of patients demanding medicines for minor problems, decided one morning that instead of prescribing for every symptom he would spend time giving advice instead.
   The new method seemed to be working well until a tribal chief appeared with headache. When refused tablets, he angrily left the clinic, warning all the waiting patients that the doctor was useless.
   A few days later the chief approached the doctor in the market place. Smiling, not angry, he explained how the headache had gone when he followed the doctor's simple advice. He was still planning to return to the clinic, not to obtain medicines but to encourage other patients to follow the doctor's advice.
3. **Do** treat causes rather than symptoms.
   If the **illness** is cured, the **symptoms** will soon improve. If symptoms alone are treated, the disease may continue as before.
4. **Do** use single preparations and not combinations of drugs.
   The few exceptions to this will include iron and folate in pregnancy and combined antituberculous drugs.
5. **Do** buy and use drugs by their generic name not their trade names.
6. **Do** make sure that all project members and doctors use the Essential Drug List.

Some **DO NOTs**:

1. **Do not** give injections when medicines by mouth will work as well.
   Thousands die each year through injection abscesses from dirty needles, and many others are at risk of catching AIDS.
2. **Do not** give drugs or injections for common colds. They don't help and they can be dangerous.
3. **Do not** give intravenous glucose for dehydration unless the person is unable to drink.
4. **Do not** use tonics or enzyme mixtures.
   Only use vitamins if the patient is dangerously ill or malnourished. Give nutrition education instead.
5. **Do not give medicines just because the people want them, expect them or say they will go somewhere else if they don't receive them.**
6. **Do not** be discouraged if this advice seems hard to follow: health workers throughout the world are all facing similar problems.

Figure 16.10 This CHW has been trained to use medicine only when essential

---

Each time we refuse to prescribe an unnecessary medicine it is another small victory for Health for All and a defeat for the forces of greed and profit.

Summary

Community Based Health Care should aim to use a health model rather than a medical model. In promoting good health and preventing illness health workers will only prescribe medicines which are really essential.

Two mistakes are commonly made in prescribing – using too much non-essential medicine and using too little essential medicine. Health workers need to be taught correct prescribing and communities shown that good health comes from a healthy lifestyle, not a dependence on pills and injections.

Each programme needs to draw up its own essential drug list which all those prescribing should follow. As the community becomes aware of the correct use of drugs initial objections give way to improvements in health and widespread satisfaction.

Further Reading

1. *The Use of Essential Drugs. Model List of Essential Drugs* (6th list) WHO, 1990.
   This is an essential list to obtain but also includes drugs needed by hospitals.
   Available from: WHO. See Appendix E.
2. 'Essential drugs: a convincing concept'. *Contact* No 107, Feb, 1989.
   This contains useful guidelines and includes the WHO list of essential drugs 1988.
   Available from: CMC. See Appendix E.
3. *Bitter Pills: Medicine and the Third World Poor.* D. Melrose. Oxfam, 1982.
   A 'classic' outlining the worldwide misuse of drugs and the pressures on the poor to become consumers of medicine.
   Available from: Oxfam. See Appendix E.
4. Essential Drugs for Church-related Rural Health Care. H. Hozergeil. *World Health Forum* **8**: pages 472ff, 1987.
   Especially relevant to West Africa.
   Available from: WHO. See Appendix E.
5. *Where There is no Doctor.* D. Werner.
   A variety of editions and languages are available from TALC and Macmillan. See Appendix E.
6. *Price Indicator on International Low-Price Sources for Essential Drugs.* Medico International, 1987.
   Price guides for essential drugs from nine different sources.
   Available from Medico International, Obermainanlage 7, 6 Frankfurt 1, Germany.
7. *Essential Drugs for Primary Health Care.* WHO/SEARO, 1988.
   This is especially relevant to Asia.
   Available from: WHO. See Appendix E.
8. *Medicinal Plants in China.* WHO, 1989.
   Lists and describes Chinese herbal remedies.
   Available from: WHO. See Appendix E.

Slides

The following teaching slides are available from TALC. See Appendix A.

- Cold Chain   CoV
- Essential Drugs   DAP

17

Evaluating the Health Programme

In this chapter we shall consider:

1. What we need to **know**
   - The meaning of evaluation
   - Who benefits from evaluation?
   - What types of evaluation are used?
   - Some pitfalls to avoid
2. What we need to **do**
   - Choose what to evaluate
   - Select the best indicator
   - Gather and process information
   - Act on the result
   - Use a sample evaluation chart

What we need to know

The meaning of evaluation

Evaluation or feedback is a system to find out how

well our health project is achieving what it set out to do.

When a programme first starts appropriate aims and targets need to be set. After regular intervals of 1, 3 or 5 years we need to know if we are achieving those targets, and if not ways in which we can improve our performance:

plan   **evaluate**   **replan**

In Community Based Health Care (CBHC) evaluation is carried out in partnership with the community, and results are carefully interpreted to community members so that they are able to replan and redirect the programme with our assistance.

Who benefits from evaluation?

The programme itself

We will often start with good ideas and high tar-

Figure 17.1 Evaluation helps everyone to see what they are doing and where they are going

gets. As time goes on these often become lost or buried in day-to-day activities or problems.

> Regular evaluations help both health workers and community members to focus aims and direct activities.

Donors and sponsors

In practice, evaluations are often triggered because donors want confirmation that their money is being well spent. This should not be the **sole** reason for evaluating.

Government

Governments will want to know what results the programme is achieving and especially if it is reaching national targets.

Research workers, visitors and students

CBHC is a comparatively new idea. Evaluations will help researchers know how it can be best be carried out, both in terms of **improving health** and being **cost-effective**. In turn, knowledge gained can be used to help and advise other projects, and give ideas to government planners.

For example: Non-Governmental Organisations (NGOs) are often able to produce real improvements in health at the community level more effectively than government health services. For this reason NGOs are increasingly being asked to run primary health care. Even more significantly, governments will often themselves adopt methods and ideas which NGOs originally set up.

In order for NGOs to have this sort of impact they need careful evaluation based on accurate record keeping.

What types of evaluation are used?

This will depend on the **size** of the project, **who** is available to do it, **what** is being evaluated and **why** it is being done.

In practice evaluations often fall into one of three groups:

1. Small scale evaluations.
   These are the routine evaluations of projects often carried out yearly as part of the annual

© Illustration David Gifford

Figure 17.2   Know the percentages

write-up or report.
They are usually done by members of the health team and the community and use standard information and records.
The **advantages** of these 'insider evaluations' are:
   - Evaluators know the local situation, people, problems and language.
   - They are cheap, and relatively easy to do.
A **mistake** commonly made is simply to list out numbers of patients seen or procedures done without recording these in context (see Figure 17.2).

2. Large scale evaluations.
   These are the occasional, 3, 5 or 10 yearly evaluations of projects often asked for by government or donors.
   They are usually carried out by **outsiders** working together with programme members.
   The **advantages** of these 'outsider evaluations' are:
   - Expert advice: those with special skills will

be able to design an effective method, and give advice on how to carry the evaluation through.

- Lack of bias: results may be more accurate as outsiders will not have such a strong personal interest in the achievements of the programme.
- More accurate feedback from the community, whose members may be more ready to share with outsiders the way they **really** feel than with health team workers with whom they are working each day.

Two **disadvantages** of outsider evaluations are their cost both in time and money, and the difficulty for visiting experts to understand language, customs and the local situation.

3. Specific evaluations.

Sometimes one particular aspect of a project needs evaluation because it is either especially good, bad, significant or interesting. This type of evaluation may be part of an investigation carried out by visiting students or research workers.

Results and findings can be helpful to the project but the possibility of any publication or publicity resulting from research must be clearly discussed beforehand.

Some pitfalls to avoid

Programmes evaluate too little

Many projects go on from year to year without proper evaluation. Annual reports are still written, and numbers listed of patients seen, immunisations given or procedures carried out. Such figures may accurately record the amount of work being carried out, but have little to say about the impact the project is having on the community.

Projects evaluate too much

Some programmes go to the opposite extreme especially if run by doctors and administrators with an interest in statistics.

In these situations collecting figures and producing good 'results' can become more important than working in partnership with the community for long-term improvements.

Sometimes donors expect projects to provide excessive amounts of information. The danger of a programme being 'run by the donor agency' needs to be recognised and resisted.

The real needs and opinions of the poor are ignored

Especially when gathering 'soft' information the articulate and well-off usually do most of the talking, while the poor have little chance to express their opinions or describe their needs. Sometimes the **overall health** of a community may improve but the health of the **poor** may stay the same or even decline.

Differences in health improvements between the rich and the poor can be highlighted by keeping separate figures for the **better-off majority** (e.g. the high caste or members of the dominant tribal group), and for the **worse-off minority** (e.g. the low-caste or landless). Similarly we can keep separate figures for men and women.

Results of the evaluation are not used at all or are wrongly used

The outcome of an unsatisfactory evaluation should be used for teaching and guidance, not for threats or personal criticisms. Equally when results are positive the community should be given the credit where possible.

What we need to do

Choose what to evaluate

When planning an evaluation select a **few things**, which are **important** to know about, relatively **easy** to find out about, and which are likely to benefit the programme.

Aspects to evaluate can be chosen from Table 17.1 depending on the priorities, aims and targets set originally by the project and the community.

A summary of how to carry out the evaluations listed in Table 17.1 appears on pages 243–4 in Table 17.2 'A sample evaluation chart'.

Table 17.1 Aspects of a project which can be evaluated

1. *Health of the community:*   *a or b*
   a) Child nutrition
   b) Immunisation
   c) Maternal health
   d) Family planning
   e) Control of infectious diseases
   f) Curative care
   g) Use of essential drugs
   h) Abuse of alcohol, tobacco and drugs
   i) Use of clean water
   j) Waste disposal

Most of these can be calculated from routinely kept project records (see Appendix F).

2. *Overall impact of the project on the community:*   *b*
   a) Infant mortality rate
   b) Under 5 mortality rate
   c) Maternal mortality rate
   d) Adult or female literacy rate

In working out these rates we will need:

- Time: it usually takes 5–10 years for a project to make a real impact and cause significant changes in rates.
- Large populations. We will need to keep records of at least 5000 families or 25 000 individuals for these rates to be valid.
- Accurate records: small mistakes in records can lead to large differences in rates. All team members must therefore be trained in accurate record keeping.

3. *Community connections:*   *b*
   a) Work of the CHWs and/or health committees
   b) Community awareness about what the programme is trying to achieve
   c) Community participation in planning and action
   d) Community satisfaction with the project
   e) Level of unwanted side-effects of programme activities
   f) Level of co-operation with the government

These are of great importance but are best done with guidance from an outside evaluator.

4. *Cost effectiveness of the project:*   *a or b*

This is easy to work out and can be done each year.

Key
a   means suitable for small-scale e.g. annual evaluation;
b   means suitable for large scale e.g. 3–5 yearly evaluation.

Select the best indicator

Having chosen **which** subjects should be evaluated, we must now decide on the most appropriate **ways** of measurement. This can be best explained by looking at this example:

We are wanting to evaluate our DPT immunisation performance over the past year as in 1(b) in Table 17.1. The indicator chosen must give the most accurate measurement of **what we really want to know**.

Here are some possible indicators we could use:

a) The **total number** of DPT injections given during the past year.
b) The **total number** of children who received DPT injections during the past year.
c) The **total number** of children who completed courses of DPT during the past year.
d) The **percentage** of children who completed courses of DPT during the past year.

We can see how moving from a) to d) the indicator is becoming **increasingly useful**.

The indicator commonly used in annual reports is a) but has only limited value. What we really want to know is how completely we have immunised our target population, the figure given by the lower indicator d). This is therefore the most appropriate even if it takes a little longer to calculate.

These four indicators (a to d) are all examples of **input** evaluation – in other words they measure the **amount** of work we have actually **put in**.

But we could use a very different indicator. We could measure: **number** (e) or **percentage** (f) of children who suffered from the diseases diphtheria, pertussis and tetanus during the past year.

These are examples of **output** evaluation and measure the **effectiveness** of the immunisation programme. Because our ultimate aim is to eradicate these three diseases from the target population, f) is therefore the best indicator of all.

Indicators are more useful still if we use them for comparisons.

For example: We can **either** compare how things are now, compared with how they were when we first started. To do this we will need an accurate baseline survey at the time the project started.

Or we can compare how things are in the project area compared with how they are in a non-project

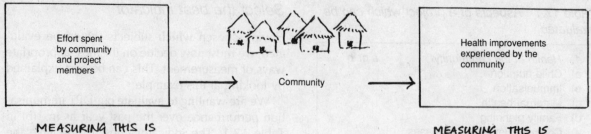

Figure 17.3   Two types of evaluation

or 'control' area which we also surveyed originally but in which we have not been working.

Gather and process information

There are two different types of information which are useful in evaluation: numerical (or hard) information and descriptive (or soft) information.

Numerical or 'hard' information

This is generally the most useful and is used to measure the subjects in categories 1, 2 and 4 in Table 17.1 above. Figures are obtained from the following sources:

- Registers e.g. vital events, disease, immunisation.
- Family folders and insert cards.
- CHW record books and diaries.
- Surveys (comprehensive, sample or specific).
- Tally sheets used by illiterate health workers.
- Other clinic and hospital records.

The Master Register or computer should contain the relevant hard information needed, tabulated out each year from the relevant project sources listed above. See Appendix F.

Descriptive or 'soft' information

This is useful in evaluating the personal and social side of the project such as morale, leadership, participation and other aspects in category 3 in Table 17.1. It is obtained from the following sources:

1. **Observations** of specific aspects of the project. *For example*: How well the leader relates to team members.
2. **Interviews** with community members which can either be unstructured or based on lists of prepared questions.
3. **Discussions** with community and team members.

Methods of **processing** information are described in Chapter 6 pages 65–8.

WRITE UP THE RESULTS OF EVALUATION BEFORE THEY ARE OUT OF DATE!

© Illustration David Gifford

Figure 17.4

Table 17.2 A simple evaluation chart

Subject	Indicators	Sources of information
1a Child nutrition	Percentage of under 5s on Road to Health	Child's growth card
	Percentage of 1 to 4s with MAC 13.5 cm or above	CHW notebook MAC Charts Family folder insert card
1b Immunisations	For each immunisation, percentage of children under 5 who have completed course (in past 1, 3 or 5 years)	Immunisation register Family folder and insert card
	For BCG, percentage of under 5s with BCG scars	Special survey
	For tetanus toxoid, percentage of women at delivery who have completed course	Maternity card Immunisation register CHW/TBA records
	Incidence rates of immunisable diseases	Disease Register Clinic and CHW records Special survey
1c Maternal heath	Percentage of mothers attending for 3 or more pre-natal checks	Maternity card TBA/CHW records
	Percentage of mothers with serious obstetric complications*	Maternity card CHW/TBA records Hospital records
	Percentage of newborns weighing 2500 g or above or with MAC of 8.7 cm or above	CHW/TBA records Maternity card
	Percentage of babies delivered by midwife or trained *TBA using sterile delivery pack	CHW/TBA records Maternity card
1d Family planning	Percentage of eligible couples using regular FP (specify which)	FP Register Family folder and insert cards
	Average space between children	Family folder
	Percentage of couples with 3 children or fewer	Family folder
1e Control of infectious diseases	Incidence or mortality rates of specified diseases	Disease Register Survey Clinic and CHW records Vital events register
	Compliance rates of confirmed TB cases	TB Register Family folder and insert cards CHW records
1f Curative care	Percentage of all patient attendances seen by CHW	CHW records Clinic attendance register
	For diarrhoea, percentage of families using ORS as first line treatment	Special survey
1g Use of essential drugs	Percentage of CHWs or health centres with regular supply of essential drugs	Inventories Spot surveys CHW records

continued

Table 17.2   continued

Subject	Indicators	Sources of information
1h Abuse of tobacco, alcohol, drugs	Percentage of population aged 10 and over who admit to use*	Family folder
1i Use of clean water	Percentage of families with clean water source within 15 minutes walk from house	Family folder
1j Waste disposal	Percentage of families using latrine*	Family folder
2a Infant Mortality Rate This is: $$\frac{\text{Number of deaths under 12 months}}{\text{Number of live births}} \text{ per year} \times 1000$$	Vital events register	Family folder CHW records
2b Under 5 Mortality Rate This is: $$\frac{\text{Number of deaths under 5}}{\text{Total number of under 5 children at mid year}} \text{ per year} \times 1000$$		As above
2c Maternal Mortality Rate This is: $$\frac{\begin{array}{c}\text{Number of maternal deaths}\\ \text{(during pregnancy, delivery and}\\ \text{up to 42 days after delivery)}\end{array}}{\text{Number of live births}} \text{ per year} \times 1000$$		Vital events register Maternity card Family folder and insert cards Clinic and Hospital records
2d Adult or Female Literacy Rate This is: $$\frac{\begin{array}{c}\text{Number of adults (or women) aged 15}\\ \text{or over who can read and write}\end{array}}{\text{Total number of adults (or women) aged 15 or over}} \times 100$$		Family folder
3a Work of the CHWs	Percentage of community homes visited on average once per week	CHW record book
	Level of CHWs knowledge about prevention and cure of common illnesses	Spot survey Questionnaire
	Percentage of families or individuals able to prevent and self-treat selected illnesses e.g. diarrhoea, scabies	Questionnaire
	Level of satisfaction of community with their CHW	Questionnaire
4 Cost effectiveness This is: $$\frac{\text{Total cost of project}}{\text{Number people covered by CBHC}} *$$		

Notes:
1. *Accurate definitions needed
2. Family folder refers to the survey or resurvey done using the family folder. Full information on each family appears on the outside of the folder (see Chapter 6 page 61). Much of the most useful information for evaluation is best collected during house to house surveys using the folders.
3. Under 'sources of information' several are suggested reflecting the different record systems used by different programmes. The most important/useful source is listed first. Clinic records refers to any records or registers kept in clinics not otherwise specified.
4. For some subjects more than one indicator is usually listed though in practice only one would normally be chosen for any one evaluation.
5. Most information, from whatever source, would be tabulated annually and stored in the master register or computer.

© Illustration David Gifford

Figure 17.5

© Illustration David Gifford

Figure 17.6 Community based health care that is well set up and effectively supervised is very cost effective

Act on the result

Unless action is taken on the findings of an evaluation the whole process is a waste of time and money.

> The results of evaluations often cause brief encouragement, or discouragement and then papers are left to gather dust on the shelves. **Evaluations** must always be followed by **action**.

In order to take effective action we will need to be:

- organised enough to do something about it,
- brave enough to face up to areas of failure,
- flexible enough to change the programme.

Health team and community members working together can then carry out:

- an analysis of reasons for success or failure,
- decisions on ways to improve results,
- replanning in detail as soon as possible,
- teaching any lessons to be learnt.

Use a sample evaluation chart

A sample chart is given in Table 17.2 with suggestions on how to evaluate each of the subjects listed above in Table 17.1.

Summary

All programmes need regular evaluation in order to discover how successfully they are achieving their aims and reaching their targets. Simple evaluations can be done each year by the programme itself as part of an annual report. More detailed evaluations can be carried out every 3–5 years with the help of outside specialists.

The most important subjects for evaluation must be decided and an appropriate indicator set up for each. Sources of information, both numerical and descriptive need to be decided well in advance. As part of the evaluation results must be analysed, and joint action for improvement taken as soon as possible.

The community itself should work in partnership with the health team in each stage of the process.

Further Reading

1. *Partners in Evaluation.* M-T. Feuerstein. Macmillan, 1986.
   An excellent and well-illustrated guide on how to evaluate in partnership with the community.
   Available from: TALC. See Appendix E.
2. *How to Measure and Evaluate Community Health.* J. McCusker. Macmillan, 1982.

A useful field guide.
Available from: Macmillan. See Appendix E.
3. *Practising Health for All.* D. Morley, J. Rohde, G. Williams. Oxford University Press, 1983.
   Descriptions and evaluations of 17 health programmes from around the world.
   Available from: TALC. See Appendix E.
4. *Development of Indicators for Monitoring Progress towards Health for All by the Year 2000.* WHO, Geneva, 1982.
   Available from: WHO. See Appendix E.
5. *Health Programme Evaluation: Guiding Principles.* WHO, 1981.
   Available from: WHO. See Appendix E.

18

Managing Personnel, Supplies and Finance

In this chapter we shall briefly consider how to manage personnel, supplies and finance.

Many programmes which start well, eventually fail through poor management. Management skills are important not only for programme directors but also for all health team and community members who share responsibility.

> In community based health care, management skills are as important as clinical skills.

HOW TO MANAGE PERSONNEL

In this section we shall consider

1. What we need to **know**
   - Models of leadership
   - Guidelines for leading
   - Ways of encouraging the health team
   - Ways of discouraging the health team
2. What we need to **do**
   - Plan project activities
   - Run the day-to-day programme
   - Write job descriptions
   - Solve disputes
   - Prepare for change
   - Delegate to others
   - Keep a sense of balance

What we need to know

> A contented, motivated team is the basis for a successful health programme. This will depend in large part on those in charge being appropriate leaders and efficient managers.

Models of leadership

Some people follow the **autocratic** or 'Do what I can approach'. They give the orders and others obey them.

Others follow the **democratic** or 'Let's work together approach' where everyone has a say; the leader is the 'first among equals'.

The choice of model will depend on two things:

Figure 18.1   The autocratic approach

Figure 18.2   The democratic approach

> IT ALL STARTED WHEN THE DIRECTOR SHOWED FAVOURITISM TO SOMEONE FROM HIS OWN TRIBE

© Illustration David Gifford

Figure 18.3

1. The **task** needing to be done
   Most community health tasks are best done through discussion and participation. Only in urgent situations such as medical emergencies will firm orders need to be issued. An autocratic style is generally inappropriate in Community Based Health Care.

2. The character of the **leaders**.

Many natural leaders are autocratic, and others often become so when put in charge. For this reason leaders will **need to learn** how to become more democratic and participatory in their style of management.

Guidelines for leading

Leaders of all levels should learn to be:

1. **Democratic** in the day-to-day running of the programme, and **dynamic** when the situation demands it.
2. **Facilitators**, helping other people **to do things themselves**. In this way each person learns new skills and grows in self-confidence.
3. **Talent spotters**, learning how to recognise and use the gifts and skills of the health team and community.
4. **Credible** – our team must trust and believe in us. This means being **competent** at the skills we are practising and **just** in our ways of handling people.
5. **Patient**, being ready to start at the place where

others are, not where we feel they ought to be. In this way people grow more quickly in self-esteem and confidence.
   There is a proverb which says: 'People like plants grow best by cultivation, not suffocation'.

6. **Unbiased** – we should avoid showing favouritism, being careful to treat everyone with equal friendliness and fairness.

Even slight favouritism towards one team member, can, through jealousy, sow the seeds of tribal and regional infighting which may later ruin the project.

---

7. **Available** and ready to spend time with the health team. Sometimes this will be at inconvenient times.
   An effective leader learns how to combine the roles of friend, pastor and manager.

Ways of encouraging the health team

These will include:

1. **Sharing** objectives. Team and community members will perform best if they are able to share in drawing up aims and setting targets.
2. **Commending** people for good achievements.
3. Giving **responsibility**.
4. Ensuring **salaries** are paid on time and that increases and promotion are given when due.
5. Arranging **in-service training** and chances for personal improvement.

```
Dear Sam,

    It was good hearing from you again. I was sad to hear your health
programme is running into trouble. Would you mind if your older
brother gave you a few suggestions?

    I'm sorry some of your junior health workers seem "sullen and
discouraged". Do you listen to them and give them a chance to share
their ideas?

    Does your team know that you believe in them and appreciate them?
They will tend to live up· to the expectations you have. Do they think
of you as someone who "lifts them up" or someone who "puts them
down"?

    I wasn't surprised to hear that your team leader threatened to
resign when you cancelled his holiday!

    By the way when did you last have a team outing or celebration
together? . . .
```

Figure 18.4

Ways of discouraging the health team

These will include:

1. Poor **administration**. Leaders who regularly forget, delay, overwork staff or plan inefficiently will annoy and discourage their teams.
2. Lack of personal and professional **respect** for others.
3. A domineering **attitude**.
4. Giving **too much** or **too little** work.
5. Giving work that is regularly **much too easy** or **much too hard**.
6. **Cancelling** leave or holidays unless there is an important reason.

> It is important to follow good leadership patterns from the beginning. It is easier to **keep** a team happy than to **make** a team happy.

What we need to do

Plan project activities

In planning new, or large-scale activities it is helpful to consider the following stages:

Obtaining information

Part of good planning is doing our homework' so that we are well informed about all aspects of the activity being considered.

One structure we can use for gathering information is based on the 4 Cs.

- **C**ommunity need and interest.
- **C**omponents or materials needed.
- **C**onstruction or how to carry it out.
- **C**ost expected.

For example: In planning a programme to install smokeless cooking hearths into village homes we will need information as follows:

1. Community:
   - Do the people want them?
   - Do the people need them?
   - How do they want them built?
   - Are they ready to do it themselves?
   - Will they need special training?
   - Are they ready to pay some or all the cost themselves?

2. Components:
   - What materials are needed?
   - Where can they be obtained?
   - How will they be transported?
   - Where will they be stored?
3. Construction:
   - What is the best way of making them?
   - What are the secrets of success which other projects have found?
   - What are the pitfalls to avoid?
4. Cost:
   - What will be the cost of components?
   - What will be the cost of labour?
   - What will be the cost of transport?
   - Will there be other hidden costs?

A similar framework of questions can be worked out for other community health activities.

Figure 18.5 Successful co-ordination between project, community and government: the first house to install a smokeless cooking hearth in a north Indian health programme

> The more carefully we plan at the beginning, the more time, energy and costs we will save later.

Setting up an action committee

This will be needed for major programme activities. It will comprise members of the health team, the community (usually representatives of the health committee) and any other agency involved.

Smaller scale activities can be based on meetings between health team members and the village health committee.

Carrying out a task analysis

This is done by subdividing the programme into stages and tasks and for each asking the following questions:

- **Who** is going to do it?
- **When** will it be done?
- **Where** will it be done?
- **How** will it be carried out?
- **What** equipment will be needed?

See also Chapter 15 page 226.

Appointing a leader or responsible person for each activity

Where appropriate a community member can work alongside a member of the health team, thereby developing management and technical skills.

Communicating with all parties involved

Lack of communication quickly leads to argument and discouragement. We must ensure that everyone involved is fully informed and notified as soon as possible if plans change.

Run the day-to-day programme

Quite apart from planning major project activities, we also need to set up a system for managing the day-to-day programme. This will involve matching the staff available with tasks that need to be done in the field. At an early stage in the programme health committee members can share in day-to-day planning.

A chart can be made which lists out the days of the month, with each day divided into columns

Figure 18.6 Ensure that everyone is fully informed and knows when plans change

either per CH team, per target area or per activity. The chart can have a plastic surface, and coloured, erasable, felt-tip pens can be used to mark different activities and personnel involved in each.

Activities planned, along with names of health and community workers involved are filled in as far ahead as possible. Full details are completed at least one week in advance with instructions about time of departure, destination and other important information.

This board is displayed in the programme headquarters.

Write job descriptions

Job descriptions usually include not only a description of duties to be carried out, but details about terms and conditions of service.

When a programme first starts it may be unhelpful to describe jobs too clearly. Later, as different team members take on specific tasks, it is useful to define them. Often this will be formalising what the team members have already been doing.

However job descriptions must have a clause which builds in **flexibility**. Health workers should be ready to do any reasonable task that needs to be carried out.

> A well written job description helps each person know what is expected both of themselves and of others. It gives a sense of security and can increase job satisfaction. Used wisely it may help to prevent or solve disputes.

A full job description includes the following:

1. Title and grade.
2. A list of duties.
3. Accountability.
4. Appraisal and promotion.
5. Length of contract and conditions of employment if any.

On first joining a project, team members will need to be given a form to sign which sets out details of their employment. This can be drawn up **either** in the form of a full job description **or** as a separate document. We should follow the practice used by our organisation or follow the normal procedure used nationally.

Job descriptions usually belong to a **person** – for an example see Chapter 7, page 74. They can also apply to a **task**.

For example: A job description for CHW supervision might include:

1. To **visit** the CHW in her community on a regular basis in order to:
   - give encouragement,
   - check that she is carrying out her duties,
   - teach skills and knowledge,
   - plan future tasks,
   - refill her medical kit,
   - complete her records,
   - pay her wages.
2. To **assess** how well the CHW is functioning and to decide on appropriate guidance for her.
3. To **inform** the project director or team leader of the CHW's progress.

Figure 18.7 Part of the job description for CHW supervision

© Illustration David Gifford

Figure 18.8   Trust between team members is one key to successful programmes

Solve disputes

> Preventing disputes is both easier and quicker than solving them.

Guidelines for preventing disputes

To prevent disputes we can follow these guidelines:

1. **Manage** efficiently and fairly.
2. **Meet** regularly so that team and community members can both plan together and express ideas and feelings.
3. **Recruit** team members who are tolerant and friendly with no excess tribal, religious or other prejudices.
4. **Write** clear job descriptions and give clear task instructions.
5. Give **spiritual input**. There can be a regular time for prayer or meditation. An appropriate sense of apology and forgiveness can be encouraged.
6. **Assure** the whole team that those in authority will not listen to any personal complaints against others, nor allow any team member 'special access' to the director.

> Even in the most contented teams conflicts will arise. If they are handled quickly and sensibly they can usually be solved. If they are ignored or mishandled their effects can continue for years.

Guidelines for solving disputes

To solve disputes we can follow these guidelines:

1. **See** each party separately.
2. **Listen** carefully, making every effort to understand each person's point of view.
3. **Ask** each party if they are willing to make peace. If they do seem willing, they are encouraged to do this on their own. If they fail or are unwilling we can offer to be a mediator or invite them to name someone else acceptable to both parties.
4. **Remain** unbiased and·slow in giving judgement.
5. **Be ready** to act as a scapegoat. One of the causes of the dispute may be our poor management.
6. **Correct** any problem which might cause the dispute to happen again.

Prepare for change

Programmes, like people often suffer stress at times of change. Such times might include:

1. The appointment of a new director or team leader.
2. Converting a project from a curative, clinical approach to a participatory community approach.
3. Starting in a new area or beginning a different type of work.
4. Uncertainty about funding, or about the programme's future.

Before any change occurs team members will be asking themselves such questions as:

- How will this affect me?
- Will I have more or less money?
- Will I have more or less status?
- Will I enjoy the job as much?
- Will I be able to do the new job?
- If the project closes where will I find employment?

Because of underlying anxiety, there may be more arguments and complaints than usual, more days lost because of illness, or a general decline of interest in the work.

We can support the team during times of change:

1. By **understanding** the stresses they will be feeling and why their standard of work may be falling.
2. By **ensuring** a good personal relationship with staff.
3. By **informing** the team as soon as possible and as fully as possible about any developments.
4. By **introducing** change at the right time.
5. By **planning and discussing** with the team. We can point out the disadvantage of the present arrangements and explain ways in which they will benefit by the intended changes.

Delegate to others

> Delegation is the art of enabling others to use the gifts and talents which they possess, and encouraging them to do as much, but not more, than they are able.

Delegation is good for **doctors**, **managers** and **leaders**. It gives them more time to do the things which only they can do.

It is good for **health workers** – it teaches them new skills and makes their jobs more challenging.

The idea of delegation is the basis of an important principle in community health: 'A job should be done by the person **least** qualified who can do it well'.

Delegation is a skill which has to be learnt. We need to practise it ourselves, then teach others how to carry it out.

In delegating a task to someone else we need to pass on:

1. **Knowledge** of how to do it.
2. **Responsibility** for the task being delegated. Although we may take the **final** responsibility a large measure is given to the person being delegated the job.
3. **Authority** to carry out the task.
   For example: If a team member is asked to organise follow-up of TB patients both he and other team members must know that he has been asked to do this.

If any of these three is left out conflict may develop in the team.

> Delegation must never become an excuse for us giving to others the jobs we don't want to do ourselves.

Keep a sense of balance

'Balance' helps to keep a project stable and its members contented. This might include balance between:

- Prevention and cure.
- Community and hospital.
- The rich and the poor.
- Work and leisure.
- Health and development.
- Working with women and working with men.

If balance is lost in any of these areas, tension may develop.

HOW TO MANAGE SUPPLIES

(see also Chapter 4, page 46)

In this section we shall consider

1. Managing the supplies
2. Managing the paperwork

Managing the supplies

Supplies includes both equipment and medicines. We have covered **ordering** supplies in Chapter 4. Supplies will now need to be **received**. We should check items for:

Figure 18.9   A delay in the system caused by inefficiency

- quality
- quantity
- expiry date in the case of medicines,
- temperature, packing and cold chain in the case of vaccines.

Supplies will need to be **stored** – in a safe, dry place with easy access. For further details on the storage of medicines see Chapter 8 page 113 and Chapter 16 page 233.

Supplies will need to be **issued**. We should ensure that they are:

- packed carefully,
- labelled clearly,
- checked to make sure we have sent the **items** ordered in the **quantities** ordered,
- placed in an ice box in the case of vaccines.

Managing the paperwork

We will have the following papers:

1. Bills (invoices) and receipts.

After payment, bill and receipt can be kept together, filed by company or type of product, in order of payment with the most recent on top.

2. A stock card or sheet.

We can keep a separate card for each recurrent item: it is divided into two sections: a **supply** section and a **balance** section (see Figure 18.10). Cards (or sheets) can be filed alphabetically, and by subject e.g. drugs in one card holder, medical supplies in another, laboratory supplies in a third etc.

Once every 6 or 12 months we will need to **stocktake**. This means checking that the balance of each item on the stock card is the same as the amount on the shelf.

In the case of medicines we should also check expiry dates, making sure the oldest supplies are issued first.

> If dangerous or restricted drugs are used, the medical advisor or project doctor must supervise safe storage and the recording of details.

Item .... Code number .... Monthly consumption ....

Supply section   Suppliers   1 ....   2 ....

                                 3 ....   4 ....

Date ordered	Rate per 1/10/100	Quantity	Total value	Date received	Supplier	Notes

Balance section   Re-order level ....

Date received or issued	Where received from/issued to	No. issued	No. received	Balance

Figure 18.10   Example of a stock card

3. The order request from the clinic.
   We simply fill in the number sent and return the request form with the drugs or equipment requested (see Chapter 8, page 112).
4. Inventory of capital items.
   A list must be kept of all capital items owned by the project including furniture, projectors, microscope, steriliser, fridge etc. This should be checked and updated at least once per year. A list or book can be kept in each centre. Alternatively a central register can be kept with details of which items are kept where. This can include dates and details of maintenance and upkeep.

HOW TO MANAGE FINANCE

Who should do the bookkeeping?

To keep accounts accurately and methodically needs skill and experience. At the beginning, the programme director will usually keep accounts. Later he may delegate this to an administrator or outside accountant who can work on a part-time basis. Sometimes the base hospital will manage the accounts.

     Anyone who takes on project accounting must

have a reputation for honesty.

     More junior members of the health team should not normally keep project accounts.

© Illustration David Gifford

Figure 18.11

When should the accounting be done?

Money received and paid out should be entered into the account books at the time and never held over until the following day. Unless this rule is followed accounts quickly become incomplete and disorganised.

Accounts should also be checked and totalled every month, every 6 months and at the end of the year.

Yearly account checking takes considerable time as books are sent to the auditor whose job is to make sure all accounts are both accurate, honestly kept and legal.

How is the accounting done?

Broadly similar systems are used world wide but there are minor variations depending on the country. Some larger projects use computers.

The person doing project accounts for the first time, will need to work with someone experienced in accounting until he completely understands the system.

Most projects will keep the following accounting books:

1. A **cash register** which records all money received and all money paid out, except petty cash (see below).
2. A **ledger** which lists **expenditure** according to the suppliers of goods and services, and **income** according to its source.
3. A **petty cash** register where minor day-to-day spending is recorded, details of which are also written on a Petty Cash Voucher and kept with any receipts.
4. A **salary** register where details and breakdowns of all salaries are recorded and where payments are signed for.

In addition books of petty cash expense vouchers, receipts, bank pay-in-slips, and cheque books will be needed.

Bank accounts should be opened and funds not immediately needed placed in an account which gathers interest. Cheques may take weeks to clear and in many countries suppliers will want to be paid in cash or by money order rather than by cheque.

An **imprest system** can be set up. Any worker who regularly spends project funds is advanced a fixed sum of money (the imprest) from which he makes any purchases. When his imprest becomes low he presents the receipts for money spent to the

PETTY CASH VOUCHER

AUTHORISED BY	RECEIVED BY	AMOUNT	
TSW	N. Weru		

DATE	DESCRIPTION	£	p
9. 1.92	Candles	2	40
"	Soap	1	30
	TOTAL	3	70

Figure 18.12 Petty cash voucher

programme director or finance officer who replenishes his imprest up to the original amount.

Foreign funds

Projects which receive foreign funds will usually need special registration.

Extra care is needed in accounting as these may be inspected at any time, and permission to receive such funds withdrawn if accounting is inadequate.

Summary

Community health programmes need skillful management of personnel, supplies and finances.

The director and other senior staff must learn how to lead democratically and fairly, making sure that their style of leadership encourages and involves the team and community. Systems need to be set up both for planning new or larger-scale activities as well as managing the day-to-day programme.

Supplies, including medicines, need careful ordering, receiving, storing and issuing. Paperwork needs to be kept simple but accurate.

Bookkeeping should be done by a senior project member or by the director. Accounting skills need to be learnt and the utmost care taken to make sure accounts are always complete, tidy, honest and accurate.

Further Reading

1. *On Being in Charge*. WHO, revised edn, 1992.
   A definitive guide on project management covering all aspects.
   Available from: WHO. See Appendix E.
2. *Management Process in Health Care*. S. Srinivasan. Voluntary Health Association of India, 1982.
   A comprehensive and practical book, which though written in India, is useful world-wide.
   Available from: VHAI. See Appendix E.
3. *Medical Administration for Front Line Doctors*. C. Pearson. FSG Communications, London, 1990.
   A remarkable book, especially useful for managers of district and base hospitals, but also of relevance to primary health care.
   Available from: TALC. See Appendix E.
4. *How to Look After a Health Centre Store*. AHRTAG, 1983.
   Available from: AHRTAG. See Appendix E.

Slides

The following teaching slides are available from TALC. See Appendix A.

- Management in Child Health   MnC

19

Co-operating with Others

In this chapter we shall consider how to co-operate with:

1. Government
2. Aid and funding agencies
3. Other voluntary programmes
4. Doctors and practitioners
5. Hospitals

Co-operating with government

What is 'government'?

As far as health projects are concerned 'Government' includes:

1. The **Health** Services or **Health** Ministry.
   These are usually set up on the following levels:

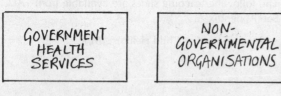

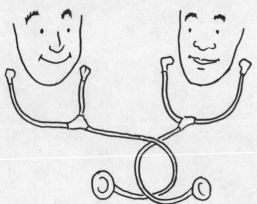

© Illustration David Gifford

Figure 19.1 An essential partnership to bring health services to the world's poor

- **Central** level: responsible for nationwide health policy and planning.
- **State**, **provincial** or **regional** level: responsible for adapting and carrying out national health policy according to the needs of the area.
- **District** level: responsible through the District Medical Officer (DMO) for organising and carrying out all aspects of health care in the district.
- **Local** level which includes the primary health centre, sub-centre, health post or dispensary (the terms used vary from country to country), to which may be attached health committees and a cadre of community health workers.

2. **Other** ministries or departments that have an influence on health such as agriculture, forestry and environment; energy and renewable resources; human resources; education; urban or rural development; water.

Who carries out health care most effectively – Government or NGO?

Government and Non-Governmental Organisations (NGOs) each have their particular strengths.
   Jobs often done best by **Government** include:

- **Planning** health services.
- **Funding** nationwide health care (though other sources are increasingly necessary).
- **Establishing** secondary and tertiary health care – district and regional hospitals.
- **Training** doctors, nurses and other senior health professionals.
- **Co-ordinating**: supplies of medicines and equipment, infectious disease control, immunisation programmes, and water and sanitation projects.
- **Replicating** nationwide, methods and ideas worked out by NGOs at local or district level.

These are all tasks which require both high expenditure and nationwide planning to be effective. Jobs often done best by NGOs include:

- **Setting up** primary health care.
- **Encouraging** the participation of the community.
- **Training**, teaching and motivating health workers and communities.
- **Meeting** local needs with programmes that are flexible and appropriate.
- **Using** money, people and resources effectively.
- **Working** in remote or difficult areas, or with neglected, backward or tribal groups.
- **Integrating** primary health care and development activities at local level.

These are tasks which spring from the strengths of the NGO – enthusiasm, flexibility, community involvement and manageable size.

How can government and NGO work together?

Historical stages

Three stages can usually be seen:

Stage 1: Voluntary programme provides health care for those most needing it, especially the poor.
Stage 2: Government uses the ideas, takes over

the service and makes it available for all. More recently, owing to increasing needs, and decreasing government resources there is sometimes:

Stage 3: Government actually hands back defined areas of health care to the NGO, most commonly responsibility for primary health services. This happens where needs are proving too great for government resources alone.

Present models of co-operation

At the present time working relationships between government and NGO usually follow one of these three models:

1. NGO and government set up a joint programme. The NGO works closely with the government, and carries out a specific programme or task which government services are not providing.
For example: In parts of Nepal the government concentrates on providing curative services at local level leaving the NGO to train community health workers.
There are **disadvantages** in this approach – it may be hard to define who does what and which organisation is responsible for which part of the project. Much time is taken in planning and meeting. The NGO may be restricted and unable to make best use of its enthusiasm and flexibility.

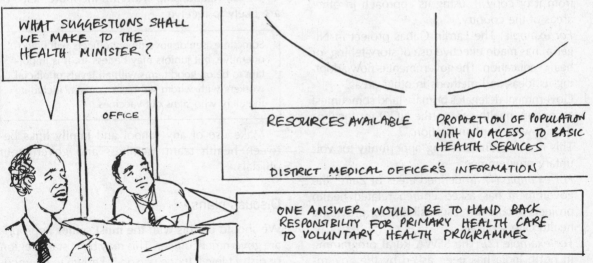

© Illustration David Gifford

Figure 19.2

Figure 19.3

2. NGO sets up a programme on its own terms. Here the NGO is free to make use of its own resources. It can respond to the needs of the local people, work in co-operation with them, and remain unhindered by bureaucracy.

If the programme proves to be effective, the government may either help to fund it, learn from it or copy it, using its approach in other areas of the country.

For example: The Lardin Gabas project in Nigeria, has made effective use of story-telling for health education. The government is now adopting its ideas and methods in other areas.

3. Government delegates primary (and sometimes) secondary health care to the NGO for local or district-wide implementation.

This is a new and exciting opportunity for voluntary programmes.

For example (1). In defined areas of Zaire, the government has asked church related health projects to take full responsibility for providing health care services.

For example (2). The SEWA Rural programme in north India has been asked by the government to be fully responsible for the primary health care in one whole district.

Practical guidelines for working with government

Build personal relationships

The most strategic person is usually the District Medical Officer or his equivalent or deputy. The better our relationship with him the more help we are likely to receive.

> Sometimes senior government officers will be co-operative, but juniors may be less so. It is important to be on good terms with all levels of official workers with whom we have contact, including the clerk who signs out vaccines.

Make use of any school and family links between health team members and government officials.

Discuss plans

We should do this with **the most senior** appropriate government officer. This may be at state, region or district level. If one person is known to be unco-operative we should try someone else.

When **first starting** a programme, we may need

advice and ideas from the DMO, both about the area we should work in and the type of project we should carry out.

As the programme **develops** we should inform the DMO of any important change of plans or expansion into new areas.

If we have been planning with a government officer other than the DMO we should make sure that the DMO himself also knows about our plans.

Send regular reports, returns and information

These are needed for national statistics. It will be to our credit if health improvements such as higher rates of immunisation are recorded from the programme area. The DMO will also be glad to have any returns to add to his own.

Define areas of responsibility

In joint programmes with government we must ensure that the exact responsibilities of both NGO and government are clearly defined.

> If the government has given us responsibility for part of the programme, we should make sure that they also give us the authority to carry it out.

Help that may be obtained from the government

Drugs and supplies

The government often provides free or subsidised supplies. These may include: TB and leprosy drugs, family planning supplies, vitamin A, iron and folic acid.

REPORT FORM

Monthly report for ....
(month)

Weighing group (hamlet) .... Village .... District ....

Date of weighing .... Field Worker .... Number of kaders helping ....

Total hamlet population .... in .... families

1. Total children under 36 months old
2. Total children with weight charts
3. Total newly entered this month
4. Total with increased weight this month
5. Total with no increase in weight
6. Total weighed with last month weight unknown (therefore, do not know if weight increased)
7. Total weighed this month

Participation score = # 2/1
Activity score = # 7/2
Growth score = # 4/(7 − (3 + 6))
Overall score = # 4/1

Use of supplies this month:
 Weight charts
 Oralyte packets
 Vitamin A high-dose capsules
 Iron folate tablets

Figure 19.4 A report form used in Indonesia for sending monthly statistics to the government

Vaccines can usually be supplied under the WHO Expanded Programme on Immunization (EPI) via the DMO or District Hospital.

We should use government supplies whenever possible, but remember that they may be **unreliable** (we will always need alternative sources), and there may be excessive **paperwork** (we may need to employ an extra staff member to deal with this).

Financial grants

These are often available, usually for a specific purpose. However they may be **late** or never arrive (meaning we should not be dependent on them) and they may have **strict conditions** (such as defining exactly how the funds should be used).

If possible we should obtain grants for **general** purposes not **specific** ones so that the programme can decide on the most appropriate way of using the money.

Co-operating with aid and funding agencies

Questions asked by projects

From time to time we may wonder:

- Why are the agency's forms so long and complex?
- Why does it take so long for funds to reach us?
- Why does the agency send representatives to question us and take photographs. Why instead don't they send experts to give us ideas and information.

It helps to answer these questions if we understand the problems faced by agencies.

Problems faced by agencies

Funding agencies themselves are often under great pressure. We should remember that:

1. The agency is **dependent** on its own supporters, who in turn will expect reassurance that their money is being well spent, and request information including stories and photographs. The more of these that supporters receive, the more money they will give to the agency.
2. The agency may have **insufficient funds**, because so many **projects** are making requests, because a major **disaster** has just occurred, or because **famine relief** takes priority.
3. There are problems in **communication** because **forms** may be incomplete or wrongly filled in, and **postal** delays hold up letters or financial support from arriving.

© Illustration David Gifford

Figure 19.5   Funding agencies themselves can be under great pressure

Ways in which projects can help

- By **sending** regular reports as requested.
- By **preparing** accurate budgets, and **keeping** costs as low as possible.
- By **replying** promptly to letters.
- By **informing** the agency of any major changes of plan.
- By **welcoming** visitors from the agency.

> If two or more agencies are supporting a project, then the area of support and contribution of each should be carefully defined and recorded.

Finally we should remember that the agency wants to be in partnership with us. Its members are genuinely interested in what we are doing, and many who visit us will themselves be experts, who have previously worked in similar programmes.

Co-operating with other voluntary agencies

We should aim to work as closely as possible with other voluntary programmes present in the target area. These will include development projects who may be tackling the root cause of ill health through forestry, agriculture, literacy and education. They may also include other health programmes.

Although we should always work in co-operation, not competition, we must carefully assess any programme with which we develop special links.

If the programme seems inappropriate we should be slow to develop formal links.

For example: A new group moves in which has plenty of money but little understanding of development. They give free handouts and distribute bottles of tonic and vitamins. The people flock to

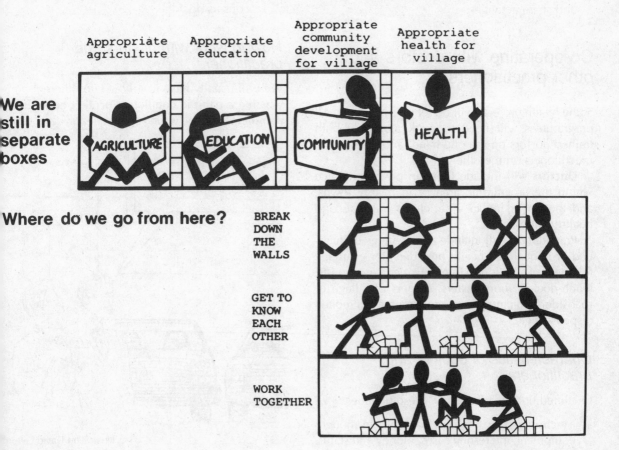

Figure 19.6

their centre not realising that such a group may have a secret motive, or be 'here today, gone tomorrow'.

If however the programme seems appropriate we can:

1. **Co-operate** together, for example by visiting each other's projects, training each other's staff, sharing expensive items of equipment, setting up a combined system for ordering and supplying drugs, sharing leisure activities.
2. **Define** project areas:

> If there is genuine overlap between projects, either in terms of the ground **area** we are covering or the **activities** we are carrying out, it will be necessary to define clearly **where** each project should work and **what** each project should do.

3. **Join** any voluntary health organisation which encourages local programmes to work together and share activities.

Co-operating with doctors and other practitioners

Some health projects will be set up by doctors. **All** programmes will need to work alongside both trained doctors on the one hand, and a variety of practitioners on the other.

Doctors will include those in private practice within the programme area or in nearby towns, and those working in a variety of hospitals and health centres.

Practitioners will include a huge range of qualified or unqualified health providers, for example: followers of traditional systems of medicine, priests, witch-doctors, bone-setters, owners of village or roadside medicine shops, government accredited dispensers etc.

Characteristics of doctors and practitioners

Qualified doctors often show these qualities:

1. **Much** interest in cure, in hospitals, in modern equipment, interesting cases, money and status.
2. **Little** interest in primary or community health care – often considered to be dull or beneath

their station.

3. **Some** interest in the community health programme, either out of social concern, out of fear that successful health prevention will reduce their patient numbers or in hope that serious cases will be referred to them.

Most doctors, unless converted to a community health approach are more interested in **medical** care than in **health care** (see Chapter 16, page 230).

Unqualified practitioners often show these qualities:

1. Genuine **concern** for the community of which they are often members.
2. **Eagerness** to make money or acquire gifts.
3. Specialist **skill** or interest in one area of expertise, for example TBAs in deliveries, witch doctors in epilepsy and mental illness.
4. An **interest** in our programme for the same reasons as doctors.

How to work with doctors and practitioners

We will usually have to follow two different aims which are often in conflict: to **protect community members** from the wrong type of health care, espe-

© Illustration David Gifford

Figure 19.7 Conventional medical schools do not prepare doctors for working in the community

cially from practices which are harmful or lead to dependence; to **co-operate** with doctors and practitioners as far as we are able.

We can follow these guidelines:

1. Build **personal relationships**.
2. Explain **who** we are and **what** we are doing, making clear that our main aim is not primarily to treat patients but to improve the health of the community.
3. Never publicly **speak ill** of a doctor or practitioner.

> Even if we strongly disapprove of the way a colleague is treating a patient, we should be slow to criticise either in public or to one of his patients. If the case is serious we should see the practitioner ourselves.

4. **Provide** health education to local practitioners. *For example*: We can **invite** practitioners to our staff training days, run local health courses or seminars, loan health books or journals, allow them access to the project library, supply them a copy of *Where There is No Doctor* or other suitable books.
5. **Include** practitioners in our health programme.

Some will be converted to community health as they observe what we are doing. Many projects have examples of local practitioners once strongly opposed to the project, who are now its staunchest supporters. Once sensitised, witch-doctors on the one hand and private doctors on the other can find a valued role in CBHC.

On the other hand doctors interested only in building their own practices can wreck a programme within months, converting it from a **health** project based in the community to a **medical** project dependent on themselves.

The doctor's role in community health programmes

Doctors can have the following roles:

Clinical medical officer

The doctor should see patients referred by other health workers. These may include the very ill or chronically sick e.g. with TB or AIDS, cases which

Figure 19.8

are difficult to diagnose or require emergency treatment or surgery.

> In Community Based Health Care the doctor should train other health workers to see patients, himself seeing only those with serious illnesses or referred by another health worker.

Teacher

The doctor's aim should be to pass on relevant skills and knowledge so that other health workers quickly learn to diagnose and treat common and important diseases.

Planner

Doctors should take part in project planning and in drawing up a suitable health programme for the needs of the people.

Supervisor

Doctors ought to supervise the clinical care of patients including their diagnosis, treatment and rehabilitation.

Compiler of an essential drug list

See Chapter 16, page 234 for details.

'THE TWO MULES'

A fable for
the Nations

CO-OPERATION

IS BETTER
THAN
CONFLICT

Figure 19.9   Everyone benefits when hospitals and primary health programmes work together

Advisor

Doctors can advise on all health related topics, including clinical care, the use of medicines, immunisation schedules, clean water, latrines, and the setting up of clinics and MCH care.

Director

> Doctors should only direct community health programmes if they are fully committed to its principles.

In practice doctors who understand community health are often in short supply. Problems occur when out of desperation projects call in private or hospital doctors because no one else is available.

It may be better to have no doctor at all than one who speaks a 'different health care language'.

Co-operating with hospitals

Some community health projects are attached to a base hospital, others are independent. Whichever arrangement is used one principle is essential: hos-

pitals and community health programmes (CHPs) must work in partnership.

Hospitals ideally provide a whole range of back-up services for the primary health care level.

The way a health service **should** work

There are usually three levels in a clinical health system. Sometimes a level may be divided into two parts and the levels may have different names depending on the country.

1. Primary level.
   This includes:
   - CHWs working in the community.
   - Health posts, subcentres, primary health centres and their staff who support the CHWs, and to whom CHWs refer patients.
2. Secondary level.
   This is the District or 'Base' Hospital which gives backing to the primary level, and takes referrals from it. It has inpatient beds, can perform routine surgery and carries out a range of investigations.
3. Tertiary level.
   This is the large well-equipped regional hospi-

? Where do we start building the pyramid of health care

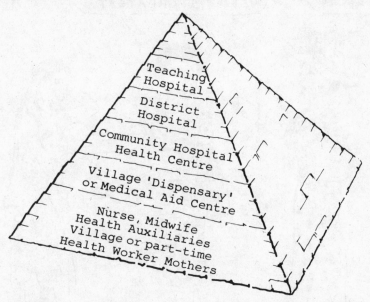

Figure 19.10   Patients should normally enter at the lowest level and only move upwards by referral

tal able to do major surgery, complex investigations and offering a range of specialist care. It takes referrals from the secondary level.

When this system works correctly (see Figure 19.10) it is good for patients, health workers and the economy.

It is good for **patients** because they usually receive care at the primary level which is near their home and convenient, so saving them time, money and worry.

It is good for **health workers** because they see patients appropriate to their level of training and receive job satisfaction, neither being swamped by problems that are too easy, nor being frightened by problems that are too difficult.

It is good for the **economy** because highly trained, highly paid doctors or nurses don't spend their time seeing patients with less serious illnesses who could be seen just as well, and at much less cost by health workers at the level below.

> As each person does the work he was trained for and each level does the job it was designed for, the health service becomes efficient and economical and all levels of health worker become more satisfied.

The way a health service usually works in practice

In practice the richer and more educated try to bypass the lower levels of the health service and go to the secondary or tertiary levels for their minor health problems. Smart people like seeing smart doctors in smart hospitals even for their headaches and itchy bottoms.

This has unfortunate results:

1. The **rich** get overtreated, demanding more expensive drugs and treatments, so setting up an inappropriate pattern which others start to follow.
2. The **poor** get undertreated or not treated at all as there is little time left for serious problems referred from the level below.
3. **Health workers** are unfulfilled: doctors spend time seeing patients with minor problems, and so get bored, CHWs and middle level workers get bypassed except by the very poor, and so get discouraged.
4. The **referral system** breaks down.
5. **Costs** increase even more and more hospitals get built.

Figure 19.11 A key question for health care in the 1990s – 'Will this health worker give in to the demands of the rich or respond to the needs of the poor?'

The correct roles of the base hospital

Acting as a referral centre

Most patients will be referred in from the primary health centre or its equivalent. Seriously ill patients in the community may be referred direct by CHWs bypassing the primary health centre. A few patients will be self-referred.

Patients requiring referral to hospital will include: emergencies; those needing surgery, Caesarian section or assisted delivery; any needing investigations (either as out-patients or in-patients).

In acting as a referral centre the hospital will have three important tasks:

1. It will **receive** patients, trying where possible to admit any patient referred especially if from a long distance.
2. It will **care** for patients in the ward, where staff will need to be taught to show kindness and special care for the poorest, the most uninformed and the most sick. Often in practice staff

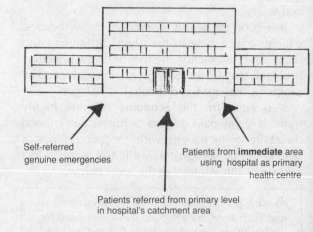

Self-referred
genuine emergencies

Patients from **immediate** area
using hospital as primary
health centre

Patients referred from primary level
in hospital's catchment area

© Illustration David Gifford

Figure 19.12 The correct use of a referral hospital

respect the rich and push the poor aside.

3. It will **discharge** patients back to the community, first contacting the primary health centre team to arrange a suitable time, and means of transport. A doctor or nurse will write a discharge summary.

> The time immediately after discharge is often a difficult one for the patient. He may not know who should be looking after him, when he should be seen again or what treatment he should be taking. To avoid this, primary and secondary levels must **communicate** and follow agreed procedures.

Whenever a patient is admitted to a ward or seen as an out-patient, he should be offered 'primary health activities' such as health education, immunisation, family planning or other appropriate services. Any procedures given should be written on the patients self-retained record card.

Acting as a teaching centre

In some programmes teaching of the health team, including the CHWs, is done in the hospital – in others it is done mainly in the community with occasional visits to the hospital.

Backing up with supplies and equipment

The hospital may be the simplest place to obtain medicines, vaccines and equipment. It may arrange to sterilise instruments and needles. It may have more expensive items which community health programmes can borrow or use such as teaching aids, projectors or vehicles.

Backing up with management

The hospital may do the CHP's accounting, prepare statistics or help produce the annual report. It may have salary structures and management systems that can be followed.

Backing up by giving the same health message

Hospitals should be using simple drugs and the same essential list (with a few additions) as the primary team. They should be giving the same basic health teaching.

> Patients will usually pay more attention to what the hospital says than to what the primary health team says. It is important therefore that both give the same message and that the hospital supports the teaching of the primary health workers.

Hospitals are also in a good position to fight those who promote illicit liquor and drugs, smoking and artificial baby foods.

Backing up by discouraging self-referrals

The role of the hospital is to treat serious cases referred from the primary level, **not** to act as a primary health centre for anyone who walks in. The hospital should discourage patients from attending unless they have a referral letter, are a genuine emergency or come from the hospital 'core area' (see below).

One way of doing this is to charge self-referred patients double rates or agree to see them only if they first go and see a member of the community health team and bring a letter with them.

Providing a 'core' primary health programme

People who live in communities very near the hospital, especially the poor, can use the hospital as their primary health centre.

The hospital can set up an appropriate programme for those in the core area and carry out community health activities just as would be done by a regular CHP. CHWs can be selected and trained, immunisations and mother and child care set up. Those needing to be seen in a clinic can be referred direct to the hospital by the CHW.

How hospitals and community health projects relate to each other

Models

There are several different models of how hospital and CHP can relate. Here are some common ones:

*Community health programme **under** hospital management*

This is the traditional plan. The hospital has been set up in the past and now for various reasons decides to start a community health programme. This may be because the funding agency has asked for it or because of genuine interest among health workers or because of a request from the community.

Community health programme **separate** from hospital

1. No fixed hospital for referral.
   Here the CHP is truly on its own and dependent on its own resources, planning and expertise. Patients needing referral will be sent to different practitioners, clinics or hospitals, with whom arrangements are made. Many urban projects follow this model.
2. Fixed hospital(s) for referral.
   The programme remains detached but builds up special contacts with one or two hospitals which act as referral centres. This pattern has much to commend it and if well set up enables

a project to be self-dependent, while still retaining use of a base hospital for referral.

Community health programme **served** and **supported** by base hospital

This radical pattern, though rarely followed is probably the best. The hospital is actually part of the community health programme and has been set with the chief aim of providing referral and support services. Staff move freely between hospital and community; patients feel welcomed in the hospital and are treated with understanding.

Problems in practice

The following problems tend to be worse when CHPs are managed by hospitals. They tend to be least when a CHP sets up its own hospital as a referral base.

Figure 19.13   Close links between hospital doctors and primary health services in China benefit all members of the community

1. Poor co-operation – misunderstandings between the hospital and CHP may be very long standing.
2. Poor care for the poor patient – hospital staff prefer looking after the rich who can pay rather than the slum-dweller or poor villager who 'can't pay and can't understand'.
3. Priority to the hospital – the hospital is seen as the most important service, the community health project as an extra. When shortages of money or staff develop, the CHP suffers.

Practical solutions

The secret of a successful partnership is the development of a friendly working relationship between the Primary level and the Secondary level, between the CHP and the base hospital. We should set this as a definite aim of our programme.

There are several keys to good CHP – hospital relations and one leads from the other:

1. Mutual **understanding** of each other's role.
   CHP members need to spend time working in the hospital, understanding how it works and getting to know its staff. Hospital staff need to spend time in the community, understanding the way of life of its members and sharing in their problems and solutions.
2. Mutual **respect**.
   As each branch of the health team understands the other so mutual respect grows, which in turn leads on to:
3. Mutual **co-operation**.
   Where everyone benefits, and through which the poor receive appropriate treatment.

Summary

Community health programmes work best when they co-operate, rather than compete with other branches of the health service.

They need to learn to co-operate with government in a well-defined partnership, with each rec-

ognising the strengths and roles of the other.

They must co-operate with donor agencies, providing the information they are asked to without undue delay. They should work with other voluntary health or development programmes in the project area, providing that goals are similar.

Community health programmes should work with both local doctors and other health practitioners, co-operating where possible and being careful to avoid antagonism.

Finally CHPs should integrate with other levels of the health service so that each tier carries out the jobs for which it was designed. This causes increased job satisfaction to health workers, provides more effective services for patients and greatly reduces costs.

Underlying all co-operation is the building of friendship and trust between colleagues in government, neighbouring programmes and hospitals.

Further Reading

1. *Primary Health Care: Reorienting Organizational Support.* G. J. Ebrahim and J. P. Ranken. Macmillan, 1988.
   Helpful background to ways in which government health services can emphasise primary health care and ways in which voluntary programmes can co-operate with them.
   Available from: TALC. See Appendix E.
2. *District Health Care.* R. Amonoo-Lartson *et al.*
   A clear description of how District Health Services function. Macmillan, 1984.
   Available from: TALC. See Appendix E.
3. *Hospitals and Health for All.* WHO, 1987.
   Available from: WHO. See Appendix E.
4. 'The role of voluntary organizations.' A. Mukhopadhyay. *Health for the Millions* **13**, Oct, 1987.
   Available from: VHAI. See Appendix E.
5. *WHO: What it is, What it does.* WHO, 1988.
   Available from: WHO. See Appendix E.
6. 'Feeling unwell? – Must you go straight to the hospital?' P. E. S. Palmer. *World Health Forum* **12**: 38–42, 1991.
   Available from: WHO. See Appendix E.

20

A Community Development Approach to AIDS Care, Prevention and Control

By Captain (Dr) Ian Campbell, Medical Advisor, and Alison D. Rader, AIDS Programme Consultant to the Salvation Army International Headquarters, London.

In this chapter we shall consider:

1. Introduction – What is AIDS?
2. Should we start a programme?
3. What resources do we need?
4. How is a programme developed?
5. Important principles for programme design
6. Evaluating the impact of AIDS

Introduction – What is AIDS?

AIDS stands for the Acquired Immune Deficiency Syndrome. This is a disease in which the body's immune system collapses, often leading to death within 2 years. It is caused by the Human Immunodeficiency Virus (HIV). At the time of writing nearly 500,000 cases have been officially reported world-wide, but actual numbers are likely

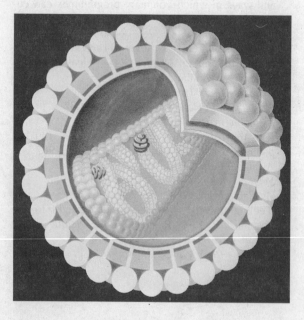

Figure 20.1 Structure of the human immunodeficiency virus (HIV)

to exceed 2 million.

Infection with HIV usually leads to AIDS. An individual becomes positive usually within 3 months of contact, but the time between sero-conversion (i.e. becoming HIV positive) and the development of AIDS is variable ranging from months to many years – with an average time of about 10 years. During this latent period the person infected with HIV is largely free of symptoms but is infectious to others. There are estimated to be over 12 million HIV positive individuals world-wide.

AIDS became generally known in the early 1980s, and since that time it has spread extremely rapidly, especially in sub-saharan Africa. Other countries of the world also have high rates including Brazil, parts of the United States and Europe. AIDS is starting to spread quickly in a number of Asian countries. Most countries have now reported cases of AIDS.

AIDS is spread largely through sexual contact with an HIV positive individual. In addition it can be passed on through blood transfusions, infected needles, breastmilk and from mother to fetus before or during birth.

> In many countries AIDS is becoming the number one health priority and there is a great and growing need for community-based AIDS programmes to be established. These can be based in a variety of settings including hospitals and health centres, clubs and churches or in the homes of the community.

Such programmes should include care, prevention **and** control. The community itself needs to own responsibility for the programme.

In AIDS related community development programmes the two most important activities will be:

1. Home based **care** of people with AIDS and HIV.

2. **Counselling** of individuals, families and communities.

These cannot operate successfully on their own but together must be integrated into other aspects of AIDS management.

Should we start a programme?

This depends largely on need which can be discovered as follows:

1. **Ask community members** what they think about the AIDS problem. Their answers usually include the way **they** feel as well as the way they think **others** feel. Here is an example of questions which can be asked:
   a) What do people know about AIDS?
      - How is it transmitted?
      - What are the symptoms and signs?
      - How does one talk to a person with AIDS?
   b) What do people feel about AIDS? – look at attitudes.
   c) What do people believe about the behaviours that cause AIDS? How should these be changed?

Collecting this information will also help to build awareness which in turn will prepare the community for a formal AIDS programme. Any features unique to the community can also be identified.

2. **Ask local health workers** – from hospitals or clinics – how they assess the problem. The presence of HIV testing will help to give accurate answers.

3. **Contact district** and **national** health authorities to seek information and guidance.

We need to respond not only to the present 'felt-need' of the community but also to the needs recognised by health authorities, who can help to predict long-term problems.

Because the prevalence of the virus in the community is often little known, we need to realise that

Figure 20.2   The headman of a village in Zambia works closely with community workers

the existence of even one confirmed case usually means that many other community members will be HIV positive. Moreover once the virus has entered a community the AIDS problem **will grow**. This means that it is usually only a matter of time before the community recognises the problem of AIDS and the need for an AIDS programme.

In these early stages we can build trust which will become the foundation for a formal AIDS programme in the future.

What resources do we need?

The most important resource will be a group of **committed people** who are concerned both for individuals and for communities. Such a group can make decisions and gather ideas more effectively than individuals working alone.

In addition we will need **links to a referral hospital** which does HIV testing, or can pass on samples to a testing centre.

As soon as HIV testing is known to take place questions will arise within the community which will need to be answered, and counselling will become necessary. In many parts of the world community volunteers are being recognised and trained to carry this out, which if done sensitively can enlarge awareness and if combined with a follow-up plan need not cause fear.

How is a programme developed?

Many people who are concerned about AIDS will have no formal health qualifications nor even any links with hospitals and clinics. This does not matter. An AIDS programme can start with one motivated individual, whether based in a hospital, a clinic, a school, a village, or any other community structure.

Step 1. Form a team

This will comprise committed and caring people, drawn either from community members or health care staff.

This team can be part time, consisting of people already working in the institution or organisation. A good starting point is to recruit people who are known to be doing well in their own jobs, but care needs to be taken not to detract from their existing tasks, and to make time for discussion and understanding with all levels involved.

In a hospital it is relatively easy for a volunteer team to be formed, without hiring a single extra staff member. This can be an effective way of setting the programme in motion. Additional staffing, office facilities, funding and administrative details can all follow later on.

Step 2. List the strengths of the community

An important first step is to understand the way communities work together and solve problems. We may be tempted to impose our own solutions but it is better to discover the community's own beliefs and weigh up their own suggestions.

Often, community members, because they are dependent on health services, believe they will not be able to manage at home. For this reason, reassurance about a support network needs to be given at an early stage. This is where home care can be helpful in building up strengths that have existed for a long time, and in promoting hope.

In 1987 an AIDS care unit was formed at Chikankata Hospital in the Southern Province of Zambia. This included a home care team. The decision to shift the emphasis from the hospital to the community was based on identifying community resources and requests. They included the following:

- That other health programmes should continue.
- That the family is the greatest long-term strength.
- That patients prefer to die at home.
- That people learn best by talking together.
- That changes in behaviour are best achieved through activating traditional leadership and helping the community to take responsibility for care and prevention.

Step 3. Set up community care

The objectives will include:

- Caring for patients.
- Supporting families.
- Promoting discussion within the wider community.

- Conducting operational research:
- Promoting AIDS control through.
  - community discussion,
  - community counselling which stimulates strategies for behaviour change,
  - practical activities such as contact tracing.

Team members can be part-time provided the **tasks** of team members are analysed, **roles** are defined, and the **structure** of the team is repeatedly examined.

> Good teams depend on relationship building. Stress within teams can be reduced provided members are prepared to help each other, and to give abilities away to one another.

Suitable **transport** will need to be arranged.

Step 4. Identify specific target groups for education

The family is the primary target others usually include school children, teenagers and contacts of those known to have AIDS or to be HIV positive.

Step 5. For those involved in hospital work, co-ordinate the AIDS programme with general processes of treatment and management within the hospital

This means:

1. Acceptance of a multidisciplinary approach. The AIDS programme will involve medical, nursing, laboratory, education, counselling, administration and pastoral care staff.
2. A hospital management plan should include:
   - Diagnosis/counselling.
   - Planned discharge, with family involvement.
   - Liaison with the community and home care team.
   - Hospital care when required.

Step 6. Write a project proposal (if there is no other funding source) see also Chapter 4 page 44

This does not need to be a complicated document. Help can usually be found from donor organisations, national AIDS organisations or from within other departments of the institution or organisation.

A **summary statement** at the beginning of the project is useful, outlining the main concept. This is best followed by an **outline** of the **project background**, giving a picture of AIDS in the district and its possible impact on other areas of development. Then should follow a **list of the objectives**. The donor needs to know about **project requirements**, a **schedule** for implementation, and a **budget** (separating capital and recurrent expenditure).

A **description of relationships** of the health organisation to other networks at district, provincial and national level will also be useful to the donor.

Important principles for programme design

The steps in programme development outlined so far follow on from one another. Running through all stages are the following **principles** which are necessary for a successful outcome:

Integration

An approach is needed that combines home care, community counselling, community development and hospital back-up when needed. This is known as Integrated AIDS Management.

Such management produces a framework for care in which genuine interest will result in action, presence and hope. A family with AIDS in the Chikankata area of southern Zambia said in 1989 'the home care team gives love and hope – they are visitors from the source of life'.

Management also contains a plan for prevention, and control: caring is the vital entry point.

This principle of integration is expressed in many ways. For example: **within** the institution it means a co-ordinated approach to the following disciplines:

- clinical/nursing/laboratory,
- education,
- counselling,
- pastoral care.

Outside the institution it means co-ordination between different programmes as between government and non-governmental organisations, church and state, field workers and policy makers.

Decentralisation

To be successful AIDS programmes need to be grounded in the community, even though any effective national policy should be followed and hospital back-up strengthened.

> Through home-based care, the community becomes motivated for prevention. This 'bottom-up' approach is one that is owned by those who suffer most, and is therefore more likely to be sustainable into the future.

Management models

Management strategies already in place should continue, especially where primary health care is included. However new programme skills and management teams will need to be developed.

Administrative structures for AIDS are necessary to enable the development of specific skills, to cover the huge work load, and to allow other programmes to carry out their tasks. Such structures can be part of existing primary health care departments, or can co-exist with them. Whatever the arrangement, an AIDS programme will often eventually need a specific allocation of people, skills and resources, for caring, prevention, control and measurement.

In a response to AIDS, future success is likely to be found in those programmes which explore principles of **community development**. These respect and preserve local community initiative, and they promote group **formation** and group **function**.

Emphasis of training

Trainees should be encouraged to share different leadership responsibilities, so remaining 'multi-purpose' within the AIDS programme. They need to be sufficiently flexible to learn about other aspects of AIDS management such as pastoral care and counselling, and to put these into practice.

As experience grows, other groups needing help will visit. Action plans can be discussed informally and possibly through formal training programmes.

These will emphasise home care, community counselling, discussion and networking, education and evaluation, hospital linkages and team building.

Behaviour change and counselling

> AIDS will **not** be controlled by health workers telling the community how to control their behaviour. AIDS **can** be controlled by a community being taught the issues and choices so it can then control behaviour on its own terms.

What exactly is meant by the word 'community'? In simple terms a community is a group that has a recognisable structure, and whose members can function effectively together.

What then is '**development in community**'? In this process the community builds up its group structure and its capacity to function. To stimulate this process counselling has a vital role.

The functions of community counselling

It is important to understand the exact meaning of this word. Counselling can be defined as an activity expressed through conversation, where **responsibility for prevention** is transferred from health personnel and other concerned helpers to individuals, families and communities. This can be extended not only to prevention but to care and eventually to a sense of **ownership of responsibility for the control of AIDS**.

Community counselling is an activity focusing on groups and communities which enables the whole community to take responsibility for behaviour change.

The stages of community counselling

These include:

1. **Selection** of the target community (this will usually be self-selected by the presence of home-care clients and increased community awareness).
2. **Relationship** building between community and counselling team.
3. **Problem exploration** by team and community.
4. **Decision making** by community, including the planning of strategies.

5. **Implementation** of strategies.
6. **Evaluation** (leads to further problem exploration and redirection of programme).

This process takes much energy, teamwork and time. It does not require much money.

The volunteer community counsellor

Community counselling is ideally carried out through a volunteer community counsellor, selected by the community and trained by the health team. Such 'insiders' often work more effectively than outsiders who are less able to understand community attitudes and beliefs.

The **role** of the community counsellor can include the following:

1. **Promoting** respectful and confidential sharing of information within the community.
2. **Linking** the community and the health services.

3. **Helping** to implement community-specific strategies.
4. **Referring** patients to the hospital when necessary.
5. **Counselling** in bereavement and other stress times in the community.

The community counsellor can sustain the commitment of the whole community to care for those who suffer, to prevent the disease in those still HIV negative, and ultimately to control the disease in the district.

Community action

Widespread control will only happen if counselling teams in one community are prepared to share their skills with other communities. Some of the ten communities studied in 1989 in the Chikanakata area are developing AIDS action groups with the objective of counselling a neighbouring village.

Figure 20.3   Community counselling helps people to take responsibility for changing their behaviour patterns

In summary we must remember that **helping a community to change its behaviour** is very different from **trying to control behaviour**. This 'facilitation of behaviour change' is the most effective AIDS control measure.

It is exciting to see that 'responsibility awareness' can begin at the 'bottom' but a realistic strategy for AIDS control also needs to contain strong community and political leadership from the 'top'.

To **summarise** the principles of programme design:

- Think inclusively.
- Think community.
- Think realistically.
- Quality is more important than quantity.
- Project hope.
- Build teamwork.
- Build in sustainability, of people, programme and finance.

Evaluating the impact of AIDS

Collecting information can be relatively easy, and is very valuable if it is systematic. At district hospital level, the information that can be easily collected is listed as it applies to Chikanakata AIDS care and prevention work in Zambia.

Gathering information

Table 20.1 outlines field and hospital data that can be collected by simply counting the numbers of people in various categories.

Impact on the hospital

If we work in a hospital or health centre, the impact of AIDS on the institution needs to be measured. An example of this is shown, where the number of people found to be HIV positive (tested because they have symptoms) has been listed year by year.

Financial impact

The financial impact on hospitals is important and the following categories can be costed:

Table 20.1   Types of data that can be easily collected

Administration	– total patients seen
	– new patients seen
	– total families seen
	– new families seen
	– patients preferring home care to periodic checks at hospital
Clinical care	– number with AIDS
	– number with AIDS related complex
	– number asymptomatic
	– number patients with nursing care felt needs
Laboratory	– total contacts tested
	– number contacts HIV+
	– results from all sources (in-patients, out-patients etc.)
Mortality	– total persons known to have died
	– number died at home
	– number died in hospital/ readmission
Education	Patient knowledge of disease (score 1–5, 1 = low) course, transmission, prevention
Pastoral care	– number funerals attended
	– number times pastoral care required in the form of prayer, scripture, counsel
Counselling	– number children of HIV+ patients
	– number families with HIV+ primary breadwinner
	– number families headed by HIV+ single mother
	– number families with abnormal atmosphere due to disease
	– number patients acknowledging life-style changes in social activity, family life, sexual behaviour

- Safety precautions (e.g. gloves, needles, plastic bags etc.)
- In-patient care.
- Drugs.
- Test kits.
- Administrative charges.

Community impact

This is most easily measured by ongoing operational research through a home care programme.

Figure 20.4 shows the number of HIV-positive patients referred to the follow-up programme over a 4-year period.

In the Chikankata area it has been significant to note over the past 4 years that:

- Most deaths occur at home.
- Most people prefer home visits.
- Very few people are rejected by the community if a support team visits regularly.
- Numbers HIV positive in the community are increasing in certain groups in the population.

One point clearly emerging from this evaluation is that the follow-up programme cannot cover all new patients on an individual basis. This has led to new aspects of programme design which motivates the community to promote basic changes in

Figure 20.5 A fragile world teeters on the brink of a 'great fall'. Only a world-wide effort will stop it.

behaviour. Home care and community counselling are effective tools for measurement of both motivation and behaviour change.

Summary

AIDS is a relatively new disease which is spreading rapidly through sub-Saharan Africa and other parts of the world. It has no cure, is spread from infected people who have no symptoms, and often affects younger members of the community. There is therefore an urgent need to set up AIDS-related development programmes. Such programmes must include care, prevention and control activities.

Unless we express **care** for people with HIV and AIDS, we will have little hope of **preventing** and **controlling** the disease. Unless the communities with which we work sense some **hope**, which usually comes through knowing someone who cares, they will not be motivated to work towards

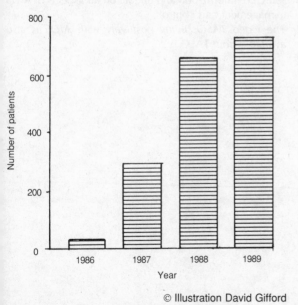

© Illustration David Gifford

Figure 20.4 Chikankata Hospital: HIV positive patients referred to the follow-up programmes

preventing the spread of HIV infection. Programmes therefore need to stress both the importance of caring for people, and of communities preventing the disease for themselves.

Home care and counselling are two essential practical **components** of a community development strategy for AIDS. These are best implemented by teams.

The key **principle** underlying a successful programme is the **transfer of responsibility** for AIDS control to the community. This is largely brought about by counselling in which a volunteer community counsellor can play a leading role.

Programmes need to evaluate the various impacts of AIDS so that strategies can be remodelled to meet ever changing and growing needs. Information needed for this can be easily gathered from the hospital and the community.

As experience grows, other groups needing help will visit. Action plans can be discussed both informally, and through formal training programmes. Such plans can emphasise home care, community counselling, education and evaluation, hospital counselling, community discussion, networking and team building.

Further Reading

1. Strategies for Hope Series: *1. From Fear to Hope*. G. Williams; *2. Living Positively with AIDS*. J. Hampton;
3. AIDS Management: an Integrated Approach. I. Campbell and G. Williams; *4. Meeting AIDS with Compassion – a study from Ghana*; *5. AIDS Orphans – a study from Tanzania.* 6. The caring community: coping with AIDS in urban Uganda. G. Williams and N. Tamale. Published by Action Aid/AMREF/World in Need, 1990/91.
These excellent and practical booklets growing out of field experience in Africa are *available from*: TALC. See Appendix E.

2. *Guide to Planning Health Promotion for AIDS Prevention and Control*. WHO, 1989.
A practical step-by-step guide for stimulating behaviour changes needed to limit the spread of AIDS. *Available from*: WHO. See Appendix E. A number of other books are published by WHO in their AIDS series.

3. *Talking AIDS: A Guide for Community Work*. G. Gordon. Macmillan/International Planned Parenthood Federation, 1990.
Available from: IPPF. See Appendix E.

4. 'AIDS care and prevention in rural communities.' I.D. Campbell. *Postgraduate Doctor* 12 (5): 108–10 and **12** (6): 134–6, 1990.

5. 'Caring for people with AIDS – it can be done.' I.D. Campbell and A. D. Rader *Africa Health* **12** (5): 46–7 July, 1990.
See Appendix D.

The free international newsletter AIDS Action is *available from* AHRTAG, see Appendix E. This is an excellent source of information and update on all aspects of AIDS management and control.
The video TASO: living positively with AIDS is also *avaliable from* TALC.

Part V
APPENDICES

Appendix A: Suppliers of equipment

General supplies, equipment, vehicles

1. ECHO: 2 Ullswater Crescent, Coulsdon, Surrey CR3 2HR UK.
   Supply a huge range of medical and surgical equipment, medicines, appliances, vehicles etc.

2. International Dispensary Association (IDA): PO Box 3098, 1003 AB Amsterdam, The Netherlands.
   Suppliers of a large range of medicines appropriate for developing countries. Also produce INFO letter.

3. Lifeline: Unit 9a, Herald Industrial Estate, Botley Rd, Hedge End, Southampton, SO3 3JW UK and PO Box 56938, Nairobi, Kenya.
   Relief and development supplies provided and shipped world-wide.

4. Mission Supplies Ltd: Alpha Place, Garth Rd, Morden, Surrey, SM4 4LX, UK.
   Supply a variety of appliances, office equipment, computers, audiovisual aids, vehicles.

5. Unimatco: Beta Works, Oxford Road, Tatling End, Gerrards Cross, Bucks, SL9 7BB, UK.
   As under (2) and (3).

Community health supplies

1. Teaching Aids at Low Cost (TALC): Box 49, St Albans, Herts, AL1 4AX, UK.
   TALC is a major community health resource centre in the UK. Supply a complete range of books on community health, plus child weighing scales, height measurers, arm measurers, growth charts, sets of teaching slides, etc.

2. Tropical Health Technology: 14 Bevills Close, Doddington, Cambs, PE17 0TT, UK.
   Supply laboratory equipment and books, microscopes, AIDS/HIV Test kits etc. Also publish appropriate laboratory manuals.

Weighing scales

1. CMS Weighing Scales: 18 Camden High Street, London, NW1 0JH, UK.
   Supply beam, clock face, tubular and other scales.

2. Continental Scale Corporation: 7400 West 100th Place, Bridgeview, Illinois 60455, USA.
   Also supply a range of weighing scales.

3. TALC PO Box 49, St Albans, Herts, AL1 4AX, UK.
   TALC supplies the Direct Recording Scale, the most appropriate model available.

Pressure cookers

See under general above. Also from:
- Wisconsin Aluminium Foundry Co Inc: Box 246, 838 S. 16th St, Manitowac, Wisconsin 54220, USA.
  Models recommended: 1925X plus aluminium container No 2162, and 1941 with aluminium container 2164.

Films

- Concord Video and Film Council Ltd, 201 Felixstowe Rd, Ipswich, Suffolk, IP3 9BJ, UK.
  An educational film library covering a variety of health and development issues. Full catalogue available.

Further information on supplies

- AHRTAG: 1 London Bridge Street, London, SE1 9SG, UK.
Supply comprehensive lists on all aspects of community health resources.
- See also Appendix E.

Appendix B: Supplies needed by a small scale health programme

General equipment for base/health centre

Storage cupboards, tables, examination couches, stools, benches and other furniture
Autoclave or pressure cooker
Drums for autoclave, cloth for wrapping instruments, labels, autoclave tape etc.
Refrigerator
Home tool kit
Chalkboard and chalk and/or overhead projector
Emergency generator
Film and/or slide projector
Variety of educational and teaching aids

Office equipment and stationery

Typewriter and spare ribbons
Supply of project and plain paper; envelopes, stamps
Ballpoints, carbon paper, paper clips, elastic bands, stapler and staples, thumbtacks, erasers, ruler (scale) glue etc.
Rubber stamps, ink pad
Order, supply and stock cards
Cash books, ledger, cheque and receipt books
Folders and files
Computer, where applicable, plus software

Medical equipment for clinics

Blood pressure machine (sphygmo)
Otoscope with speculums and spare bulbs: ophthalmoscope
Clinical thermometers
Stethoscope
Fetoscope (obstetrical stethoscope)
Tongue depressors
Weighing scales for adults and children (with stirrups)
Height measurer
Portable weight/height chart
Tape measure
Tourniquet
Eye testing charts (near and distant)
Eye testing lenses
Ear syringe
Vaginal speculums
Family planning supplies including IUDs
Abscess/suture set
Scissors straight/blunt
Forceps Kocher no teeth
IV cannulas and giving sets
Child feeding tubes
Dental forceps and other instruments
Dressing tray stainless steel *c.* 30 × 15 × 3 cm
Kidney dishes stainless steel *c.* 26 × 14 cm
Syringes Luer 2, 5 and 10 ml resterilisable and/or disposable
Needles Luer IM 21 G, SC 25 G, IV 19 G
BCG syringe

Renewable medical supplies

Rubber gloves
Urinary catheters, Foley, varying sizes disposable
Blades, cord ligatures and other midwifery supplies
Suturing material
Absorbent cotton wool
Adhesive tape 2.5 cm × 5 m roll
Elastic bandage (crepe) 7.5 cm × 10 m roll
Gauze bandage 7.5 cm a 10 m roll
Gauze compresses 10 × 10 cm 12 ply non-sterile
Tourniquet
Bar of soap
Nailbrush (autoclavable)
Sugar, salt, spoons, cups etc. for demonstrating use of homemade ORS

General equipment for clinics

Cold boxes for storing, carrying vaccines
Storage boxes for equipment, records etc. (animal, ant, weather–proof)
Waste bins
Water buckets and dippers
Soapdishes and soap
Keys, locks
Brooms, dust pans etc.
Batteries
Lights, lanterns, cooking stoves, kettles and utensils and supply of fuel
Matches, candles
Insect sprays, mosquito nets
Water filter with replacement filters or 'candles'
Drug lists, standing orders, textbooks
Money box

Cardboard or other numbers for patients
Teaching aids including drama props, flashcards, leaflets etc.
Medicines, laboratory equipment etc. See Appendix C.

Registers and record cards for clinics

Strong registers: master, immunisation, patient attendance, TB, salary, CHW attendance etc.
CHW notebooks or other records
Self-retained records – general, under 5, school child, TB, maternity, each with plastic envelopes
Family folders and insert cards
Referral letters and list of suitable referral centres, doctors and clinics
Supply of government required forms

Appendix C: An essential drugs list

This is a suggested list of commonly used medicines at the community health centre level. **Each project will need to make its own modifications** drawing up a list with the help of a doctor or medical advisor.

Drug lists may differ considerably from one area or one programme to another. Factors influencing choice include local patterns of disease, drug availability and expense, population covered and level of training of health personnel. Equivalent drugs can be used depending on what is available and current price levels. Drugs included are in the WHO *Model list of essential drugs* (6th edition 1990).

Many smaller projects with no regular doctor in attendance at the clinic, or those with good hospital back-up would be able to use a shorter list (suggestions are marked*)

A list suitable for use by CHWs is included in Chapter 7.

Anaesthetics
Ketamine injection 50 mg/ml, 10 ml (general anaesthetic)
Lidocaine injection 1% or 2% (local anaesthetic)

Analgesics and anti-inflammatories (pain-killers)
* Acetylsalicylic acid tablet 300 mg (aspirin)
  Ibuprofen tablet 200 mg
  Morphine injection 10 mg/1 ml (drug subject to international control)
* Paracetamol tablet 500 mg and 100 mg or paediatric syrup 125 mg/5 ml

Anti-allergics
* Adrenalin injection 1 mg/ml (Epinephrine)
* Chlorphenamine tablet 4 mg (Chlorpheniramine)
* Chlorphenamine injection 10 mg in 1 ml
  Dexamethasone injection 4 mg in 1 ml
  Prednisolone tablet 5 mg

Anti-amoebics, antigiardials
Diloxanide tablet 500 mg (for amoebic cysts)
* Metronidazole tablet 200 mg or 400 mg or Tinidazole 500 mg tablet

Anti-anaemia drugs
* Ferrous sulphate tablet equivalent to 60 mg iron
* Folic acid tablet 1 mg
  (Ferrous sulphate and folic acid often in combined tablet)
* Iron dextran injection 50 mg in 2 ml

Antibacterials
* Amoxicillin tablet or capsule 250 mg or ampicillin tablet or capsule 250 mg
* Chloramphenicol capsule 250 mg
  Chloramphenicol injection 1 g/vial
  Phenoxymethylpenicillin tablet 250 mg
* Procaine benzylpenicillin injection 1 g (1 million IU)
* Sulfamethoxazole 400 mg + trimethoprim 80 mg tablet (co-trimoxazole)

Anti-epileptics
* Diazepam injection 5 mg in 2 ml
* Phenobarbital tablet 30 mg, 50 mg or 60 mg (phenobarbitone)
  Phenytoin tablet 100 mg

Antifungals
* Griseofulvin tablet 125 mg or 250 mg
* Nystatin tablet 500 000 IU and pessary 100 000 IU

Anthelminthics (for worms)
* Diethylcarbamazine tablet (DEC) 50 mg (for filaria)
  Ivermectin tablet 6 mg (for onchocerciasis)
* Mebendazole tablet 100 mg
  Niclosamide tablet 500 mg
* Praziquantel tablet 600 mg (for schistosomiasis)

Antileprotics

Clofazimine capsule 50 mg or 100 mg
Dapsone tablet 50 mg or 100 mg
Rifampicin tablet or capsule 150 mg or 300 mg
(also in antitubercular list)

Antimalarials

* Chloroquine tablet 150 mg base, or syrup
* Quinine tablet 300 mg
  Quinine injection 300 mg/ml, 2 ml
* Sulfadoxine 500 mg + pyrimethamine 25 mg
  tablet ('Fansidar')

Antiseptics

* Chlorhexidine 5% solution

Antituberculous drugs (depending on project policy)

Ethambutol tablet 200 mg or 400 mg
Isoniazid tablet 100 mg or 300 mg (INH)
Pyrazinamide tablet 500 mg
Rifampicin tablet or capsule 150 mg or 300 mg
Streptomycin injection 1 g
Thiacetazone + isoniazid tablet 50 mg + 100 mg
or 150 mg + 300 mg

Cardiovascular drugs

Digoxin tablet 0.25 mg
Furosemide tablet 40 mg (Frusemide)
Hydrochlorothiazide tablet 25 mg or 50 mg
Propranolol tablet 10 mg, 40 mg or 80 mg

Dermatological drugs (for applying to skin)

* Benzyl benzoate lotion 25%, bottle 1 litre
* Calamine lotion
* Gentian violet aqueous solution 1%
  Hyrocortisone cream or ointment 1%
* Lindane cream or lotion 1%
  Miconazole ointment or cream 2%, or Whitfield's
  ointment
* Neomycin and bacitracin ointment

Gastro-intestinal drugs

* Aluminium hydroxide tablet 500 mg
* Atropine tablet 1 mg or equivalent
  Cimetidine tablet 200 mg
* Metoclopramide tablet 10 mg
* Oral rehydration salts, powder 27.9 g/l
  Senna tablet 7.5 mg or equivalent

Gynaecological/Obstetric/Contraceptive preparations

* Condoms preferably with spermicide nonoxinol
  Copper-containing intrauterine device
* Ethinyloestradiol + levonorgestrel tablets (30 µg
  + 150 µg or 50 µg + 250 µg) **or** ethinyloestradiol
  + norethisterone (50 µg + 1 mg) (contraceptive
  pills)
* Ergometrine tablet 0.2 mg and injection 0.2 mg
  in 1 ml

Immunisations/serum

Anti-venom sera
* BCG vaccine
* Diphtheria–pertussis–tetanus (DPT) vaccine
  Diphtheria–tetanus (DT) vaccine
* Measles vaccine
* Poliomyelitis vaccine
* Tetanus vaccine
  (Others as indicated locally e.g. hepatitis B, rabies, typhoid, yellow fever vaccines)

Intravenous solutions

Compound solution of sodium lactate injectable
solution
Glucose injectable solution 5%

Ophthalmic drugs (for eyes)

Atropine eye drops 0.1%, 0.5% or 1%
Pilocarpine eye drops 2% or 4%
Tetracaine eye drops 0.5%
* Tetracycline eye ointment 1%

Psychotherapeutic drugs (for mental disturbance)

Amitriptyline tablet 25 mg
* Chlorpromazine tablet 100 mg and injection
  25 mg/ml in 2 ml
  Diazepam tablet 5 mg

Respiratory drugs

* Aminophylline tablet 100 mg or 200 mg
  Aminophylline injection 25 mg/ml in 10 ml
  ampoule
  Salbutamol tablet 2 mg or 4 mg or aerosol inhaler

Vitamin preparations

* Vitamin A capsule 200 000 IU or oily solution
  100 000 IU (retinol)

* Vitamin C 50 mg (ascorbic acid)
  (Other vitamins and minerals will depend on
  local deficiencies.)

* **Water for injection**

> Formulations of some drugs will differ from
> one country to another.

Appendix D: Useful journals and newsletters

Addresses in most cases are given in Appendix E which lists resource agencies.

General community health topics

Contact
International magazine, each issue concentrating on a particular community health topic, or giving a write-up of an outstanding programme.
Order from: Christian Medical Commission, WCC, 150 Route de Ferney, 1211 Geneva, Switzerland.
Bimonthly: English, French, Spanish, Portugese

Footsteps
Free international newsletter on practical aspects of community health and development. Specially designed for leaders and members of community health teams, but also of value to doctors, nurses and project leaders.
Order from: TEAR Fund, 100 Church Road, Teddington, Middlesex TW11 8QE UK.
Quarterly: English, French, Spanish

Directions
Free international journal, each issue focusing on one aspect of health care, and the appropriate technology needed.
Order from: Programme for Appropriate Technology in Health (PATH). 4 Nickerson Street, Seattle, Washington WA 98109, 1699, USA.
Twice yearly English

Specific community health topics

AIDS Action
Free international newsletter and information on AIDS prevention and control.
Order from: AHRTAG.
Quarterly: English, French, Spanish, Portugese

ARI News
Free international newsletter on acute respiratory infections.
Available from AHRTAG.
Three per year: English, French, Spanish, Chinese

Child-to-Child Activity Sheets
A free add-on series on how children can teach health care to others.
Order from: Child-to-Child, Institute of Education, 20 Bedford Way, London, WC1H 0AL, UK.
Various languages; write for details.

CBR (Community Based Rehabilitation) News
Free international newsletter on practical care of the disabled and community rehabilitation.
Order from: AHRTAG.
Three per year: English

Community Eye health
Free international newsletter on all aspects of eye care.
Order from: International Centre for Eye Health.
Two per year: English

Dialogue on Diarrhoea
Free international newsletter on practical management of diarrhoea and dehydration.
Order from: AHRTAG.
Quarterly: English, French, Arabic, Portugese, Spanish, Tamil, Urdu, Bengali and Chinese

Partners
Free newsletter giving clear, practical coverage on leprosy, with diagrams.
Order from: The Leprosy Mission, Goldhay Way, Orton Goldhay, Peterborough PE2 0GZ, UK.
Two per year: English, French, Hindi.

Journals with community health emphasis mainly written for doctors or administrators

Tropical Doctor
A useful journal for doctors and nurses working in community health programmes and rural hospitals.
Available on subscription from: Royal Society of Medicine, 1 Wimpole Street, London, W1M 8AE, UK.
Quarterly: English, Spanish edition in planning

World Health Forum
Comprehensive coverage on a variety of community health related topics. Each issue about 100 pages.
Available on subscription from: WHO.
Quarterly: English
WHO also publish other journals. Write to address in Appendix E for further details.

Medicine Digest
Abstracts and updates on all aspects of medical care with emphasis on tropical medicine.
Order from: York House, 37 Queen Square, London, WC1N 3BH, UK.
Monthly: English

Regional Publications

Africa Health
Covers all aspects of health care with special reference to primary health care.

Free to countries in Africa from: Vine House, Fair Green, Reach, Cambridge, CB5 OJD, UK.
Bimonthly: English

EPI Newsletter
News and reports on immunisation programmes in the Americas.
Order from: Pan-American Health Organization.
Free, bimonthly: English.

Future
Health care issues related to children in South Asia are covered in this regional publication.
Order from: UNICEF, 55 Lodi Estate New Delhi 100001, India.
Quarterly: English
An edition for Pakistan is available from UNICEF, PO Box 1063, Islamabad, Pakistan.
Quarterly: English, Urdu

Health for the Millions
Information, articles and forum for sharing ideas. Especially relevant for India and other South Asian countries. Free to paid up members of the Voluntary Health Association of India.
Order from: VHAI, 40 International Area, South of IIT, New Delhi 110 016, India.
Bimonthly, English, probably soon also in Hindi

MCH News
A journal on health care for the Pacific Basin.
Order from: Pacific Basin Maternal-Child Health Resource Centre, University of Guam, PO Box 5143, UOG Substation, Mangilao, Guam 96923.
Quarterly: English

Appendix E: Addresses of resource and information centres

1. African Medical Research Foundation (AMREF), PO Box 30125, Nairobi, Kenya with offices in various other countries.
Publish books, journals and other literature. Run training courses and seminars. Act as a comprehensive advisory centre on primary health care.

2. AHRTAG, 1 London Bridge Street, London, SE1 9SG, UK.
Publish a variety of useful publications (see Appendix D). Have available lists of community health resources, publications and equipment world-wide. Provide an information consultancy and issue an annual directory of training courses in community health.

3. CHESS (Community Health Support Services) Department of International Community Medicine, Liverpool School of Tropical Medicine, Pembroke Place, Liverpool, L3 5QA, UK.
For a small subscription they will advise about setting up programmes, writing proposals and evaluating projects.
The Liverpool School with which they are associated runs a variety of training programmes and degree courses in community health.

4. International Centre for Eye Health, Institute of Ophthalmology, 27–29 Cayton Street, London, EC1V 9EJ, UK.
Advises and publishes information on all aspects of eye care, including prevention of blindness.

5. International Planned Parenthood Federation (IPPF), PO Box 759, Inner Circle, Regent's Park, London, NW1 4LQ, UK.
Advises and publishes information on all aspects of family planning and child spacing.

6. Macmillan Press, Houndmills, Basingstoke, Hants, RG21 2XS, UK.
Macmillan publish a large range of textbooks on all aspects of health care, education etc, many appropriate for community health programmes. Regional Macmillan offices exist throughout the world.

7. MEDEX, John Burns School of Medicine, University of Hawaii, 1833 Kalakaua Avenue, Suite 700, Honolulu, Hawaii 96815, USA.
Publish a definitive teaching course on primary health care. Also act as resource and advisory centre, and publish a regular newsletter.

8. Medical Assistance Programme (MAP International), Box 50, Brunswick, Georgia, 31520, USA.
A resource and information consultancy. MAP also supplies drugs and equipment for health projects, and runs training courses.

9. OXFAM, Oxfam House, 274 Banbury Rd, Summertown, Oxford OX2 7DZ, UK.
Oxfam also has regional offices in many countries. It advises about community health, development and funding and publishes a variety of useful books and manuals.

10. Pan-American Health Organization, 525 23rd Street, NW, Washington DC, 20037, USA.
A health resource centre for the Americas.

11. Save the Children Fund (SCF), 17 Grove Lane, London SE5 8RD, UK.
This large international organisation dedicated to bringing lasting benefits to children is totally committed to the principles of CBHC. They help to set up long term health and development programmes world-wide.

12. TALC (Teaching Aids at Low Cost), PO Box 49, St Albans, Herts, AL1 4AX, UK.
    Their impressive resources can be viewed by appointment at the Tropical Child Health Unit see below. These include a wide range of books, slides and equipment relevant to all community health programmes. They supply an updated resource list to those on their mailing list.

13. Tropical Child Health Unit, Institute of Child Health, Guilford Street, London WC1, UK.
    An outstanding resource centre on all aspects of community health. Has an extensive library of books, journals, slides etc. Runs many practical and appropriate training courses of varying lengths. Is linked with the University of London and has its own specialist medical and nursing staff. It works in close association with TALC.

14. UNICEF (United Nations Children's Fund) UN Plaza 4/1234C, New York, 10017, USA.
    Advises governments and agencies on programmes for children. Provides a large range of resource materials, journals and books. Their regional offices will provide advice on all aspects of child health care, and they also publish regional journals.

15. Voluntary Health Association of India, 40 Institutional Area, South of IIT, New Delhi, 110 016, India.
    Publishes journals, educational materials in regional languages. Runs training programmes, acts as resource and advisory centre on all forms of community based health care. Have associated branches in each state of India.

16. Water, Engineering and Development Centre (WEDC), Loughborough University of Technology, Leicestershire, LE11 3TU, UK.
    A resource centre and consultancy on all aspects of water supplies and sanitation.

17. World Health Organization, Distribution and Sales, 1211 Geneva 27, Switzerland.
    The definitive United Nations Agency which advises governments world-wide on all aspects of health care. WHO publishes a huge number of books, journals, reports and other publications, and has specialists available to advise on almost any health related subject.

    Their regional offices are as follows:
    - *Africa*: PO Box No 6, Brazzaville, Congo (Tel. 83 3860 65).
    - *Americas*: Pan-American Sanitary Bureau, 525, 23rd Street, NW, Washington DC, 20037, USA (Tel. 861 3200).
    - *Eastern Mediterranean*: PO Box 1517, Alexandria, 21511, Egypt (Tel. 48 202 230).
    - *Europe*: 8 Scherfigsvej, DK-2100, Copenhagen O, Denmark (Tel. 29 01 11).
    - *Southeast Asia*: World Health House, Indraprastha Estate, Mahatma Gandhi Rd, New Delhi, 110002, India (Tel. 331 7804).
    - *Western Pacific*: PO Box 2932 Manila 2801 Philippines (Tel. 521 84 21).

    WHO and UNICEF are the agencies behind the 'Health for All (by the Year 2000)' initiative.

Appendix F: Summary of programme records

Level	Type of record	What recorded	Chapter and page
1. Patients seen for curative care			
Community	CHW notebook Patient card	Name, disease and brief details	Chapter 7, page 88
Health centre	Family folder insert card (if serious)	Brief details	Chapter 8, page 113
	Patient card	Brief details	
	Disease tally or register	Disease only by word or symbol	
	Attendance register	Name and age of each patient	
Base	Master register	Numbers and percentages of patients and diseases seen by CHW and in centre	
2. Children seen for weighing			
Community	Child's growth card	Weight, cause if below Road to Health	Chapter 9, page 129
	CHW notebook	Weight, cause	
Health centre	Child's growth card	Weight, cause if below Road to Health	Chapter 9, page 129
	Family folder insert card	Weight, cause if below Road to Health	Chapter 8, page 113
Base	Master Register	Numbers and percentages of under 5s on or below Road to Health	
3. Children receiving immunisations			
Community	Simple list or	Name, type of immunisation, date	Chapter 10, page 151
	Immunisation register	Type of immunisation by number and name: date	
	Child's growth card	Type of immunisation, date	
Health centre	Immunisation Register	Type of immunisation by number and name: date	Chapter 8, page 113
	Child's growth card	Type of immunisation, date	
	Family folder insert card	Type of immunisation, date	
Base	Master Register	Numbers and percentages of children for each community who have completed each type of immunisation	

Level	Type of record	What recorded	Chapter and page
4. Mothers given maternity care and family planning			
Community	CHW's or TBA's notebook or tally sheet	Name, details of pre-natal checks, delivery, family planning	Chapter 7, page 88 Chapter 12, page 186
	Patient's record card (general or maternity)	Details of pre-natal checks, delivery or family planning	
Health centre	Family folder maternity card	Details of pre-natal checks	Chapter 12, page 179
	Family planning register	Details of family planning	Chapter 13, page 195
	Patient's record card	Details of pre-natal checks and family planning	Chapter 12, page 179
Base	Master Register	Numbers and percentages of patients attending 3 or more pre-natal clinics, completed tetanus toxoid, delivery by trained attendant, live births, birth weight 2500 g or above, referred	
5. Patients with TB, leprosy and other communicable diseases			
Community	CHW's notebook or diary	Treatment given, date next treatment due	Chapter 7, page 88
	Patient's record card	Treatment given etc.	Chapter 14, page 209
Health centre	Family folder insert card	Progress, tests, treatment, compliance	Chapter 14, page 209 Chapter 8, page 114
	TB register	As above	
	Patient's record card	As above	
	Government form	Details as requested (if government supplies drugs)	
Base	Master Register	Numbers and percentages of patients per community on regular treatment, or who have completed treatment	
6. Births, marriages, deaths			
Community	CHW's notebook	Names and details	Chapter 7, page 89
Health centre	Family folder	Names and details	Chapter 8, page 114
	Vital events register	Names and details	
Base	Master Register	Names and details	

Summary of health records kept

1. At **community** level:
CHW or TBA fills in:
- Notebook, diary or tally
- If literate, patient record card
2. At **health centre** level:
Health worker fills in:
- Family folder insert card where relevant
- Relevant register (e.g. TB, family planning)
- Patient record card
3. At **base**
Doctor or director fills in:
- Master register or computer

Note on the master register

The Master Register is **kept** in the project office and information from all programme activities is recorded in it.

It can be **updated** every 3 or 6 months or every year. The information it contains is used for compiling reports, evaluating progress, drawing up indicators, and for research.

The Register **contains** statistics of the following:

- House-to-house surveys
- Patients seen. See 1 above
- Childhood immunisation and nutritional status. See 2, 3 above
- Maternal health and family planning. See 4 above

- Communicable diseases especially TB and leprosy. See 5 above
- Details of public health inputs, activities, improvements

Information is **transferred** regularly either through tally sheets from each health centre or by calling in health centre registers once or twice per year.

Some projects use a computer instead of a register to store this information.

Appendix G: Family folder survey form

a) NAME OF HEAD OF FAMILY _____ OCCUPATION _____ FOLDER NO. _____

VILLAGE/TOWN/COLONY _____ DISTRICT _____ REGION _____ STATE/PROVINCE _____ DATE OF SURVEY _____

b) Felt Problems – see inside folder

c) FAMILY PROFILE   d) DISEASES   e) IMMUNISATION   f) FAMILY PLANNING   g) ADDICTION   h) EDUCATION

No	NAME	AGE + D.O.B. IF UNDER 5	SEX	RELATION TO HEAD	RELATION TO EACH OTHER	T.B.	LEP ROSY	STD VD	MALE UNDER 5	BCG	DPT	POLIO	TET TOX	TUB	VAS	O/C PILL	COL	IT IUD INS EP	ELY NAN EP	MID TOB POS	ALCO	HIGH SCH LIT	ILL	REMARKS
01																								
02																								
03																								
04																								
05																								
06																								
07																								
08																								
09																								
10																								
11																								
12																								
13																								
14																								

VITAL EVENTS SINCE SURVEY

BIRTHS				DEATHS				MIGRATION					
NAME	SEX	FATHER'S NATURE	DATE OF BIRTH	NAME	AGE	CAUSE	DATE OF DEATH	NAME	AGE	SEX	DATE OF MIG.	RELATION TO HEAD	In/Out REASON

i) DEATHS IN THE LAST 12 MONTHS

NAME	SEX	DATE OF DEATH	AGE AT DEATH	CAUSE OF DEATH

(space for other data needed)

b) FELT PROBLEMS
what are the main problems affecting your family

1. _____
2. _____
3. _____

j) USE OF EXISTING SERVICES

1. Who and where does the family attend when sick?

2. Who delivers Babies? _____
   TBA _____ FAMILY MEMBER _____ OTHER _____

k) WATER SUPPLY

1. Type of supply _____
2. Distance from house _____
3. Average No. of months per year operating _____
4. Type of alternative supply if any _____

L) SANITATION

1. Method used _____

ESTIMATED SOCIO-ECONOMIC STATUS

1.   2.   3.   4.   5.

Index

List of Commonly Used Abbreviations

AIDS	Acquired immune deficiency syndrome
ARI	Acute respiratory infection
CBHC	Community based health care
CHW	Community health worker
EPI	Expanded Programme on Immunization
DMO	District medical officer
EDL	Essential drugs list
FPP	Family planning provider
HIV	Human immunodeficiency virus
HRF	High risk factor
IUD	Intra-uterine device
KAP	Knowledge, attitude and practice
MAC	Mid-upper arm circumference
MPW	Multipurpose health worker
NGO	Non-governmental organisation
ORS	Oral rehydration salts
ORT	Oral rehydration therapy
STD	Sexually transmitted diseases
TALC	Teaching Aids at Low Cost
TBA	Traditional birth attendant
TB	Tuberculosis
UNICEF	United Nations Children's Fund
WHO	World Health Organization